AN INTRODUCTION TO NATURE

Birds ★ Wild Flowers ★ Trees

BY JOHN KIERAN

Illustrated by

DON ECKELBERRY · TABEA HOFMANN · MICHAEL H. BEVANS

HANOVER HOUSE · GARDEN CITY · NEW YORK

HANOVER HOUSE

Library of Congress Catalog Card Number: 55-9501

Printed in the United States of America

INDEX

INTRODUCTION

This is a book that was produced on the installment plan. It is, in appearance and in effect, three books in one. But the three parts that were published in sequence were merely divisions of a general project that was planned as a whole and that now reaches completion with the consolidation of *An Introduction to Birds, An Introduction to Wild Flowers,* and *An Introduction to Trees* into this volume, AN INTRODUCTION TO NATURE.

It is a book for beginners, young or old, and has been made as simple as possible. The fact that it is illustrated with color plates by noted artists in their various fields might lead to the conclusion that it is a "picture book" primarily for children. This is not so. It is designed to help the ordinary person of any age who would like to know and name the more common birds, flowers, and trees of our cities and villages, our woods and fields, our seashores and mountain slopes.

Birds, flowers, and trees, to be sure, call for a different approach in each case. Most of our birds are migratory. They come and go with the change of seasons, and you have to be on the alert to see them at the right time or place. Most of our wild flowers have only a brief blooming period. You must look for them at a certain time of year if you hope to find them in all their beauty and fragrance. But the trees we have always with us. They stand there Winter and Summer, year in and year out, in all kinds of weather. Many have been standing for a century or more. There are Douglas Firs standing today on the Pacific Coast where they stood when Columbus landed on San Salvador in 1492. Some of the Sequoias of the Sierras are older than Christendom. Trees are not only useful and beautiful but the oldest and largest living things on earth.

One rule holds true about birds, flowers, or trees. To learn to know them you must look at them. I put it that way because I remember the time I discovered that I had been going about the woods and fields for years without seeing things that were all around me. It was when I was just out of college and was teaching school in Dutchess County, New York. I had a one-room schoolhouse in the woods and six pupils from nearby farms. Among other things, I was supposed to teach the children how to recognize a few common birds. I had been supplied with colored pictures of four birds and under each picture was a short account of the bird – its name, its size, its habits, and when and where to look for it.

The first one of these bird cards I looked at pictured an odd bird in a queer position. The bird was gray and black on top and clear white underneath, and it seemed to be going down a fence post headfirst. That surprised me! I never had seen any bird going down a fence post or a tree trunk headfirst. I read what was on the card. It said that the bird was the White-breasted Nuthatch, a common bird about 5½ inches long that was noted for its habit of going down tree trunks, telegraph poles, or fence posts headfirst and that most farm children knew it well.

I was puzzled. The bird was absolutely unknown to me though I had been walking along the roads, over the fields, and through the woods of that region since I had been a small boy. I thought I knew something about birds in a general way. I certainly knew a Robin and a Bluebird and a Crow and a Baltimore Oriole and a few more. But here was a "common bird" – the card said so – that I never had seen in my life! I made up my mind to look for it, since the card also stated that it was a "permanent resident," a bird that stayed around all year. I said nothing to my pupils about birds that afternoon. I went home to sleep on the matter.

I slept out on the open porch of our farmhouse and, about 10 feet away from my cot, there was a Black Cherry tree on the lawn. The next morning when I woke up, the first thing that caught my eye was something moving on the shiny trunk of the Cherry tree. It was this bird, the White-breasted Nuthatch, and it was going down the trunk headfirst just as shown on the fence post in the picture! I had to walk a mile to reach the school and on the way that morning I kept my eyes open and saw four more of these birds moving up, down, and around the trunks or large branches of trees. By the time I reached the schoolhouse door I realized that the birds always had been there but I never had looked at them. In short, I had been blind. I made up my mind to look at things around me after that. I am still looking and finding things that to me are a never-ending delight.

One discovery leads to another. While looking for the White-breasted Nuthatch I found that there were many other "common birds" in the area that I never before had noticed. When I began to pick up an acquaintance with birds, I also took note of many flowers for the first time. I grew curious about their names. I borrowed a book from the library and looked them up. I was often in the woods looking for birds and, being no longer blind, I looked at the trees and took a lively interest in distinguishing one species from another. I found strange and beautiful insects of all kinds on trees and flowers. I bought an insect guide and an amazing new world was opened to me. There is no end to this sort of thing — no end to the things you can learn, and no end to the fun of learning them.

Do not be discouraged if you make mistakes at first. All beginners make ludicrous errors. It takes time to learn anything, particularly the birds, which are known to be flighty creatures. The bird pictures in this book are, for the most part, of the males in breeding plumage, which is their brightest dress. Meeting them this way is merely the first step in getting to know the birds at all, but it is, I think, the easiest step and at the same time the most important step. Once you have taken this step, you may go as far as you please. Incidentally, the actual size of the birds you will find in this book is indicated by the length in inches printed under the name of each bird. The measurement is from the tip of the bill to the tip of the tail when head, tail, and body are placed in a straight line, as they are in the "bird skins" that are preserved for study in museums. The measurements that are helpful in identifying trees and flowers are given in the text.

The knowledge of a few basic points about trees and flowers will give the beginner a start on firm ground. Trees, shrubs, and flowers belong to that great division of botanical life called Flowering Plants. The distinction is mostly a matter of size. It may come as a surprise to some readers that all healthy mature trees have flowers of some kind, the Elm as well as the Magnolia, the Oak as well as the Cherry. Not all individual trees, however, bear fruit. In some species there are male and female flowers — or "staminate" and "pistillate" flowers, as the botanists prefer it — that are produced on separate trees, and in such cases only the trees with the female or pistillate flowers can bear fruit.

"Fruit" is a term that needs explaining for beginners. Whatever contains the seed of any tree is the fruit, and it may be a nut, a berry, a cone, a capsule, a bean, a "pome" such as an apple, a "drupe" of the plum type, an acorn, or any number of other things depending upon the kind of tree that produces it. For instance, there are many different species of Maple but all Maples have one thing in common and that is the fruit that children call "keys" and botanists call "samaras." The acorn is the sign of the Oak family. Aside from that, most trees have distinctive features that are easily seen, at one season or another, even by a novice in the field. It may be the bark, the leaf, the flower, or the fruit, or a combination of such features. In the White Birch and the Beech the bark is distinctive. The mitten-shaped leaves of the Sassafras are distinctive and so are the star-shaped leaves of the Sweet Gum. The flowers of the Horse Chestnut, the Buckeyes, the Magnolias, and the Tulip Trees are distinctive and so are the fruits that follow in each case. Once you have recognized a tree by its distinctive features, take note of less striking details at different times of the year. You wouldn't know a man very well if you didn't recognize him when he changed his suit. You will not know a tree well until you recognize it in Winter as well as Summer.

Birds and flowers should be looked at in the same way. It is not difficult to recognize the lovely Mountain Laurel when you find it in bloom, but you must take note of the leaves, the bark, and the buds to know it at other seasons. The brilliant hues of the male Bobolinks and Scarlet Tanagers in the Spring change to the sober plumage of the females and young later in the year. The "gold" of the Goldfinches is much tarnished in Winter. Even so, the sweet call note of the Goldfinch remains the same throughout the year and the catkins hanging from leafless branches help us to find the Alder in the January swamp. When you have struck up a friendship with a bird, a flower, a shrub, or a tree, it will not be long before you will be able to recognize that friend in any guise.

The way the birds, flowers, and trees are described in this book is not the way in which a scientist would describe them, nor is the order in which the birds and flowers are shown the order in which a scientist would list them. The birds are listed more or less in the general order in which you might expect to see them if you stepped outside the door and began to look around for common birds. The flowers are presented in the approximate order in which you may find them coming into bloom if you begin to look "when the hounds of Spring are on Winter's traces" and continue your search to the frosty edge of November. Later on, when the beginner has learned something of Nature in this simple fashion, he or she will be better able to understand why the scientists list birds, trees, and flowers as they do, placing them in what they call Orders, Families, Genera, and Species.

There are many fine handbooks and field guides on birds, flowers, trees, insects, fish, and other divisions of Natural History, with detailed descriptions of practically all the species that are to be found in North America. They have been written by noted experts. But the very wealth of material in such field guides or weightier works may baffle or — worse still — discourage the beginner. The modest aim here is to provide the novice with an elementary guide to a friendly acquaintance with some birds, flowers, shrubs and trees as a first step in a fascinating field. After that, the reader whose interest is aroused may move ahead to wider and richer researches in Natural History with more capable guides. This book will serve its purpose best if it is not only An Introduction to Nature but an introduction to other books of greater scope by authors of recognized authority in their various fields. There is no lack of such books and authors for any region of temperate North America.

John Kieran

An Introduction to Nature

PART 1

BIRDS

ILLUSTRATED BY DON ECKELBERRY

ROBIN

(About 10 inches)

Everybody knows the Robin Redbreast, a familiar bird all over North America. In Canada and most of the United States except the Gulf Coast area they are "Summer residents." That is, they come with the warm weather of Spring and leave when "the North Wind doth blow and we shall have snow." Some hardy Robins may stay through the season of snow and ice, but if we look out the window in late February or early March and see a Robin on our lawn, most of us are inclined to shout: "Spring has come; the Robins are back!" They are friendly, trusting birds and feel quite at home on our lawns. Notice that they do not walk when they move about the ground; they run. Male and female are alike in general color but the female is usually a little duller than the handsome male Robin and young Robins have spotted breasts like their near relatives, the Thrushes. Robins have a rolling carol that is cheerful and melodious. They like to take baths and a bird bath on your lawn will bring Robins to bathe in it. Note that the length of the Robin—from the tip of its bill to the tip of its tail—is about 10 inches. Since the Robin is so well known, it can be used as a guide to help identify other birds by the difference in size or plumage between the stranger and the Robin.

ENGLISH SPARROW

(About 6 inches)

This bird is called the English Sparrow because it was brought here from England about 100 years ago, but it is common all over Europe, just as it has become common all over this country. It is a familiar sight in cities and suburbs and around our farmyards where it chirps, chatters, fights and builds its nests in all sorts of places, high and low, in boxes, under eaves, in cornices, in old shoes, drain spouts, gutters and other odd lodgings. Its plumage is often discolored by dust and smoke in cities, but around a farmyard it is surprising how nice the male looks in its clean suit. The male is the one with the large black bib tucked under its chin. The female and young are duller in color. English Sparrows are hardy, chunky, noisy, rowdy and cheerful. They have driven off many of our Bluebirds and Purple Martins by taking their nesting sites but otherwise are settling down as regular residents and accepted members of the bird community.

STARLING

(About 8 inches)

The plumage of the Starling varies according to the time of year, but the shape and actions of this bird are enough to distinguish it from such other blackish birds as Grackles, Cowbirds and Rusty Blackbirds that also walk about our pastures and lawns. At all times the Starling is the chunky, heavy-shouldered bird with the short tail and the longish bill. In the Spring the bill of the male is yellow, which easily sets it apart from our other black birds. The plumage of the birds at that season is a shining mixture of brown, black, green and dark blue that glistens in the sunlight. In the Autumn and Winter the Starlings have speckled or mottled plumage. They are not natives of this country. They were brought over from Europe, and the descendants of Starlings that were imported in 1892 and liberated in Central Park in New York City have spread from the Atlantic Coast to the Rocky Mountains. In time they will cover the whole country, because nothing seems to stop them. They feed in flocks, walking about in zigzag fashion as if they didn't care which way they were going. They breed in holes or cornices of buildings, raise two or three broods a year and are looked upon as nuisances where they become too numerous. They have a wonderful variety of whistles, squeaks and call notes and can imitate the songs of dozens of native birds.

BLUE JAY

(About 12 inches)

The handsome, swaggering, noisy Blue Jay wears a striking costume of sky-blue oversprinkled with stripes and patches of midnight black and clear white. It has a sharp crest, a sharp voice and a sharp eye for everything that goes on in the neighborhood. It patrols the highways and byways, bullying smaller birds, heckling stray cats, shrieking at any hawks or owls it may spy and generally looking into the business of any stranger in the vicinity. The ordinary note of the Blue Jay is a jeering cry but it can produce many other sounds, including some flute-like notes, a nut-cracking noise and a perfect imitation of the whistling cry of the Red-shouldered Hawk. There are half a dozen kinds of Jays in different parts of the country, but the Blue Jay is the most common and the most widespread. It ranges from the Atlantic Coast to the Rocky Mountains and there are few birds with which it might be confused. The Belted Kingfisher is probably the closest in appearance to the Blue Jay. Both birds are largely blue and white and both have crests. Also, they are about the same size. But the Belted Kingfisher is a short-tailed, short-legged, heavy-bodied bird with a jagged crest and a very heavy bill, whereas the Blue Jay is a graceful, sharp-crested, long-tailed bird that is much more common around our fields and woods. The Belted Kingfisher sticks pretty close to ponds, lakes and rivers.

CROW

(About 19 inches)

The "black Crow" is all black—wings, body, head, feet and beak—and some persons go on to say that it has a disposition to match its color. Farmers put up "scarecrows" to keep these birds out of their cornfields and there are organized "Crow shoots" in some localities to reduce their numbers, but Crows flourish just the same. Probably that's because they are wary birds. When Crows are feeding in a field they usually have at least one sentinel posted on a lofty perch to give warning of any approaching danger. They can say "Caw" in a dozen different ways, and each variation has a different meaning to them. They can make other sounds, too, including a cracking, stuttering sound like the creaking of a heavy barn door on rusty hinges. They have the bad habit of robbing cornfields and they are also charged with the crime of raiding the nests and eating the eggs and young of smaller birds. It is probable that this crime is more often attempted than carried out because Crows often are seen being driven away from nests of infuriated small birds. Crows definitely do much good by eating many slugs, beetles and caterpillars that do damage in gardens, grainfields and orchards. Whether they are a helpful or a harmful bird is a great subject of debate. Perhaps they are helpful in some regions and harmful in others.

What is certain about Crows is that they are very interesting birds. They are the watchmen of the woods and the open fields. They gather in wheeling and cawing flocks whenever one of them spies a Hawk, an Owl, a fox or a jackrabbit. They will follow a fox across open country like a pack of winged hounds and drive an Owl from one evergreen tree to another by continued swooping at it. In return for this noisy attention, a fox will gladly eat a Crow if it can catch the bird off guard on the ground, and more than one Crow has been caught napping by a Great Horned Owl. Young Crows make good pets and are easily tamed but they are great thieves and will fly off with anything they can carry. It is not true that they can be taught to speak if you split their tongues. The Crow never uses its tongue in producing any sound that it can make.

Crows are birds of the fields and woods and it is hard to get near them. They usually nest in a high tree in the woods and it is believed that both parents share in the labor of hatching the eggs and bringing up the young birds, but it's hard to be sure because the male and female look exactly alike and it's difficult to know which one is on the nest or bringing in food at any particular time. Apart from the breeding season Crows often gather in great flocks and move to favorite roosting places in long lines at dusk. If disturbed on such roosts at night, the departing birds with their flapping wings sound like a great rush of water. All Crows look alike, but individually they are really odd characters.

BALTIMORE ORIOLE

(About 8 inches)

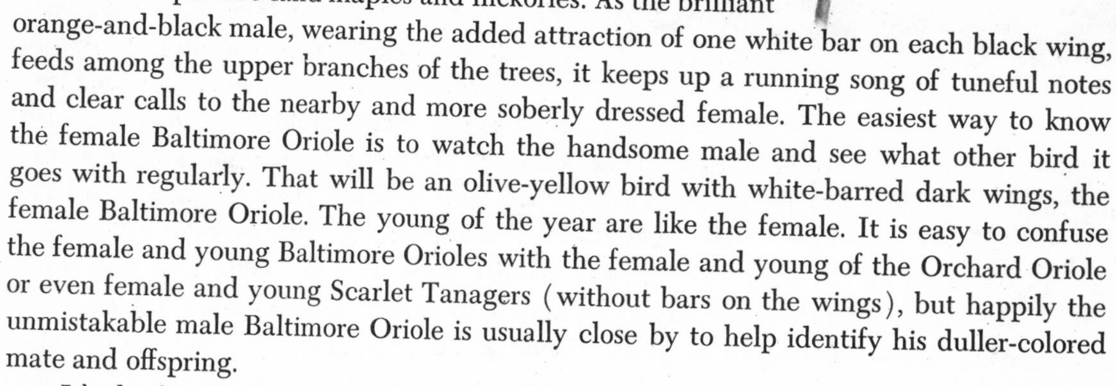

The beautiful, friendly and melodious Baltimore Oriole is easy to know because of its striking color combination of orange and black and its habit of feeding in the trees of our lawns, roadsides and orchards. It is a Summer resident of the eastern half of the United States and it is frequently in sight in the open all over its Summer range. It is not a bird of the deep woods. It likes the company of men, women and children and domestic animals like horses and cows. It loves to hang its wonderful woven nests in the outer foliage of our dooryard elms and our pasture-land maples and hickories. As the brilliant orange-and-black male, wearing the added attraction of one white bar on each black wing, feeds among the upper branches of the trees, it keeps up a running song of tuneful notes and clear calls to the nearby and more soberly dressed female. The easiest way to know the female Baltimore Oriole is to watch the handsome male and see what other bird it goes with regularly. That will be an olive-yellow bird with white-barred dark wings, the female Baltimore Oriole. The young of the year are like the female. It is easy to confuse the female and young Baltimore Orioles with the female and young of the Orchard Oriole or even female and young Scarlet Tanagers (without bars on the wings), but happily the unmistakable male Baltimore Oriole is usually close by to help identify his duller-colored mate and offspring.

It's the female that builds the remarkable hanging nests of this species and she does it by weaving plant fibers together so skillfully and efficiently that, long after the young birds have grown up and left home, the abandoned nests cling stubbornly to the bare branchlets through the rain, the snow, the sleet and the wild winds of Winter. Sometimes the birds conceal their nests so cleverly that we never find the woven cradle until the leaves come tumbling down in Autumn and bare the secret to the world at large. Many birds will accept contributions with thanks when they are looking for nesting material. Robins will take string or yarn of almost any color, but the female Baltimore Oriole prefers plain white yarn to weave into her nest along with grass and plant fibers. The 4 to 6 eggs hatch in about two weeks and there is only one brood a year as a rule.

Many years ago the poet Edgar Fawcett put in rhyme his admiration for the flashing Baltimore Oriole and asked:

At some glad moment was it Nature's choice
To dower a scrap of sunset with a voice?

But his final and delightful explanation of the origin of such a brilliant bird in our clime is that an orange-and-black tulip in an ancient garden

Yearning toward Heaven until its wish was heard,
Desired unspeakably to be a bird.

BROWN THRASHER

(About 11 inches)

The Brown Thrasher is a first cousin of the Mockingbird and Catbird and has the same general shape and good singing voice. It is the largest of the three and quite different in color from the others. The Brown Thrasher is a rich light brown with a reddish tinge above, and its cream-colored under parts are heavily marked by what look like dark dotted lines. It appears to be a "longish" bird because it has a long tail and a rather long bill that curves slightly downward. It can be found all over the United States in Summer, but in Winter the majority of the northern birds move southward to get away from the ice and snow. The Brown Thrasher is a bird of our lawns, shrubbery, village outskirts and farmlands. It is a fine singer with a loud clear voice and it picks a prominent perch—often the topmost branchlet of a tree or shrub—from which to perform. Some who have listened think they hear it say in Spring: "Plow now—plow now—plant it—drop it—cover it up—cover it up—good boy—three cheers!" It differs from the Thrushes in that it is a longer bird, has straw-colored eyes, has light wing bars and is much more a bird of the open fields and hedgerows.

CATBIRD

(About 9 inches)

The Catbird—general color a dark slate gray with a black cap and tail for those who look closer—is the poor relation of the Mockingbird. There are some who think that all a Catbird can do is mew like a cat and they refuse to believe that a bubbling song from the shrubbery can be produced by any Catbird. But the truth is that, while not quite up to the famous Mockingbird, it is a talented and tireless songster. It is not bold like a Blue Jay or easily familiar like a Robin. But it likes to live in the vicinity of houses and keep an eye on what people are doing. The Catbird is a skulking busybody, prying into everything, always lurking in the underbrush or peering out of the shrubbery. It builds a rather ramshackle nest in a thick bush and two broods a season are the rule. In the Summer there are Catbirds all over the United States east of the Rockies, but when the Autumn leaves come whirling down, most of the birds in the North pack up and go South to avoid the snows and wild winds of Winter. Catbirds feed mostly on insects but they will take a few berries in season. Still, we can't begrudge a few berries to such a beneficial and melodious bird.

RED-HEADED WOODPECKER

(About 9 inches)

Many Woodpeckers have some red on their heads, but this is the only one with an all-red head from the shoulders up. It is rare in eastern New York and New England and along the Pacific Coast, but elsewhere it is common and almost unmistakable because of the color combination, the bright red head and the contrasting black-and-white pattern—in large chunks—of the wings and body. The young have mottled brown heads but the large white patches in the black wings easily identify them. The older birds certainly are handsome and by no means shy. Male and female look alike and they catch the eye—or ear—as they fly from one dead branch to another or cling to a telegraph pole and utter their loud rattling calls. The golf courses of the country have turned out to be the favorite haunts of these brilliant birds. In fact, golf courses have become "bird sanctuaries" in general but the Red-headed Woodpecker, because of its size, color, loud cries and habit of alighting on dead limbs or fence posts, is one of the most easily noticed. Like other Woodpeckers, they breed in holes in trees or posts

HOUSE WREN

(About 5 inches)

There are more than a dozen different kinds of Wrens in North America, but you will have no trouble getting to know the House Wren. All Wrens have a family resemblance. They are small, stocky, brownish birds with lighter under parts, perky tails and small sharp bills, some of which curve slightly downward. To find most of them you have to go to special places such as the woods, the marshes, the canyons or the cactus lands. But the House Wren is well named. It likes to live in dooryards and, over the eastern half of the United States at least, rarely strays as far away as the orchard to build its nest. It will build in a convenient hole of any kind around the house or barn. It will build in the pocket of an old coat or in a mailbox or in a clothespin bag left hanging on the wash line. It carries twigs and grass to its nesting place and two or three broods a year are raised. The House Wren sings its rattling, rolling, bubbling song from daylight until dark. It is a bustling little bird, a spitfire. It is always feeding, fussing around, singing or driving away bigger birds that come near its nest. Our House Wrens move southward to spend the Winter near the Gulf of Mexico, but April or May always finds them back in our dooryards again.

CARDINAL

(About 8½ inches)

You couldn't mistake a male Cardinal for any other bird in North America. It is a flaming red bird—indeed, it is often called the Redbird—with a distinct crest and, around the base of its short and heavy red bill, it has a patch of black that extends back through the eye and down the throat a little way. The female Cardinal and the young of the year are much duller in color but they have the crest, the red bill and more than a hint of red in their cinnamon-yellow plumage to make them known as the wife and offspring of the more brilliant Cardinal. There is in the Southwest a bird, the Pyrrhuloxia, that is much like the female Cardinal (and young of the year) in size, color, shape and crest, but it has more gray in its plumage and it has a yellow bill, whereas all Cardinals have red bills. In addition to that, the Pyrrhuloxia is confined to the mesquite and cactus regions of the Southwest, whereas the Cardinal is a cherished resident of most of the United States from the Canadian Border to the Gulf of Mexico and from the Atlantic Coast to the Rocky Mountains. It is uncommon in New England and rather rare on the Pacific Coast, but over the remainder of the country you may find it around villages or farms or any kind of open country, often whistling loudly and clearly from a perch on a telephone wire, a fence rail or the topmost branch of a tree. It sounds much like a boy whistling sharply for his dog. The female joins in the whistling, which is unusual among birds. Another mark of distinction for the Cardinal is—what most boys know—that it has a major league baseball club named after it; the St. Louis Cardinals.

Since the Cardinal usually is an all-year resident over its range, it has to live through the snows of Winter in the northerly part of the United States, and there is no prettier sight in Nature than a male Cardinal in a snow-covered setting, the fiery color of its plumage contrasting so vividly with the soft white background. Cardinals are beneficial as well as friendly and beautiful birds. They eat many weed seeds and no small amount of injurious insects of one kind or another, including the seventeen-year cicada or "locust." The female and young often lurk modestly in the shrubbery while the proud male is whistling loudly from an exposed perch, but the hidden members of the family give their presence away by the sharp "tsik" call note they utter from time to time. It is quite distinctive and is easily recognized as a Cardinal trait after it is heard a few times.

The nest is made of twigs, leaves and grass and is placed in vines, shrubs or trees, seldom very high above the ground. The female does all the brooding of the 3 or 4 eggs that hatch in about twelve days. The male Cardinal is a good husband and a fond parent, however. He feeds the female while she is on the nest and he takes entire care of the feeding of the young when they have left the nest and the female is going about the business of laying more eggs to rear another brood. Sometimes the parent birds bring up three broods in a year.

There was a time when Cardinals were trapped in large numbers and sold as cage birds, but restrictive laws put an end to that trade.

SCARLET TANAGER

(About 7 inches)

You will know the Scarlet Tanager as soon as you set eyes on it. That is, if it's a male in its best dress—a flaming scarlet body with black wings and tail. But the female is easily overlooked. It is nothing like its gorgeous mate. It is an olive-green bird with darker wings and tail. Even the gaudy male takes on the sober olive-green traveling costume when it is time to go southward in the Autumn. It is a curious-looking bird when it is changing from its scarlet coat to its traveling suit. At such times it often looks like a greenish bird that had been spattered with red paint. The young birds of the year are olive-greenish, much like the female. The Scarlet Tanager is a woodland bird but it also likes shade trees on lawns and often will call or sing from an exposed perch on a dead branch. The easiest way to find Scarlet Tanagers is to get to know the song and the call note. They are persistent singers through Spring and Summer. The song is a vibrant continuing warble something like that of the Red-eyed Vireo but with more of metallic buzz in its quality. The call is a snappy "Chip-churrr!" that can be heard at a distance. Once you know the song or the call notes you will be able to find any Scarlet Tanagers that happen to live in your neighborhood—and probably there are more than you suspect. The Scarlet Tanager is a Summer resident over most of the United States east of the Great Plains.

BLUEBIRD

(About 7 inches)

Here is a beautiful, friendly, modest bird with a lovely liquid note and a plaintive song. It has the blue of the sky on its back, the warm color of a hearth fire on its breast and the clear white of soft snow underneath. Whether it is perched on a dead limb or dreamily floating through the air, it keeps up a soft warble all through the day. James Whitcomb Riley, describing the arrival of the first Bluebird of Spring, wrote:

In acrost the orchard come,
Soft as an angel's wing,
A breezy, treesy, beesy hum,
Too sweet for any thing!

Others say that it warbles "Ber-muda, Ber-muda" as it flies daintily over our fields and along the roadsides. It is definitely a bird of the open country and likes to build its nest in bird boxes or holes in fence posts or dead trees around dooryards or barnyards. It is gradually being pushed out of city parks and suburban areas by such imported interlopers as the English Sparrow and the Starling that also nest in holes.

MOCKINGBIRD

(About 10 inches)

This is the favorite bird of the South, famous in song and story. Like the Nightingale of Europe, the Mockingbird is a plain bird with a beautiful song. It is a generally grayish bird about the size of a Robin, except that it is thinner. When it flies it shows flashes of black and white in its wings and tail. Sitting on a wire, a fence or the branch of a bush or tree, it looks much like its cousin the Catbird but is much lighter in color. The only other bird with which a Mockingbird might be confused is a Shrike. The Loggerhead Shrike is also a grayish bird slightly smaller than the Mockingbird and it is common in many places where the Mockingbird is found, but the Shrike is a chunkier bird with a heavy bill and a black line through the eye. And no Shrike can sing like a Mockingbird. As soon as the singing starts, the Mockingbird never could be mistaken for a Shrike or a Shrike for a Mockingbird.

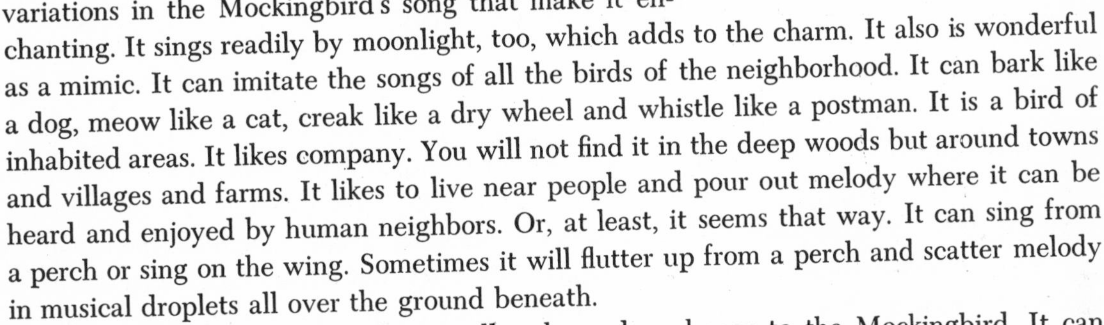

It is not only the lovely liquid quality but the variations in the Mockingbird's song that make it enchanting. It sings readily by moonlight, too, which adds to the charm. It also is wonderful as a mimic. It can imitate the songs of all the birds of the neighborhood. It can bark like a dog, meow like a cat, creak like a dry wheel and whistle like a postman. It is a bird of inhabited areas. It likes company. You will not find it in the deep woods but around towns and villages and farms. It likes to live near people and pour out melody where it can be heard and enjoyed by human neighbors. Or, at least, it seems that way. It can sing from a perch or sing on the wing. Sometimes it will flutter up from a perch and scatter melody in musical droplets all over the ground beneath.

No wonder the poets and storytellers have done honor to the Mockingbird. It can sing its own song or the song of any other bird it hears. It sings by sunlight or moonlight. It can give a concert from a perch like a tenor singing from a stage, or it can flutter through the air and let a shower of music fall over the landscape. Not only that, but it sings through almost the entire year! The Mockingbird is courageous and in the breeding season is fearless in attacking cats or other raiders that may seem to be threatening its young in the nest. It is bold with other birds and tolerates no impudence from upstarts at the feeding tray or the bird bath. The Mockingbird demands first place there and takes vigorous measures if there is any dispute about it. Though it does eat some cultivated fruit, the Mockingbird is beneficial around the farm or garden because of the great number of injurious insects that it eats.

The nest may be placed anywhere in vines or shrubbery or trees from just off the ground to a branch 50 feet up. There are usually from 3 to 6 eggs and two or even three broods may be raised in a year. Mockingbirds are common over the southern section of the United States east of the Great Plains and may range as far north as eastern Canada.

SONG SPARROW

(About 6 inches)

There are many kinds of Sparrows in all corners of this country and almost all of them are rather plain brownish birds with or without streaked breasts. But if you will look a little closer and also listen to the different songs of the common species, you will easily come to know at least a dozen different kinds. The Song Sparrow, for instance, is found all over North America pouring out its cheerful song that sounds something like "Tea-tea-tea! Polly-put-the-kettle-on!" It is a friendly bird of dooryards, roadsides and open country generally. It varies slightly in color and song in different sections of the country but it can be known by its confident rattling little song and three spots in a triangle on its streaked throat and breast. There are other Sparrows that are brownish above and streaked on the breast, but the Song Sparrow has a dark spot on each side of its throat and a heavy spot in the middle of its breast where the streaks seem to meet in a bunch. Most Song Sparrows go South for the Winter, but a few remain all year in northern territory where snow blankets the ground.

MEADOWLARK

(About 10 inches)

True to its name, the Meadowlark is a bird of the open fields with a clear whistle for a song. It is a stumpy gray-brown bird with a bright yellow breast that has a black crescent across it. It has a striped head and its tail is white on either side, which is a fine mark as the bird flies away when flushed from the grass. The Flicker also has a black crescent on its breast, often feeds on the ground and also shows white on its back as it flies away. But the Flicker's breast is pinkish-brown instead of bright yellow and the white spot it shows flying away is a single patch on its rump. The two white patches that show in the tail of a departing Meadowlark are separated by a dark middle line. The Meadowlark walks when feeding on the ground. Or perhaps it would be better to say that it waddles. Its eggs are laid in a grass-lined depression on the ground. In fact, the bird rarely leaves the ground except when it is disturbed or when it takes some perch from which to sing. It flies with stiff wings and a fluttering style, alternately sailing and beating its wings quickly. Most Meadowlarks are merely Summer residents with us, but a few may stay over Winter.

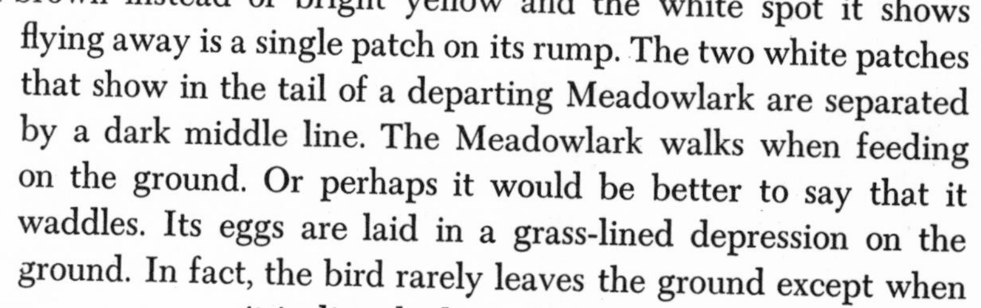

GOLDFINCH

(About 5 inches)

The male Goldfinch in its bright Summer costume is one of the prettiest and daintiest of our native birds, and also one of the easiest to identify with its shining yellow body, its black wings with white bars and its jaunty little black cap pulled down low over its forehead. The female is a much duller color all over and lacks the black cap. These are the birds that many persons call "wild canaries" because they are little yellow birds about canary size and they seem quite friendly as they chatter and twitter when feeding on the lawn or in the garden. They eat seeds for the most part and often come to our lawns for dandelion seeds, which they gobble down with a musical accompaniment. Except in the breeding season, they go about in small groups or flocks, making music as they go. They fly with a long bounding motion, as though they were riding great waves in the air, and at each dip in flight they seem to say "Per-chick-o-ree, Per-chick-o-ree" in musical tones. Their regular and long song is canary-like, a tuneful chattering warble. Even their call notes are musical and sweet. It is easy to know when Goldfinches are in the vicinity because they are rarely silent. They chatter when feeding or resting. Their flight notes come as regularly as their wing movements when they are bounding through the air. They call sweetly to one another all through the day.

There are Goldfinches all over temperate North America and, for the most part, they are permanent residents wherever they are found, though some of them may wander a little in a southerly direction when the Winter winds are at their worst in snow-covered northern territory. The males lose their black caps in Winter and the bright yellow of their Summer plumage turns to the olive-yellow of the female, but the birds lose none of their cheerfulness with this loss of color. They are tuneful and chattering in the dried weed patches of Winter as they are when eating lettuce seeds in the garden in Summer. It is wise to watch the Goldfinch flocks in Winter because these friendly and familiar little birds act as decoys for other and less familiar birds such as Pine Siskins and Redpolls that come down from the more northerly regions to spend some part of the Winter with us.

Goldfinches, Pine Siskins and Redpolls are much alike in shape, size and habits, but the Pine Siskins and the Redpolls are more or less heavily striped and Goldfinches never have stripes. But because even the male Goldfinches are dull of color in Winter, it's wise to inspect any flock of Goldfinches that may be feeding cheerfully on birch cones or weed seeds in Winter. Only a close inspection will show whether or not there are Pine Siskins or Redpolls in with the Goldfinches.

The nest is placed in a fork in an outer branch high up in a tree and it is usually July before the 4 to 6 eggs are laid in a thistledown cradle. Some say the reason for the late nesting is because the female waits for the thistledown to ripen before she builds. The male feeds the female while she is brooding and is a good provider for the young until they leave the nest. Then off they go, parents and young, to join others of their kind and form the tuneful, cheerful, friendly flocks of Goldfinches that are so pleasant to hear and to see.

TOWHEE

(About 8 inches)

This is a bird of many names—Towhee, Chewink, Joe Reed Bird, Ground Robin—the last being a good name for it because the bird sticks close to the ground and often is heard scratching in the underbrush in search of food. There are other Towhees in different parts of the country—the Spotted Towhee and the Green-tailed Towhee of the Far West and Southwest, for instance—but the plain Towhee (or Eastern Towhee, as it is sometimes called) is a common Summer resident over the eastern half of the United States and southern Canada. It ranges as far west as the Great Plains and is the most widespread and best known of the Towhees.

The Towhee is a bird of the underbrush. It lives in thickets, in the bushes that fringe roadsides and along the edges of woods. It is rarely seen on a lawn or on the ground in an open field. It is not common in thick woods. A field that is beginning to grow wild with gray birches, dogwoods, alders and viburnums is a great place for it. It will flit from one bush to the other, showing much white with flirts of its tail as it flies. It will call "Chee-wink, Chee-wink!" from the center of a thicket. Or it may perch atop some shrub or on some limb of a small tree to give its full "Toe-whee" song that is sometimes written "Chuck-burr, pilla-willa."

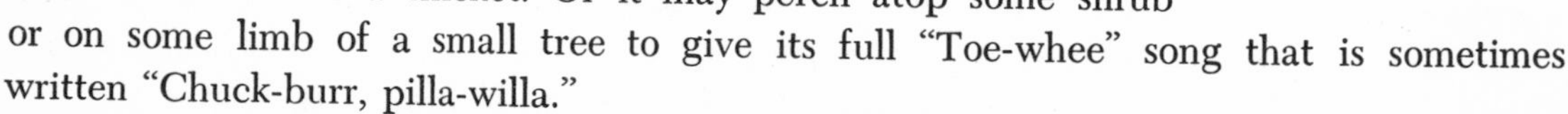

There is no difficulty in recognizing the Towhee when it does come out of the underbrush or thick shrubbery. Also, it is easy to see why some persons call it the Ground Robin. It does have the dark head of a Robin and it wears something like the red of the Robin's breast on its sides. But the black hood of the Towhee runs well down the breast to meet the clear white of the under parts and the Towhee has much white on the outer edges of its rather long tail. The female and the young have brown where the male Towhee wears black, but the general pattern is the same and the flashing white in the tail as the bird moves about in the underbrush is a sure sign of the Towhee. It almost seems to fly by fits and starts, or in jerks, always with a display of the contrasting colors in its tail. It makes so much noise scratching the leaves aside to find food on the ground that, unless you knew the bird, you might think it was a much larger bird or perhaps some animal at work in there. It feeds on seeds, insects and berries and, on the whole, is considered a beneficial bird.

The Towhee nests on or close to the ground. There are 4 to 6 eggs in a clutch and usually two broods are raised. The second brood frequently comes so late that parents are seen feeding young when it is time for all of them to pack up and be off on the southward migration to avoid the ice and snow of a northern Winter. Sometimes a Towhee will remain through the snows of a northern Winter, but most of our Towhees prefer to move below the Mason-Dixon line when the leaves begin to whirl down with the Autumn winds. If you learn to know this Towhee or the much similar Spotted Towhee of the West, it will be easy to identify other Towhees like the Green-tailed Towhee or the Brown Towhee of the Southwest because of a family likeness in appearance and habits.

RED-WINGED BLACKBIRD

(About 8½ inches)

Here's another common bird that is easy to know. All you have to do is to go to a swamp or marsh and look for a black bird with "red wings". Actually only a small part of the wing is red, but it is enough to identify the bird and give it the name it bears. The bright color is really a shoulder-patch and if you look closely you will see that it is a two-color patch on the grown males. There is an area of deep orange-red fringed by a band of yellowish-red or buff. Anyway, the bright patch stands out against the general black plumage of the male, especially when it is flying or when, from a perch on a cattail or buttonbush, it half-spreads its wings as it gives its cheerful and challenging Spring song of "Kon-keree!" The females and young are dusky striped birds and the gaudy male himself loses much of his lustre in Winter, but the red shoulder-patch always shows when the bird flies. The nest is usually a few feet above water in a low bush, reeds or patch of grass. Some Red-wings stay in the North all year but most of them go South in the Winter.

FLICKER

(About 13 inches)

This is a common bird of many different local names: Flicker, High-hole, Yellow-hammer, Golden-winged Woodpecker, Yaffle, Wicky-up and more. It is a Summer resident over much of North America and one that can hardly escape notice if you keep your eyes and ears open outdoors because it is a good-sized bird of bright colors, is often on the move over cleared ground and utters loud cries from time to time, including the piercing "flickering" call from which it derives its official name. It's an odd as well as a beautiful bird. It's a woodpecker that spends most of its time on the ground, largely for the purpose of eating ants. Often it flies up from the grass and goes off in strong bounding flight, showing the "gold" in its wings and a good-sized patch of white on its rump. The Flicker is a rich tan-brown in general color, with a small red patch at the back of its head and a black crescent on its breast. It also has dark cross-streaks on its back and many black spots on its underparts. It has a variety of loud and repeated calls that give notice of its presence in any neighborhood. It nests in a hole in a tree and if one is on the nest and you knock on the tree below, the Flicker will stick its head out of the hole to see who is "knocking at the door".

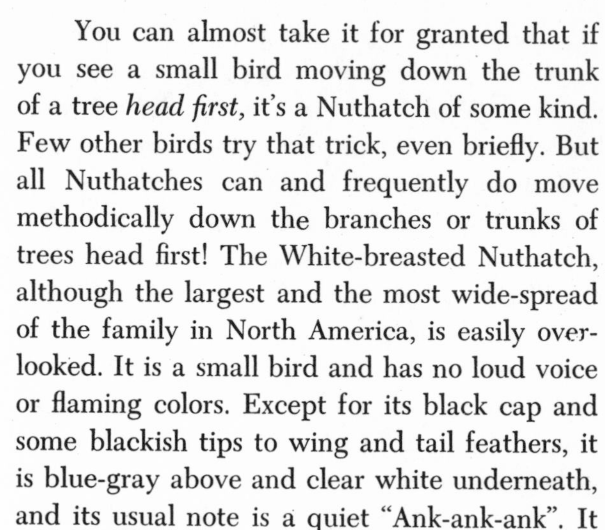

WHITE-BREASTED NUTHATCH

(About 5½ inches)

You can almost take it for granted that if you see a small bird moving down the trunk of a tree *head first*, it's a Nuthatch of some kind. Few other birds try that trick, even briefly. But all Nuthatches can and frequently do move methodically down the branches or trunks of trees head first! The White-breasted Nuthatch, although the largest and the most wide-spread of the family in North America, is easily overlooked. It is a small bird and has no loud voice or flaming colors. Except for its black cap and some blackish tips to wing and tail feathers, it is blue-gray above and clear white underneath, and its usual note is a quiet "Ank-ank-ank". It will eat nuts and seeds but it lives largely on insects that it finds in the bark of trees. It often travels in company with Downy Woodpeckers and Black-capped Chickadees and, being a permanent resident even in cold regions, it will join with them in eating suet if you tie it to a dooryard tree in Winter. Once you have come to know the White-breasted Nuthatch, you will soon learn to know the Red-breasted, the Brown-headed or the Pygmy Nuthatch, depending upon where you live in the United States or Canada.

BLACK-CAPPED CHICKADEE

(About 5 inches)

It's too bad that all birds aren't as polite as the Black-capped Chickadee that identifies itself by saying cheerfully "Chickadee-chickadee-chickadee-dee-dee". It has another "peto" call or song but it's the "chickadee" or simply "dee-de-dee" that is most frequently heard as the little bird bustles about its business of dining on small seeds, insects and insect eggs that it finds in the bark or on the twigs and leaves of shrubs and trees. There are other small birds of black and white pattern but this one you will know by its black bib as well as its black cap, the bib being tucked neatly under its chin where a good bib should be placed. It travels in groups except in the nesting season and the group is often escorted by one or more Downy Woodpeckers or White-breasted Nuthatches. The Chickadee is a permanent resident over most of North America and is common around dooryards and farmlands in Winter, but it retreats to the woods in the warm months where it nests in holes in trees. If you put out suet or peanuts or sunflower seeds—or even a hard crust of bread—in Winter, you will not have to wait long for a grateful group of Chickadees to come to dine regularly.

BOBOLINK

(About 7 inches)

For a good description of the male Bobolink we can turn to William Cullen Bryant and a poem that many children learn in school:

Robert of Lincoln is gayly dressed,
Wearing a bright black wedding coat;
White are his shoulders and white his crest,
Hear him call in his merry note:
Bob-o-link, bob-o-link,
Spink, spank, spink;
Look what a nice new coat is mine,
Sure there was never a bird so fine.
Chee, chee, chee.

Robert of Lincoln's Quaker wife,
Pretty and quiet, with plain brown wings,
Passing at home a patient life,
Broods in the grass while her husband sings:
Bob-o-link, bob-o-link,
Spink, spank, spink;
Brood, kind creature; you need not fear
Thieves and robbers while I am here.
Chee, chee, chee.

The Bobolink, which is a Summer resident of the lush meadows of hay or clover over most of the United States and southern Canada, differs from most birds in that it wears its brightest colors on its back. There are many birds that are dark in color above and clear white below, but the bubbling Bobolink is just the opposite; black below and white—in good part—above. It has a variety of liquid call notes and it pours out a perfect shower of bubbling mélody as it flutters upward from the grass in which is hidden its "plain brown wife" on the nest of speckled eggs. The "white cloak" of the handsome male is thrown over its shoulders and down its back in swaggering fashion, but the patch that begins at the back of the head and runs down the neck is a rich cream buff. In late Summer the male changes this "wedding garment" for the streaked yellow-brown costume of the female and young of the year. Then there is a great gathering of the Bobolink clan and they begin the long Autumn migration to Brazil and the Argentine where they spend the Winter. On this 8,000-mile journey all they utter is a metallic "chink" that is, however, so distinctive that, once you know it, you can tell on clear Autumn nights that Bobolinks are on their way to the pampas of South America by the scattered "chinks" that drop down through darkness. Or you may hear the "chinks" by day and catch sight of the Bobolinks high overhead, hurrying southward. But back they come to our meadows in May and once again Robert of Lincoln, quivering with joy, flutters aloft in the sunlight and pours the bubbling melody of his love song over the green grassland that is to be the Summer home of a happy family of Bobolinks.

GRACKLE

(About 12½ inches)

Roughly speaking, Grackles are large Blackbirds with extra long tails. Through all but the coldest months of the year they are spread over most of central and eastern North America in large numbers that are often grouped in great noisy flocks. The experts say there are two species of Grackle that confuse the ordinary observer; the Purple and the Bronzed Grackle. They are approximately the same size. They look much alike. They are difficult to tell apart except when seen fairly close up and in a good light. Their ranges overlap and the species interbreed, producing offspring that even the experts often have trouble classifying.

Let us solve this difficulty by calling these birds—both species—just Grackle. The common (Purple or Bronze) Grackle has a long diamond-shaped tail, much broader in the middle than at either end. That's how you will know the Grackle when you see it walking around on the ground in company with other blackish birds such as Starlings, Cowbirds, Rusty Blackbirds and Red-winged Blackbirds. The Grackles will be noticeably larger than any of these others and, in the sunlight, will have more of a sheen on their plumage. They may be a shining purple around the head and shoulders or the whole back may be a shimmering bronze color. But at any time and in any light, their long tails will make it plain that they are Grackles. Sometimes these tails may be V-shaped, with a "crease" down the center. It is said that the males in Spring "crease" their tails as part of the display in courting the female.

The voice of the Grackle sounds like the name. It's a cross between a creaky "chuck" and a prolonged loud crackle. Except when nesting, they go around in flocks and flood a neighborhood from ground level to treetop, and when hundreds of these birds descend on a lawn or an open field to feed, the din is deafening. They will eat almost anything, including the eggs and young of smaller birds. They do some good by eating harmful insects but they are so numerous in many localities that they are regarded as annoyances if not downright pests. There may be thousands of birds in a single flock in Autumn when the Grackles get together before their southward migration. The migration merely consists in a movement of the birds from southern Canada and the northern part of the United States to the warmer area below the Mason-Dixon line. Some few birds may remain in the North through the Winter but on the whole they do not like snow and ice. As the snow disappears in Spring, the Grackles move northward again and take possession of the country. They like to nest in a pine tree and fairly high above the ground. There are 4 to 6 eggs in a clutch and one brood a year is the rule.

In addition to these common Grackles there is the Boat-tailed Grackle of the Southeast and the Great-tailed Grackle of the Southwest. They are much larger birds with deeply V-shaped tails and there is no danger of confusing them with the ordinary Grackles that are spread so widely and so noisily over this country.

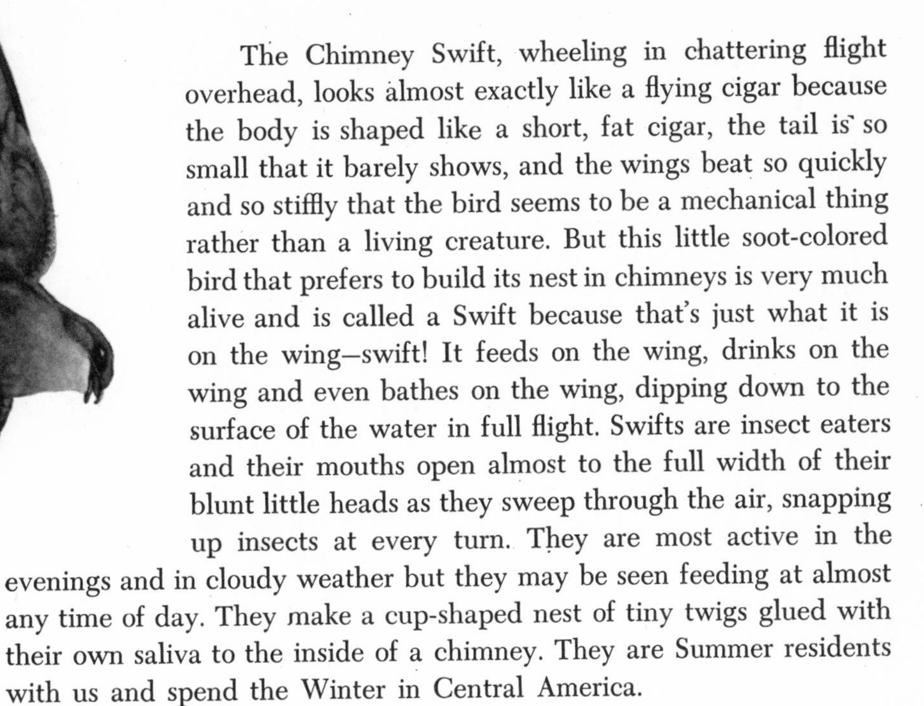

CHIMNEY SWIFT

(About 5½ inches)

The Chimney Swift, wheeling in chattering flight overhead, looks almost exactly like a flying cigar because the body is shaped like a short, fat cigar, the tail is so small that it barely shows, and the wings beat so quickly and so stiffly that the bird seems to be a mechanical thing rather than a living creature. But this little soot-colored bird that prefers to build its nest in chimneys is very much alive and is called a Swift because that's just what it is on the wing—swift! It feeds on the wing, drinks on the wing and even bathes on the wing, dipping down to the surface of the water in full flight. Swifts are insect eaters and their mouths open almost to the full width of their blunt little heads as they sweep through the air, snapping up insects at every turn. They are most active in the evenings and in cloudy weather but they may be seen feeding at almost any time of day. They make a cup-shaped nest of tiny twigs glued with their own saliva to the inside of a chimney. They are Summer residents with us and spend the Winter in Central America.

BARN SWALLOW

(About 7 inches)

Probably the most abundant, the most familiar and the most beautiful of our native Swallows is the Barn Swallow. It is truly a deserted farm building that doesn't have a Barn Swallow's nest in it. Under the eaves, along the beams, or high up on an inner wall of barn, silo, ice house, woodshed or wagon house, these birds plaster their nests of mud and grass, lay their 3 to 6 eggs and rear their young. The only other native swallow with which it might be confused is the Cliff Swallow, but from the Cliff Swallow as well as all others it may be known by its deeply forked tail with the spines of the two outer feathers sticking out like stiff wires. All Swallows are insect eaters, catching their prey on the wing in the chattering, sweeping, graceful flight with which we all are familiar. There are many species in this country, all of them beneficial and beautiful birds. When you know the Barn Swallow, you can begin to know the others by watching to see how the less familiar ones differ from the lovely Barn Swallow that is always on the wing around our farmyards in the Summer. They raise two broods with us and then fly off swiftly to spend the Winter in South America.

PHOEBE

(About 7 inches)

The Phoebe is probably the most common Flycatcher over the eastern half of North America. Flycatchers—and there are numerous species in different parts of the country—usually dart from a perch to snap up insects in the air and then return to a perch, often the same perch from which they started. It is frequently difficult to know one Flycatcher from another because of similarity in size, color and general markings, but happily their songs or call notes are quite different and the Phoebe is among those easy to identify by voice. Its regular and frequently repeated double note is "Phee-bee, phee-bee," from which it derives its name. It is a small bird that is grayish-brown above, growing darker on the head, and white underneath. It has the habit of wagging its tail while perched. It likes to build in and around houses, barns and farm buildings of any kind. Any projection under cover will do as a support for its nest. It has no eye ring or wing bars or outstanding mark of any kind. It is dull-colored but friendly and, if you are in doubt about its identity, it will speak up and name itself.

KINGBIRD

(Nearly 9 inches)

The flashing Kingbird is one of the larger and more noisy members of the Flycatcher family. It is dark gray above, clear white underneath and it has a white band across the tip of its tail. This band is quite easy to spot as the bird flies overhead in pursuit of insects or for the purpose of heckling the larger birds of the neighborhood, a habit that gives the Kingbird its common name. It perches on the topmost limb of small trees and launches itself with a chattering cry to drive off any Crow or Hawk that happens to sail into sight. It is a bird of the open country and is usually found halfway between the farmhouse and the woods. It likes orchards and it nests happily in the topmost branches of small trees or tall shrubs. Since insects are common over ponds, the Kingbird will sometimes pursue insects down to the surface of the water and look almost like a Kingfisher plunging for fish. Like the other Flycatchers, it heads southward in Autumn. The Kingbird is alert and courageous and if you see a small bird impudently making passes at a Hawk and uttering shrill cries, it probably will be a Kingbird.

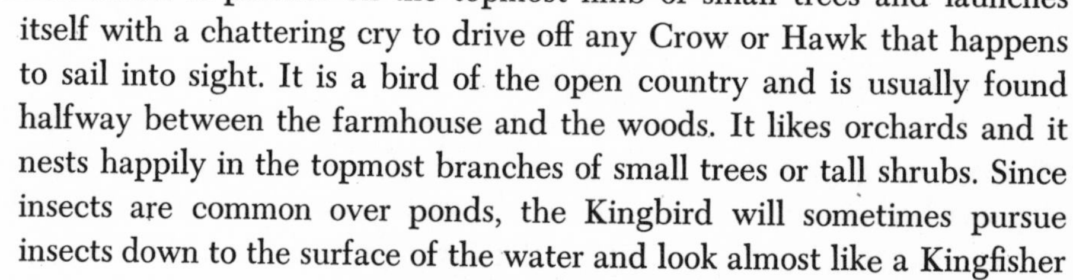

BELTED KINGFISHER

(About 13 inches)

The Belted Kingfisher is a good-sized blue and white bird that flies along ponds, streams, rivers and lakes with a rattling cry and occasionally dives headlong into the water in pursuit of some small fish. If it is successful in its plunge, you will see the fish in its bill when the Kingfisher comes up and you will hear a rattle of triumph as the bird flies off with its prey. The Kingfisher is larger than a Robin and has a rough dark crest that sticks up like hair that the bird neglected to comb. The male is blue-gray above and clear white underneath except for a broad band of blue-gray that runs from the bird's shoulders across its breast. The female is the same except for an extra chestnut-rufous band that runs below the blue-gray band across its breast and down its flanks. Kingfishers are odd birds in that the female has more color than the male and they are odd in another way, too. They nest in holes in banks, either along water or as near water as possible. The birds tunnel into the banks—sometimes a distance of ten feet or more—and lay their 5 to 8 eggs at the inner ends of the tunnels. Kingfishers are common residents all over North America and will spend the Winter as far north as they can find open water on ponds, lakes and rivers.

The only other bird with which the Kingfisher might be confused is the Blue Jay and there are decided differences, beginning with the bill, which is conspicuously long and heavy in the Kingfisher. The Blue Jay has a neat crest, white wing bars, a flashy tail and graceful lines. The Kingfisher has a raggedy crest, no wing bars, a short tail, short legs and a generally chunky or stubby appearance. The Kingfisher is almost invariably found perched above or flying along a body of water, whereas the Blue Jay is a bird of hill and dale, of suburban lawns, of the open fields and the wooded hillsides.

There is a lovely Greek legend about the origin of Kingfishers. The story is that beautiful Halcyone, daughter of Aeolus, King of the Winds, married the young and handsome Ceyx, King of Trachinia, and that Ceyx shortly thereafter went on a voyage and was drowned. Not knowing this and longing for the return of her husband, Halcyone walked the seashore each day until one morning the waves washed her husband's body to her feet. She was so overcome with sorrow that she threw herself into the sea. But as she did so she and her dead husband were changed into Kingfishers and flew off happily together. Now we refer to bright sunlit days on the water as "halcyon days" because of a Greek legend.

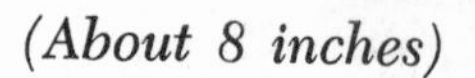

COWBIRD

(About 8 inches)

There are many persons who insist that the Cowbird is a villain but the first thing to do is to identify the alleged culprit and then take up the case of the crime charged against it. The Cowbird is the smallest of our native Blackbirds. The male is a shining black except for its head, which is a rich brown when seen in a good light. The female and young are gray-brown, just about the size and somewhat the same color as female and young Starlings but there is little difficulty in telling them apart. The Starlings are chunkier birds with long bills and short tails. The Cowbirds have short conical bills like English Sparrows, are slimmer than Starlings and have what you might call a tail of standard size. Female and young Red-winged Blackbirds are dark brown but they are heavily streaked, so there is no danger of confusing them with the unstreaked female or young Cowbirds. Where mixed Blackbirds are walking about in flocks and feeding together, the Cowbirds will be the smaller, round-headed, short-billed birds at all times. The Cowbird has a pleasantly liquid "glug-glug" call note but the Spring song of the male is a most ridiculous performance, a rasping gurgle delivered with swelling throat and half-spread wings and tail as though the bird were choking in agony. It's a combination of bubbles and squeaks on a sliding scale and anything but musical.

Now we come to the high crime charged against the Cowbird, which is that they never build nests of their own but foist their offspring on other birds. Like the European Cuckoo, the female Cowbird sneaks through trees and shrubbery until she finds a suitable nest with eggs in it and the owner absent. Then the female Cowbird deposits an egg in the nest and hurriedly departs, leaving the egg to be hatched and the young bird to be reared by the real owner of the nest, usually a smaller bird than the Cowbird. Thus the young Cowbird, at hatching or shortly thereafter, is the biggest and strongest of the youngsters and soon overwhelms the other young birds in the nest. It is a rare thing for any young except the Cowbird fledgling to survive in a group like this. It is almost certain that every Cowbird that you see was hatched and reared at the cost of a whole brood of some smaller bird and it is astonishing what a wide variety of victims the female Cowbird picks out when she goes about laying eggs. It is said that more than a hundred different kinds of birds have been swindled in this manner by the Cowbird but their favorite victims seem to be the Warbler family, Phoebes, Song Sparrows and Red-eye Vireos. Sometimes the real owner of the nest will discover the swindle and do something about it. Robins have been known to notice the Cowbird eggs in their nests and destroy them. Yellow Warblers sometimes note the strange egg with their own, abandon the whole clutch, and build another nest atop the first one in which to lay other eggs. But, alas, sometimes the Cowbird comes around to lay another foreign egg in the second-story nest, too. Or even a third-story nest.

RED-EYED VIREO

(About 6 inches)

The Vireos in North America are a group of about a dozen species of small and, for the most part, greenish-yellow birds that are seen going over the branches, twigs and leaves of shrubs and trees in more or less deliberate and methodical search for insects. They are not colorful or fluttery birds. The Yellow-throated Vireo is a bird of the upper branches of trees and the White-eyed Vireo is a haunter of the thickets, hedgerows and alder swamps, but the abundant and cheerful Red-eyed Vireo hunts high and low by hill and dale all over the United States and southern Canada, moving steadily along the branches and among the leaves of shrubs and trees and singing a pleasant but slightly monotonous song all the while. It seems to be saying "I see you—you see me—I see you—so what?" The Red-eyed Vireo is more greenish than yellow above, clear white below, and has a darkish gray cap beneath which is a white eye stripe outlined in black above. The deliberate movements, the gray cap of this greenish bird and its persistent song through the Summer are the best marks by which to identify it. Once you have come to know the Red-eyed Vireo, it will be easier for you to make the acquaintance of the other and less familiar and abundant members of the family.

WOOD THRUSH

(About 8 inches)

This is probably the most abundant and the most familiar of our Thrushes—except the Robin and the Bluebird, which are members of the Thrush family—east of the Mississippi River. Like most members of the family, this is a bird of the woodlands and a beautiful singer. But the Wood Thrush is a little more friendly than some of its shy relatives and often inhabits suburban lawns and builds its nest in cultivated shrubbery or shade trees. It is smaller than a Robin, generally brownish above and white beneath, with a heavily spotted breast. Viewed close up, the bright reddish-brown of its head gradually fades into the olive-brown of its tail. Some of the brownish Thrushes are difficult to tell apart but the heavy dots on the white breast of the Wood Thrush are a good mark, as is the reddish head. Since it often comes on lawns and readily takes to a bird bath, it is easier to have a good view of it than of the more timid wood-haunting species. Finally there is the song, which is lovely and liquid, a two-part song that is repeated again and again.

HERMIT THRUSH

(About 7 inches)

You have to go to the woods to see or hear this bird, and the chances are that you will hear it before you see it. In fact, you may have a hard time finding it even when you hear it, because it is a shy bird that keeps flitting away through the trees and the undergrowth when intruders appear in its shady domain. We have in temperate North America some seven brownish-backed Thrushes with spotted breasts and it isn't always easy to know them apart. It takes time to discover the little differences among them in color, spotting and shading. And it may take some traveling, too, because the Olive-backed Thrush of the East is practically the same bird as the Russet-backed Thrush of the West, just as the Willow Thrush of the West is merely a distant twin of the eastern Veery.

The Veery is the reddish-backed Thrush with little spotting on its breast and a rippling, ringing song that spirals downward. Its haunt is the low wet woods or the shadier part of a swamp. The Wood Thrush is the one with the large and numerous blackish spots on its breast and a reddish color on its head that fades to brownish-olive toward its tail. The Hermit Thrush shading runs just the opposite way—it is olive-brownish on its head and shades to reddish on the tail. Its breast spots are not as numerous or as large as those of the Wood Thrush, and it has a habit of flicking its tail every now and then when it is perched or standing still on the ground. The Wood Thrush, of course, comes readily to our lawns and nests in our dooryard shrubbery or shade trees. And its clear, sweet but unvaried song beginning "Ee-o-lee" is a definite distinguishing mark even when the singer is unseen. The song of the Hermit Thrush is something else. It has a dream-like quality. It begins gently and floats upward "like clouds of incense ascending" The notes are liquid and delightful with just the hint of a bell tone to some of them. The bird has several phrases and sings in different keys in gentle succession, but it is never the exact same song that the bird sang before. There is just enough variation to give the impression that it is all improvised, a bird pouring out its heart in melody. In the shadier parts of the woods it may be heard singing at any time of day; but most of its singing is done at dawn or in the hush of evening. It is wonderful to hear it in the woods at twilight—a lovely, liquid, dreamy, ethereal song floating upward through the darkening woods.

The Hermit Thrush spends much of its time feeding on the floor of the woods, turning over dead leaves in search of insects or their eggs or grubs. It nests on the ground or close to it. It often ventures out into clearings or along the edge of the woods to build its nest, which usually is made of mosses, grasses and pine needles. There are usually 4 greenish-blue eggs in the cup-shaped nest and there may be two or more broods a season. It is the last of our Thrushes to retreat before oncoming snow when the northern Winter approaches and it is the first of the family to slip northward again in Spring. It has a harsh call note that almost grates on the ear, but it's always good to hear it because, in the woods of Spring and Summer, it means that the Hermit Thrush is there and sooner or later we will enjoy its marvelous melodies.

VEERY

(About 7 inches)

The Veery is a Summer resident of the greater part of North America and a persistently vocal one in a nice way. It is easily found and easily recognized. It is the reddest or, at least, the tawniest of our brownish-backed Thrushes with spotted breasts. It has fewer and lighter spots on its breast than the others in the group. It is the most water-loving of the family. It loves swamps or low wet woods or even wet meadows that are beginning to be overrun by alders, willows, gray birches and viburnums. It has a lyrical, rippling, circling song that spirals downward and easily marks it apart from any of its group except the Willow Thrush of the West. Anything that is said of the Veery or its song might just as well apply to the Willow Thrush. Only the expert ornithologist would know one of these birds from the other by the slight difference in shading. To the ordinary observer the only difference is that the Veery is found over the central and eastern half of the country and the Willow Thrush is a Summer resident of the Northwest. For convenience, here we can stick to the Veery. It is far more widespread over the country. To find the Veery, go to the edge of any swamp from May to July and listen. Soon you will hear a flute-like rippling series of notes that begin high and spiral downward. That will be the Veery. But seeing the bird may be more difficult, and may take some time.

MAGPIE

(About 20 inches)

There never is any question about the identity of a Magpie if you see one. There is no other bird like it, except another species of Magpie. In this case our bird is the common Black-billed or American Magpie that may be found anywhere from Texas to Alaska in a broad belt of country extending from the foothills of the Rockies as far east as Kansas and Nebraska. There is another smaller species, the Yellow-billed Magpie, that is found in the valleys of central California. But wherever they are found, Magpies are large and conspicuous birds with glistening black heads, much black and white on wings and body, and enormous tails that stream out behind them when they fly. Except in the breeding season, they travel about in flocks like Crows, to whom they are related, but they are bolder than Crows when it comes to descending upon barnyards and dooryards and kitchen gardens. The Magpie has all the curiosity, impudence and knavish tricks of the Blue Jay—another of its relatives, by the way—and will steal practically anything it can carry off. It makes a huge nest of mud and twigs that is roofed over and entered from the sides. The nest is usually placed in a thorn bush to make it hard for any enemy to get near it. Magpies are regarded as permanent residents over much of their range but some of the more northerly residents may take southern trips in Winter.

WHITE-CROWNED SPARROW

(About 7 inches)

Many persons never bother to look at Sparrows, thinking that they are all little brownish birds of no particular distinction. The truth is that we have a wonderful assortment of Sparrows in North America and many of them are useful, handsome and melodious birds. They are small, to be sure. And most of them are brownish above and lighter below, with or without streaks on their breasts. But if you look closely you will see that there are many Sparrows in your neighborhood that differ very much in their markings, and if you hear them sing you will immediately note the wide differences in their songs. The White-Crowned Sparrow, which is found all over temperate North America either as a Summer resident or a seasonal migrant, is a really handsome bird with an aristocratic air about it. It is much more common in the West than it is in the East. There are slight differences in some of their markings and the experts divide them into "races" with added names such as "Gambel's Sparrow" and "Nuttall's Sparrow", but this need not concern beginners.

WHITE-THROATED SPARROW

(About 6¾ inches)

This is the only bird that might be confused with the White-crowned Sparrow because it is almost the same size and has its head similarly marked with brilliant black and white stripes, but the White-throated Sparrow is well named and its white bib tucked under its chin stands out clearly against the rather dull gray of its breast. Furthermore, the White-throated Sparrow has a yellow spot where the white eye-line runs into the bill. The yellow spot is brighter in Spring than in the Fall but at almost any time of year there is enough yellow there to be noticeable. The adult "White-throats", as they are commonly called, have unstreaked gray breasts like the slightly larger White-crowned Sparrows, but young "White-throats" generally have obscure streakings on the breast and flanks in the Autumn. The White-throated Sparrow is much more common in the eastern part of North America than the White-crowned Sparrow. It is known in some regions as the "Peabody bird" because of its song in which it is supposed to say: "Old Sam Peabody, Peabody, Peabody" Like the White-crowned Sparrow, it breeds in Canada and the higher ground of the northern United States, and is a common roadside bird on migration.

CHIPPING SPARROW

(About 5¼ inches)

The abundant and friendly little "Chippy", found all over North America in the warmer months, is another of the clear-breasted Sparrows and one of the smallest members of this large family. It wears a dark reddish-chestnut cap below which is a clear white line fringed along the lower edge by a thinner black line running through the eye to the base of the little dark conical bill. Its small size and the clearly marked and neat pattern of its "side face" help to distinguish the Chipping Sparrow from some of the other small and clear-breasted Sparrows. Another distinguishing mark is its song (if you can call it that), which is a monotonous succession of metallic-sounding "chips" strung together so rapidly that it almost amounts to a trill. The Chipping Sparrow usually is seen on the ground but often it goes aloft to a perch to deliver this song. It certainly isn't musical but it is a loud song for such a small bird.

The Chipping Sparrow is a familiar dooryard denizen all across the country. It hops about lawns, feeding on grass seed and weed seed. It also gobbles up many insects "in season" and is said to be an efficient destroyer of gipsy moths, canker worms, grasshoppers and weevils. On migration the Chipping Sparrow may be found almost anywhere but in the breeding season it makes itself at home on open ground and cleared land. It is not usually found in the woods or even in meadows where the grass is thick and high. It likes pasture lands that cattle have grazed close and it will be found along the roadsides and around barnyards and gardens. But most of all it likes a well-kept lawn and the company of human beings. It builds readily in dooryards, often in vines climbing over porches. It places its neat but frail nests anywhere from just off the ground to fairly high in a tree and the little cradle of woven grasses is usually lined with hair from a horse's tail. With tractors replacing horses on so many farms, the Chipping Sparrow may soon encounter a shortage of building material. There are 3 to 5 eggs in a clutch and there may be one or two broods a season. The female does most of the brooding of the eggs while the male does the foraging and brings food to the female on the nest.

The Cowbird finds the Chipping Sparrow an easy victim of its trick of depositing a Cowbird egg in another nest and letting a foster-parent hatch and rear the Cowbird youngster. It's funny to see a little Chipping Sparrow feeding a much larger clamoring young Cowbird in July or August. But the Chipping Sparrow is no exception among small birds in that way. It is always interesting when young Cowbirds are heard squealing in Summer to wait around to find out just what kind of bird has been victimized. The assortment of victims is astonishing.

As soon as cold weather creeps over Canada and the northern section of the United States, the Chipping Sparrows of that region begin a retreat toward the South. There is a concentration of these birds below the Mason-Dixon Line in Winter and they are in no particular hurry to go back north again, either. It isn't until warm weather has really arrived "up North" that the Chipping Sparrow will be found back on the front lawn again in our Northern States and Canada.

SLATE-COLORED JUNCO

(About 6¼ inches)

Look for the Junco in cold weather. It is a bird of the North and for most of us it is a Winter visitor to our dooryards. It breeds in Canada and on high ground in our Northern States. On its breeding range it is a bird of lonely pastures, of cool woods, of stark country where tree growth is stunted and barren ground stretches away toward the Arctic Circle. But about the time of the first frost, the Juncos come drifting down daintily all over the United States and remain with us until the call of Spring sends them back to their breeding range again. Many persons call them "Snowbirds", which is a good name for them because they come to us for the colder months, are common sights around a snow-covered dooryard and, with much white in their plumage, are as light as snowflakes on the wing.

There are half a dozen species of Junco to be found at some season in some parts of the United States but the Slate-colored Junco is by all odds the most abundant and the most widespread over the United States and Canada in general. Once you learn to know the Slate-colored Junco, you can keep your eyes open for the other species, especially if you live in the West where they are more frequently to be found. In the East, any Junco except a Slate-colored Junco is a rarity. It is well-named, being slate-colored above and a soft grayish-white below, but the mark that most easily catches the eye is the flashing of the white outer tail feathers as the bird flits away from the observer. The bird also has a light-colored bill and a characteristic "tsip" that sometimes is extended into a weak buzz or trill as it feeds or flits about the shrubbery, but look for a little dark gray bird that goes off in short flights with a display of white outer tail feathers and that will be the Junco.

Often a flock of Juncos will start scattering and flitting away almost from under your feet, for they are not particularly shy and they spend most of their time on the ground, feeding in our dooryards, our barnyards, our shorn harvest fields and the weed patches in neglected corners. They flood the country roadsides and every passing person or vehicle sets them flitting along the ground with a great display of white outer tail feathers. They are found in the woods, too. In fact, Juncos are everywhere in Winter and nowhere in Summer—or, at least, not where most of us can see them. To find the Junco on its breeding range we would have to go to Canada or the cool woodlands of the high ground of our Northern States. There in Summer we might hear the song of the Slate-colored Junco, a monotonous trill somewhat like and not much more musical than the "song" of the Chipping Sparrow, and there on or a little above the ground we might find the nest of the "Snowbird" with 4 to 6 eggs in it any time from May to July. But if you can't visit its breeding grounds, just wait for Autumn and with the falling of the leaves, the Junco will be back in your dooryard. If you put out seeds and water for them, they will be regular visitors at your feeding station. Cold weather and snow never seem to bother them at all, and they are cheerful and delightful visitors to have for the Winter.

CACTUS WREN

(About 8 inches)

Those who know Wrens in other parts of the country will be surprised if they ever come upon the Cactus Wren of the Southwest. It is the giant of the Wren family in this country and so shaped and marked that it looks more like a small Thrasher than it does a large Wren. But it is a true Wren that may be found almost anywhere in the cactus country pouring out its rackety-rax song all day and, for that matter, almost all year. It perches atop some cactus plant where it can be easily seen when singing. It is a brown color above and white below, with many numerous heavy spots on its throat and breast. It has a clearly defined white eye-line and it shows much white spotting in its outer tail feathers when it flies. It is famous for its large round nest with a tunnel entrance that it builds of plant fibers and lines with bird feathers. It is usually placed in a cactus plant in such a way that the thorns defy marauders to attack the premises. Not all the nests have eggs in them. There are extra nests that perhaps are built as decoys. It is said that, after the breeding season, Cactus Wrens may take refuge in these nests during rainstorms or spells of cold, windy weather.

BROWN CREEPER

(About 5½ inches)

This is one of the easiest birds to overlook. It is about the size and general color of a small Sparrow—brown on its back and white underneath—but it doesn't act or live like any of the Sparrows. It is rarely if ever seen on the ground. It goes about with Chickadees, Woodpeckers and Nuthatches and makes a living the way they do. It creeps up tree trunks, often in a spiral, beginning at the base of the tree and winding its way up out of sight. It searches for insects, insect eggs and larva in the crevices of the bark. When it has worked its way as high up as it cares to go on one tree, it drops off and flies down to the base of another tree to work its way up again. It clings so close to the tree and goes over the bark so thoroughly that it looks almost like a brown mouse climbing a tree. It has a beady "screeping" note that it sometimes utters as it winds its way up a tree trunk. We see it mostly in cold weather when it comes around with the Chickadees, Nuthatches and Kinglets—a little brown bird with a curved bill that creeps spirally up the trunks of trees.

MOURNING DOVE

(About 12 inches)

The Mourning Dove, shaped like a small thin Pigeon, is a rich tan-brown in general color, with some black spots on its back, glints of pink, blue and chocolate shading here and there, and a long pointed tail with white showing plainly on the outer feathers as the bird rises from the ground and flies off. It is almost an exact copy of the much larger Passenger Pigeon that once covered this country's skyways in enormous flocks and is now extinct, the victim of almost incredible slaughter by relentless market hunters. There were few or no game laws in many sections of the country when Passenger Pigeons were being shot, trapped, netted or actually clubbed down from tree branches by the millions each year, and the few game laws enacted were rarely enforced. So the Passenger Pigeon was harried to extinction in a land where its great flocks once darkened the skies. Conditions are much different now and though the Mourning Dove is considered a game bird and is much shot at in the hunting season, especially in the South where the flocks are numerous and widespread in Autumn and Winter, it seems to be holding its own across the country.

The Mourning Dove is commonly a ground feeder, walking about like a domestic Pigeon picking up food. It consumes many weed seeds and grass seeds and you will often find Mourning Doves coming to the grain fields for the leavings after the harvesters have come and gone. The birds also come like gleaners to the bare fields of Autumn from which crops of corn, peas, buckwheat and beans have been taken. Often they will be encountered on hard ground or roads surfaced with gravel, picking up the little stones and bits of gravel that are needed in their gizzards to aid digestion. But Mourning Doves often are seen in trees, too, or perched on telephone wires. They are fond of the blue berry of the Sour Gum (or Tupelo, as the tree is called in many sections) and will eat wild berries of various kinds. One of the things that is soon noticed about Mourning Doves is the peculiar noise made by the birds in flying. It has been called a "winnowing sound", for want of any better description. But it will strike any listener almost immediately and it is a sound made by no other bird in flight. Aside from that, the Mourning Dove makes no noise other than its long-drawn, moaning coo that is heard more frequently in the Spring. This is the mournful sound that gives the bird the name of Mourning Dove. On the whole it might be said that the Mourning Dove is one of the most quiet of our birds as the Blue Jay is one of the noisiest.

Sometimes the Mourning Dove will lay its two eggs in a mere depression on the ground but in general it builds a skimpy nest of twigs in a tree or moves into an old nest left by some other bird like the Robin, Brown Thrasher, Mockingbird or Blue Jay. For the first few days the fledglings receive "predigested food" like young Pigeons, reaching into the throats of their fond parents for it, but soon they go on the regular Dove diet of a few worms and berries and many, many seeds and grains.

GOLDEN-CROWNED KINGLET

(About 4 inches)

Kinglets are tiny olive-greenish birds that come to us as Autumn migrants or Winter residents after the Warblers have gone southward, and they leave for cooler regions about the time that the Warblers come back to us in Spring. The Kinglets breed in Canada and high altitudes in the United States. They like to forage in evergreens but they also work over other trees and shrubs and if you see a tiny olive-greenish bird with whitish wing-bars flitting about a bush in Warbler-fashion in cold weather, it probably is a Kinglet. If it has a golden patch running back from its forehead over its head, it will be the Golden-crowned Kinglet. The golden patch is bordered with black and the bird has a distinct white eye-stripe. The Ruby-crowned Kinglet is similar in size, shape and general color, including the wing-bars, but it lacks the golden crown patch and the eye-line. Do not look for any ruby crown by which to identify the Ruby-crowned Kinglet, because that sign is like the red flag on a taximeter; it only goes up when the operator puts it up. The ruby crown is invisible most of the time. It is worn and displayed only by the male on special occasions when it is courting a female or challenging another male. If you see a Kinglet with a golden-crown patch and a distinct eye-line, it must be the Golden-crowned Kinglet. If you see a Kinglet with no crown patch and a side face unmarked except for a tiny white circle around the eye that gives the bird a frightened look, that will be the Ruby-crowned Kinglet. In the Spring before the Kinglets disappear to cooler regions you may—if you are lucky—see the "red flag" of the Ruby-crowned Kinglet and hear its wonderful bubbling song.

BLACK AND WHITE WARBLER

(About 5¼ inches)

Warblers are, for the most part, small and brightly-colored birds of many species that are seen in the United States and Canada as Summer residents or migrants. Many of the species breed in the Canadian forests and winter in Central America or South America and these species are seen in the United States on their migrations to and from their breeding grounds. But there are dozens of species that are Summer residents of the United States and some few species that remain in various sections of the country throughout the year. One of the most widespread of these dainty little birds is the Black and White Warbler, which is sometimes called the Black and White Creeper because of its actions. It does "creep" about the trunks and branches of trees in the manner of the Brown Creeper, but it "creeps" in all directions instead of following the standard upward spiral of the Brown Creeper. There are several other Warblers that are colored black and white—the Blackpoll and the Black-throated Gray Warbler—but those birds have solid black caps whereas this bird's head is streaked.

YELLOW WARBLER

(About 5 inches)

The Yellow Warbler is a Summer resident of practically all of North America to the edge of the Arctic country. It is well named and easily identified, a small bird that seems to be bright yellow all over, for which reason it is often called a "Wild Canary" along with the Goldfinch. But the Goldfinches always have dark wings and tails whereas the Yellow Warbler is completely yellow except that the male has cinnamon-reddish stripes on its under parts. The female has few or no stripes below. Yellow Warblers are found most commonly in rather open country with scattered trees and thickets. They like swamps that include a fair supply of maples, elms, ashes, willows, alders and dogwoods whose leaves and branches they inspect in search of insects on which they dine. The Yellow Warbler has a loud song of the "switch-switch-switchy" type and is one of the most persistent singers of all the Warblers. The female does most of the nest-building, weaving a neat cup-shaped structure of grasses and plant fibers for her 3 to 5 eggs. The nest is usually in some low growth from a foot to ten feet above ground and if the female discovers that a Cowbird has laid an unwanted extra egg in the nest, she may abandon that nest and build another one right on top of it. There is a report of a case where that process was repeated six times; a 6-story Yellow Warbler structure, with a Cowbird's egg in each nest, including the top one! So that attempt to foil the Cowbird was vain.

MYRTLE WARBLER

(About 5½ inches)

The Myrtle Warbler is a blue-gray little bird that, on closer inspection, shows streaks and patches of black, white and shining yellow. The female is duller but most of the distinguishing marks are clear enough to be observed, particularly the yellow rump that is such a mark that the species is sometimes called the Yellow-rumped Warbler. In addition to the yellow on the rump, the Myrtle Warbler has a yellow crown patch and yellow patches on each side of the breast. The bird has a white throat and a black patch across the breast, with the black running down the flanks and breaking up into spots and streaks. It is one of the most abundant Warblers over the central and eastern section of the United States and in the West it is replaced by Audubon's Warbler, which is quite similar in marking except that it has a yellow throat instead of the white throat of the Myrtle Warbler. The bright yellow patches on the crown and breast in Spring plumage may be barely noticeable in the Fall traveling costume but the yellow rump is the identification tag of the bird in any plumage. Myrtle Warblers breed from the Canadian Border area northward to the tree line. They are early arrivals among the Spring migrants, sometimes seeming to fill every bush and tree in the neighborhood.

OVENBIRD

(About 6 inches)

If you go into the woods in May or June you probably will hear from the undergrowth a series of notes sounding something like "teacher-Teacher-TEACHER-TEACHER-TEACHER!", the series rising to a loud climax at the end. If you trace the sound to its source, you will find that it comes from a small olive-greenish bird walking calmly about the ground like a chicken. This is the Ovenbird or Teacher-Bird or Golden-crowned Thrush. It is known by all three names for three good reasons. It is called the Ovenbird because its nest is oven-shaped and the mother bird enters it from the side. It is called the Teacher-Bird because that's what listeners think they hear it saying in emphatic tones. It is called the Golden-crowned Thrush because it looks much like a small Thrush and it has an orange-brown patch running from its forehead back over its crown in the manner of the Golden-crowned Kinglet, except that the Ovenbird's crown is somewhat darker and not so glowing in hue.

The Ovenbird is one of the Warbler family but it is quite unlike most members of that family in appearance and habits. It does not flutter quickly and nervously through the foliage of shrubs and trees in search of its insect food and it is not bright-colored. The general tone of the bird above is olive-greenish except for its orange-brownish crown. Underneath it is white with dark stripes that look like spots placed so close together that they formed streaks. The real mark of distinction about this bird, however, is the solemn way it stalks about the ground while its more brilliant cousins—meaning most of the Warblers—flit through the greenery like so many feathered butterflies. It is almost exclusively a bird of the woods and, except on migration, is rarely encountered in open country. It is a Summer resident of most of the woodlands of central and eastern North America and rather easy to find because of its loud song.

It is much more difficult, however, to locate its curious nest because the Ovenbird takes great pains to hide the structure. It is built on the ground and usually on a slope. It may be at the base of a sapling Hemlock or Juniper or perhaps along the "shoulder" of a wood road. It's a roofed-over structure of grass, bark, plant fibers, dead leaves and other such material and the entrance is on the side so that, when you peer in at the 4 to 6 eggs, it really does seem that they have been tucked away in an oven. If the bird is frightened from the nest, it does not fly off but scurries away like a mouse over the ground.

In September the Ovenbirds begin their Autumn migration southward to Central America and on this trip they are often seen in public parks and patches of shrubbery on suburban lawns, but in the Summer they are birds of the woods and that's where you have to go to see them walking about the forest floors. The only birds with which they might be confused because of similarity in size, shape and habit of walking about the ground in the woods are the Water Thrushes and, if you get a good look, there are differences that are quite easily noted. The Water Thrushes stick fairly close to water; they twitch their tails nervously; they have distinct eye-lines. The Ovenbird has the orange-brown crown patch, no eye-line and may be found anywhere in the woods. But the easiest way is to listen for its "teacher" notes and track down the performer.

REDSTART

(About 5½ inches)

Seen against the light greenery of the Spring woods, the Redstart is like a tiny darting flame. It is a striking combination of black above, white below and flashing patches of brilliant orange-red in its wings and tail. There is also some orange-red on its breasts and flanks but the bright patches in the wings and the tail flare out and catch the eye as the bird flits from one tree or one branchlet to another. It is the most active of our Warblers, forever on the move in quick darts against a green background. The female is much less brilliant. It is rather olive-greenish above where the male is black and its wing, tail, breast and flanks are decorated with yellow where the male wears the brilliant orange-red. The young of the year are like the female and in late Summer and early Autumn, as the birds gather for the southward migration, most of the Redstarts that you will see will be of the less colorful kind, the females and young of the year. But even these females and young attract attention as they flutter about the trees and shrubs because of the yellow patches in their tails. The patches stand out because Redstarts have longish tails for such small birds and they are always spreading them like fans as they dart about in search of insects. But the shining male in Spring is really the Redstart in its glory, a bird of the woods that is as bright as any lily of the field. It is a Summer resident of most of temperate North America and you should be able to find it if you go into the woods and watch for a tiny flash of flame amid the green foliage of the trees.

YELLOWTHROAT

(About 5¼ inches)

This sprightly little bird probably should be called the "Bandit Warbler" because it lurks in the shrubbery and underbrush and pops out suddenly with a black mask over its face. It is olive-greenish above and it shades from a bright yellow on its throat to a pale yellowish wash on the remainder of its under parts, but its attractive and striking feature is the black mask that looks exactly as if the bird had tied it on to take up an outlaw career. The upper edge of the black mask is fringed with a light gray border of varying width in different individuals. The female and young do not have the black mask but the yellow throat that gives them their name is a good guide to their identity. The Yellowthroat is a Summer resident of eastern North America and it likes lowlands that are well watered. It is found in wet meadows, swamps, bushy pastures and roadsides not far from water. It is plentiful along brooks and the fringes of lakes, ponds and rivers. It has a fairly loud chip and a triple-note song that some interpret as "Witchery, witchery, witchery". It is a distinctive song, easily learned, and when you know it you will have no trouble finding Yellowthroats in the thick grasses and the low bushes in May and June.

YELLOW-BREASTED CHAT

(About 7½ inches)

The Chat is an odd bird of striking appearance and astonishing vocal ability. At first glance it might look like an overgrown Yellowthroat because its throat is a brilliant yellow and it is blackish around the face as well as olive-greenish along the remainder of its upper parts. But the blackish tinge running back from the bill a brief distance over the cheeks and crown of the bird is lightened by a white line over the eye, a white circle around the eye and a short white line on each side of its chin. It doesn't have the "masked" look of the Yellowthroat and it is a much larger bird. Furthermore, the Yellowthroat keeps repeating "Witchery, witchery, witchery" to identify itself whereas the Chat gives off an astonishing and bewildering variety of whistles, squeaks, chuckles, bubbles, and squawks. Like the Catbird, Mockingbird, and Starling, it can imitate all the birds of the neighborhood, but the Mockingbird and Starling do it in the open while the Catbird does it from a bush and the Chat usually does it from some hidden nook in a tangle of catbriar. A Chat nearby in a thicket can make a noise like a dog barking at a distance. It is a feathered ventriloquist and it seems to take delight in tricking listeners into looking at the wrong places for the source of those strange sounds. It can caw like a crow, meow like a cat, croak like a Cuckoo, scold like a Blue Jay, whistle like an Oriole and chuck like a Red-winged Blackbird. And it plays hide-and-seek with anyone who tries to locate it in a jungle of thickly clustered low trees and high bushes.

Look for the Chat in wet meadows that are running wild, with bushes and saplings cluttering it up and blackberry vines catching the foot to make it harder going for any invader of the Chat's domain. It is a Summer resident of the eastern United States and the Ontario section of Canada and it will advertise its appearance when it has settled in any locality for the season. It is not a bird of the woods nor a bird of cultivated land, but lives in between, favoring fields that once were cleared and cultivated but have escaped from bondage to the plow, harrow, mowing machine, and bush-hook to sprout gray birches, junipers, viburnums, dogwoods, black alders, gray alders, dogwoods, sumachs, bayberry bushes and assorted saplings all over the place. Where there is a leafy tangle of young trees, vines, and bushes on low ground or a well-watered hillside, there you will find the Chat—and hear it too. Sometimes it will give a vocal performance from a perch in the open and every so often in its enthusiasm it will let go with a bubbling roulade of melody in flight over its nest in the breeding season.

YELLOW-HEADED BLACKBIRD

(About 10 inches)

To see the Yellow-headed Blackbird is to know it and to name it is to describe it. But you have to live where it is a Summer resident or along its migration route to see it. It is distinctly a bird of the western part of North America, from the Great Plains to the Pacific Coast. Of course, birds have wings and can wander widely, but a Yellow-headed Blackbird is an uncommon sight east of the Mississippi River. In addition to the bright yellow head and vest that gives the bird its name, it has a white patch on its wing that is another clear mark of identification when it flies. The female is slightly smaller and duller, has no white wing patch, but does have a distinctly yellowish throat above its streaked underparts. It has about the same haunts and habits as the better known and more widely distributed Red-winged Blackbird and frequently they nest together in the same marshes in the West, but in such cases the two species usually occupy different portions of the swamp. The Yellow-headed Blackbird tries hard to sing but usually gets out nothing but squeals, grunts, and a sound something like that of escaping gas. Some of the migrating flocks pillage grain fields but the birds also eat many injurious insects to strike a respectable balance.

WESTERN TANAGER

(About 6¾ inches)

The Western Tanager is a bird that wanders widely in North America and might turn up almost anywhere in Summer but the male, at least, easily would be known wherever it appeared. It is a bird with a yellow body, black wings and tail—and a red face! You might even think of it as an extra large Goldfinch with a red face. The female is a light olive-green, with slightly darker wings, and looks much like the female Scarlet Tanager except that the female Western Tanager has two distinct wing bars. The male has two wing bars also, the forward one yellow and the hind one white. The male bird loses most (or all) of its red on the face in Winter but the two wing bars distinguish the Western Tanagers from other Tanagers in any plumage. Its song is a buzzing warble something like that of the Scarlet Tanager but rougher, and its call note of "pit-ick" or "pit-er-ick" is much different from the "chip-churr!" of the Scarlet Tanager. The Western Tanager is a woodland bird for the most part, and a regular Summer resident of a broad belt running from southeastern Alaska to Texas through the western part of the United States. It does venture east of the Mississippi, however, and has straggled eastward as far as New England, which means that it's quite possible to come upon this handsome bird anywhere in the United States.

BULLOCK'S ORIOLE

(About 8¼ inches)

There are a few odd species of Oriole that may be found in the far Southwest but the two common Orioles that are Summer residents of most of North America to the fringe of the Arctic wastelands are the Baltimore Oriole and Bullock's Oriole that practically divide the continent between them, the Baltimore Oriole taking the eastern half and Bullock's Oriole the western portion. However, the Baltimore Oriole is inclinded to infringe on its cousin's territory and the ranges overlap on the Great Plains, where both species may be found regularly in the breeding season. The general color scheme of the brilliant males is the same in both species, a glowing orange body with much black on the head, wings and tail, and some white barring on the black wings. But there is little difficulty even where the species overlap in knowing the Bullock's Oriole male from the Baltimore Oriole male. The dull female and young are admittedly difficult to distinguish one from the other but the gaudy male Baltimore Oriole's head is all black, whereas the Bullock's Oriole has the bright orange of its body color on its side-face, too. Note that, from a side view, Bullock's Oriole has a black crown, an orange side-face with a black line running across it from the bill back through the eye, and a black throat. The Baltimore Oriole has a white bar on its black wing but Bullock's Oriole has a great white patch in its wing that is another distinguishing mark of the species.

In general, however, it's Bullock's Oriole that is found from the Great Plains to the Pacific Coast and it occupies the same places in that landscape and in the hearts of the inhabitants as the Baltimore Oriole does throughout the East. It is a Summer resident of the river valleys, the farmlands, the village shade trees and the woodlands, breeding as high as 6,500 feet above sea level on some of the mountainsides. It hangs its nest like the Baltimore Oriole from the outer branchlets of a shade tree, usually high above the ground and well concealed in thick foliage.

Anywhere east of the Rocky Mountains you might find a bird that looks something like the Baltimore Oriole or Bullock's Oriole but is smaller and darker than either. That would be an Orchard Oriole male, which is marked much like the male Baltimore Oriole except that it has brick red plumage where the Baltimore Oriole displays glowing orange. However, the Orchard Oriole is not nearly as abundant as the Baltimore Oriole and Bullock's Oriole, especially in the northern parts of their range, so it will be something of a prize if you see one.

INDIGO BUNTING

(About 5½ inches)

Although small, the Indigo Bunting is a conspicuous bird that sings a loud song persistently from a prominent perch, so it should be an easy bird to find if there is one in your neighborhood in June. It is a common Summer resident of central and eastern North America as far north as the Canadian border region. It's the male that you will see and hear. The female and young are dull olive-brownish birds, faintly mottled, that are always skulking along hedgerows or hiding in bushes. However, they have the same sharp call note as the male—a cross between a brief buzz and a metallic chip—and once the male is known, the female and young are soon known by association. The Indigo Bunting is a bird of the orchard, the bush country and the roadsides. It feeds regularly in thickets but the male chooses a telephone wire or the top of a fence post or small tree from which to pour forth a loud song that sounds like "sweet-sweet-sweeter-sweeter" running downhill. If the light is bad or you are not in a good position to see it, the singer may look like a black Sparrow, but a touch of sunlight on its plumage will bring out the deep blue or shining indigo that gives the bird its name.

PINE SISKIN

(About 5 inches)

The Pine Siskin looks like a small dull-colored Goldfinch with many dark stripes running over it from bill to tail, above and below. It breeds from the Canadian Border region northward and is a cold weather visitor to the United States, coming in flocks and often drifting about the country in company with the Goldfinches that it so much resembles in size, shape, flight, and general habits. Even its voice is like that of the Goldfinch except that the Siskin's voice has a wheeze or huskiness that is easy to detect and by which the bird may be known from the Goldfinch in flight overhead. The Siskin feeds mostly on seeds and may be found extracting them from pine cones, tulip tree pods, or ragweed husks. Often a walker in Winter will come upon a Black Birch that seems alive with Goldfinches and Pine Siskins pillaging the "birch cones" of the seed and, in the process, scattering a shower of dusky particles on the snow-covered ground beneath the tree. Or perhaps the Goldfinches and Siskins will be picking away on the ground at the seeds of the Sweet Gum that the winds have shaken from the pods still clinging to the bare branches above. Always look at a flock of Goldfinches in Winter. They may turn out to be Pine Siskins. Or there may be Siskins in with the Goldfinches, as is frequently the case.

ROSE-BREASTED GROSBEAK

(About 8 inches)

The male Rose-breasted Grosbeak can be offered as a model bird in every way. It is beautiful, melodious, easy to identify, beneficial to agriculture, and good to its family. It is a common Summer resident over eastern North America, more or less abundant in our woodlands, groves, orchards, and even the shade trees of suburban lawns, yet it is always a thrill to come upon this striking black and white bird with the short, thick, whitish bill and the lovely rose-colored triangle—like a bleeding heart—on its white breast. The female and young are streaked brownish birds but they are fairly easy to identify by their "gross beaks," their broad white wing bars, their white eye-lines and chin-stripes and the general shape and look of a Grosbeak about them. Furthermore, the male Grosbeak is a very affectionate mate and fond parent and if you watch the male it will not be long before he will lead you to the female or young or both. The male helps build the crude nest and takes turns with the female in sitting on the eggs. He also brings food to the female when she is on the nest and he is a good provider when the fledglings are yammering for food.

The Rose-breasted Grosbeak has a lovely song, a warbling carol with a slight baritone touch to it. The song is somewhat like the rolling carol of the Robin but sweeter and richer. Once you know the song, you will find more Rose-breasted Grosbeaks in your neighborhood than you ever suspected. They are birds that usually feed fairly high in trees and, as you walk through the fields or woods, you may hear Rose-breasted Grosbeaks singing when it is impossible to see them because of the foliage. Happily the male Rose-breasted Grosbeak often chooses a dead branch or the top branchlet of a tree as a perch from which to sing for minutes at a time, and thus you have a chance to catch up with it and see as well as hear the delightful singer.

Another obliging feature about Rose-breasted Grosbeaks is that male and female—and young, too, later in the season—frequently utter a call note that is absolutely distinctive among our native birds and an easy guide to locating any Rose-breasted Grosbeaks that may be in the vicinity. It's hard to describe bird songs or call notes so that another person will recognize them as you do, but even a hint is often a great help. In the case of the Rose-breasted Grosbeak some listeners hear this call note as a sharp "ick," while others hear it as "hic!" uttered like the first part of a hiccup. Either way, let us hope you hear it and find the bird before the male exchanges his brilliant courting costume for the streaked travel suit of Autumn and goes off with the streaked female and young to spend the Winter in Central and South America.

ROAD-RUNNER

(From 20 to 24 inches)

There seems to be general agreement that the Road-runner is quite a character. Certainly the residents and tourists of the Southwest consider it such. There is no other bird quite like it in all of North America. Here's a streaked bird that is nearly two feet long, with an odd glint in its straw-colored eye, a crest that looks like hair standing on end from fright, a long neck, a short body, powerful legs, and an absurdly long tail that the owner often raises and lowers slowly like the boom of a derrick. Of course, there is never any difficulty about identifying a Road-runner. The difficulty is to see it. You have to live in—or visit—the cactus and mesquite country of the Southwest to see and hear this strange bird. The sounds that it makes are as strange as its appearance and habits. It may purr like a cat, coo like a Dove, "cuck" like a Cuckoo, squawk like a Jay or make a loud rattling sound by "clacking" its bill rapidly.

The Road-runner is found all through the arid regions of the Southwest but it is not easily found at all times. If you go out looking for a Road-runner, either because you want to see one yourself or you wish to point out this odd bird to some distinguished visitor, you will discover that the sometimes bold and even impudent Road-runner can be a very shy and evasive bird at other moments.

These picturesque birds pick a living from the ground, eating grasshoppers in large quantities and gobbling down such other desert tidbits as centipedes, lizards, mice and small snakes, including some poisonous species. They build large nests of twigs about a foot or two above the ground in some cactus cluster or scrub growth of bush or tree, and the female lays 4 to 6 eggs in a clutch. It's a comparatively rare thing to see a Road-runner on the wing, though the birds can fly well enough and occasionally do. But they much prefer running to flying and they have been timed ahead of automobiles running as fast as 18 miles an hour. When chased by man, beast, or car, they lean over like sprinters, hold their long tails level behind them and bound away on apparently tireless legs. When a bird is ready to stop, it throws up its long tail and uses it as an "air brake."

Though it has been proved by examination of their stomachs that Road-runners are beneficial birds, they may take a few Quail eggs from time to time. This has led some thoughtless hunters to demand that Road-runners be shot on sight. On the other hand, most inhabitants of the area where these birds are resident look upon the Road-runner as a vastly amusing and picturesque bird and a notable addition to the wildlife of the Southwest.

PURPLE FINCH

(About 6 inches)

Purple Finches are abundant and delightful little birds that are resident over much of the continent of North America and may be encountered anywhere at any time in this country and Canada, but they are not always easy to recognize at first glance for several reasons. One reason is that most of the Purple Finches you may come upon will have little or no purple on them, and another is that there are other birds with which they might easily be confused. Only the male Purple Finch in good plumage has much purple about it and then it's more of a raspberry or "old rose" color that looks as though it had been poured over the birds head and allowed to trickle down over the body and wings. The female and young are gray-brown birds with dark streaks. They are chunkier than Sparrows, have thicker bills and may be recognized by their heavier heads and a rather heavy grayish line on the side-face running backward from the eye.

There will be no problem at all as soon as you learn the song of the Purple Finch, a delightful rolling warble that differs much from the songs of any other birds with which it might be confused by sight except the House Finch of the West. The Purple Finch also has a call note that is even more decisive, because no other native bird—not even the House Finch—makes a sound like it. The call note sounds like a metallic "tick" or "click," thin but clear. Once that is learned, the Purple Finch will be no problem.

HOUSE FINCH

(About 5½ inches)

The House Finch of the West—most abundant in the Southwest—is much like the Purple Finch in appearance and also in its warbled song. However, there are little differences that are easily noted where the ranges of these birds overlap because the House Finch is well named, likes to nest in vines on porches, and is easily inspected at close range. It doesn't take long to note that the House Finch is a smaller and more finely streaked bird than the Purple Finch. The color on the male Purple Finch usually is deepest on the head, whereas the color on the male House Finch is deepest on the throat and upper breast. Also the color on the male House Finch is a brighter red than the "old rose" of the Purple Finch. The rather broad grayish line on the side of the head of the female or young Purple Finch will help to distinguish it from the female or young House Finch. Another point is that the Purple Finch does not have such a fondness for dooryards, telephone wires and human companionship. The House Finch of the West is like the English Sparrow in its desire to make itself at home where people live, but the native bird has much better manners and a much finer song than the interloper from Europe.

YELLOW-BILLED CUCKOO

(About 12½ inches)

We have two species of Cuckoo that are Summer residents the length and breadth of the land. They are the Black-billed Cuckoo and the Yellow-billed Cuckoo. They are the same size and color and have the same haunts and habits, yet it is not difficult to know one from the other if you can get a clear view of the birds because the Yellow-billed Cuckoo has some "positive identification marks" about it. Both Cuckoos are long slim birds with slightly curved bills and long tails. They are a soft olive-brown above and clear white underneath except that their tail feathers are dark on the underside, with some white spotting. One point of difference between the species is that the tail of the Yellow-billed Cuckoo is darker on the underside and has large round white spots in it. The underside of the tail of the Black-billed Cuckoo is more grayish and the white spots are more like ovals or half-moons than circles. If the bird is in a tree overhead, this difference may be noted. If you see the bird's bill you will know the species because the lower half of the Yellow-billed Cuckoo's bill is yellow, except for the black tip. In many cases it is a bright yellow that edges over to the upper bill near the base and it can be noted at a fair distance. If the Cuckoo is in flight, the Yellow-billed Cuckoo will show a bright cinnamon patch in its wing. Our Cuckoos are beneficial birds that build their own nests and eat many harmful caterpillars.

CEDAR WAXWING

(About 7½ inches)

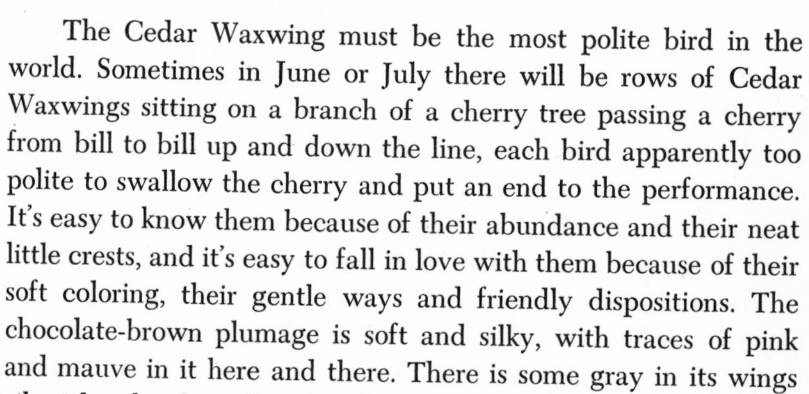

The Cedar Waxwing must be the most polite bird in the world. Sometimes in June or July there will be rows of Cedar Waxwings sitting on a branch of a cherry tree passing a cherry from bill to bill up and down the line, each bird apparently too polite to swallow the cherry and put an end to the performance. It's easy to know them because of their abundance and their neat little crests, and it's easy to fall in love with them because of their soft coloring, their gentle ways and friendly dispositions. The chocolate-brown plumage is soft and silky, with traces of pink and mauve in it here and there. There is some gray in its wings and darker gray in the tail with a bright yellow band at the end. The bird has a black chin and a brief black line running up from the base of the bill through the eye to the edge of the crest. Cedar Waxwings are found all over North America but in cold weather most of the birds of the northern area drift southward for comfort. They are sometimes called Cedar Birds or Cherry Birds but the reason for the name "Waxwing" is that at the ends of some of the wing feathers (called secondaries) there are tips of a substance that looks exactly like bright red sealing wax. The one thing these lovely birds lack is a fine song. All they can offer is a slurred series of soft notes that sound like "a string of beads."

GREAT HORNED OWL

(From 18 to 23 inches)

Owls are birds that are more often heard than seen. There are many species in North America, one of the largest and most powerful species being the Great Horned Owl. Among the Owls and the birds of prey in general the females usually are larger than the males; a female Great Horned Owl may be nearly two feet in length, with talons like hooks of steel. The "horns," of course, are merely ear-tufts that serve as definite identification marks for the Great Horned Owl. No other North American Owl of that size has such conspicuous ear-tufts. The Long-eared Owl is far smaller and its "long ears" are much closer together on top of its head.

The Great Horned Owl is one of the fiercest hunters of the wildwood. It will attack birds as large as Canada Geese and it catches Grouse, Pheasant, and Quail, as well as many other birds. Perhaps the easiest way to find a Great Horned Owl is to go to any spot where Crows are circling and swooping wildly around an evergreen tree, cawing loudly all the time. They heckle and badger the larger Hawks in that manner, too. The Hawks usually are more in the open, either on a conspicuous perch or soaring in circles with the flock of cawing Crows in cautious pursuit. But if the excited Crows are swooping at something in an evergreen; it's probably an Owl of some kind that is the object of their noisy attention and it may be that terror of the woods, the Great Horned Owl, sitting on a branch close to the trunk of the tree staring disdainfully at the swooping and circling mob of Crows.

It's a mistake to think that Owls are blind in the daytime. They see very well in broad daylight, but their eyes are better adapted than the eyes of other birds and most animals for seeing in dim light, and that's why they hunt in the dusk and the dark of night. Under such conditions they have a decided advantage over their prey. Other things that favor them when hunting in the dark is that they have remarkably keen hearing and their flight is practically noiseless. They often drop on their hapless victims unseen and unheard. They pursue all kinds of small mammals and apparently smell is a trifling thing in the lives of Great Horned Owls because they seem to relish skunks as much as they do rabbits. Owls swallow bones, pelts, and all, and the bones, fur, teeth, and claws of mice, rats, and other such prey are later ejected from the Owl's mouth in the form of pellets. A searcher for Owls often will go through the woods with his eyes on the ground, looking for Owl pellets under trees that might harbor such birds. The pellets of the Great Horned Owl are three or four inches long and an inch thick.

These large, fierce and hardy birds often begin nesting in late February or early March when snow is still on the ground and in the air.

SCREECH OWL

(About 10 inches)

This is the bird with the ghostly tremulous wailing cry that Henry David Thoreau, hearing in his nights at Walden Pond, described as the voice of a lost soul crying: "O-o-o-o that I had never been bor-r-r-rn." It runs along on one pitch for a few notes and then descends in a quavering scale to fade out in the silence and gloom of the night. It is one of the small members of the Owl family—about the size of a Robin—and is a common permanent resident throughout North America. The really odd thing about the Screech Owl is that it comes in two colors—red and gray. There are many birds that change color from Summer to Winter and there are many species in which the males are one color and the females another color. But Screech Owls do not change the color of their plumage from one season to another, nor does the male wear one color and the female another. The simple fact is that some Screech Owls are reddish-brown with lighter and darker dots and streaks that give them a mottled appearance and other Screech Owls are grayish-brown with the same assortment of dots and streaks to give the mottled appearance. But whether it is a Screech Owl of the "rufous phase" or the "gray phase," as the scientists put it, it will be known from other small Owls by its distinct ear-tufts. Sight unseen, of course, it may be known by its mournful, quavering, descending, wailing cry.

Screech Owls live in woodlands and groves and orchards and the shade trees of village streets and suburban lawns. Usually they nest in holes in trees but they will also occupy cavities in barns or other buildings and they will accept bird boxes with suitable openings if they consider the locations favorable. Furthermore, they will often use these same boxes, cavities, or holes in trees as dwelling places or retreats from enemies and bad weather at any time of year. Screech Owls have been seen sunning themselves on bright Winter days in the doorways of their retreats, and it's curious to note that most of the holes in trees that the Screech Owls choose for themselves have a "southern exposure," presumably for that purpose as well as to escape some of the Winter snow that so often is carried along by a wind whipping down from the North.

Because they do most of their hunting in the dusk or at night, Screech Owls often are unsuspected neighbors around our homes. But if they venture out in broad daylight we will hear about it from other birds that will gather around to shriek at any member of the Owl family. Occasionally a Blue Jay, inspecting a hole in a tree as a source of supply of acorns stored away by a squirrel, will find a Screech Owl tenant at home and sound an alarm to wake the neighborhood. We should be glad to have Screech Owls as neighbors because they are beneficial birds whose chief items of diet are insects and mice.

NIGHTHAWK

(About 9½ inches)

The Nighthawk is no Hawk at all but an insect-eating bird that is a first cousin of the Whip-poor-will that it much resembles in appearance and general habits. In flight both species look like great dark Swallows but there is an easy way of knowing one bird from the other. The Nighthawk has a conspicuous white patch toward the outer end of each wing that shows clearly in flight. If there are Nighthawks around—and they are Summer residents of most of North America—you will not only see them but hear them in the dusk, which is their time for hunting insects on the wing. Whether it be over crowded cities, little villages, or lonely stretches of open country, of a Summer eve these wonderful acrobats of the air wheel, whirl, dive down and zoom upward through the twilight and dusk, catching insects at every turn and uttering a loud, buzzing, nasal "be-e-eent!" all the while. They make no nests. In the country they lay their 2 eggs on the bare ground and in cities they deposit their eggs on flat graveled roofs. In the Autumn the Nighthawks gather in great flocks for the southward migration, heading down the broad river valleys, whirling about the skies with their white wing patches for positive identification marks but looking more than ever like gigantic and magnificent Swallows.

WHIP-POOR-WILL

(About 10 inches)

It seems almost a waste of words to describe a Whip-poor-will because so few persons ever see it compared to the many who know it by the weird vibrant call that gives the bird its name. It is, however, much like the Nighthawk in appearance and habits, a chunky, dark, wide-mouthed, insect-eating bird with a short curved bill, a white band across its lower throat, and white patches on the outer feathers of its tail. Unlike the Nighthawk that whirls through the upper air for its prey, the Whip-poor-will stays close to the ground in river valleys or watered meadows and gathers insects in short low flights. It drifts like a shadow through the gloom, rarely rising to a height so that its form can be seen against the sky. It may give its throbbing call from the bare ground, from a smooth stone, or from a lengthwise position on a fence rail or limb of a tree, with a preliminary "chuck" and a deep nod at each "WILL" of its repeated call: "Whip-poor-WILL! Whip-poor-WILL! Whip-poor-WILL!" Sometimes of warm moonlit night it will call and fly about to feed from dusk till dawn. It lays its 2 eggs in a depression on the ground in the woods or on a brushy hillside. It drifts southward almost unnoticed on migration, an unseen bird that is known to many only as a throbbing call in the hush of Summer eves.

DOWNY WOODPECKER

(About 6½ inches)

This is probably the most common, friendly, and widespread representative of the Woodpecker family in all of North America. It may be found in our woods, on our farms, in our parks, and around our homes Winter and Summer. It is one of the midget members of its great family and a plain black and white bird except in one respect; the male wears a red patch on the back of its head. There is another member of the family that looks almost exactly like the Downy Woodpecker but in a larger size. That's the Hairy Woodpecker, which is also found the length and breadth of the country but is not so abundant or so friendly a bird as the little Downy.

If the two birds are seen together, the Hairy will look almost twice as large as the Downy, though the real difference is not nearly that much. But when the birds are seen alone, it is sometimes difficult to estimate the exact size. In such a case, look at the bill of the bird. The Hairy Woodpecker has a much heavier and longer bill in comparison with the size of the bird itself. After a few trials, this difference will be clear to the eye. There is a difference in the notes, too. The call note of the Hairy is much firmer and louder and the clattering cry of the bigger bird is sustained in pitch, whereas the notes of the Downy are descending at the finish. The little Downy is much the friendlier and will be a daily dooryard visitor in Winter if a supply of suet is offered as a lure.

YELLOW-BELLIED SAPSUCKER

(About 8½ inches)

Despite its name, this is a Woodpecker and looks and acts much like other members of the family except that, over much of its range in eastern North America, it is a Summer resident or migrant where other Woodpeckers are sedate and respectable permanent residents. If you see a Woodpecker between the size of the Downy and the Hairy Woodpecker with a red forehead, a black band across its breast, yellowish on its speckled under parts and a vertical white patch in its wing, that will be the Yellow-bellied Sapsucker. There are other kinds of Sapsuckers in the western part of the country that differ in plumage but all the males can be identified by the yellow on the under parts and the vertical white patch in the wing. The Yellow-bellied Sapsucker is the only smallish Woodpecker over its range with a red forehead patch. The male also has a red throat where the female wears white. The bird gets its name from its habit of drinking the sap that oozes from the regular rows of holes that it drills in the bark of trees, particularly apple trees. It also eats insects that come to drink the sap, and has a squealing, whining cry that it utters frequently.

PILEATED WOODPECKER

(About 18 inches)

Think of a Woodpecker as large as a Crow! A great black and white bird with a flaming red crest! That's the Pileated Woodpecker that is still to be found throughout the wooded regions of North America. Once upon a time the even larger Ivory-billed Woodpecker might have been seen or heard in the big timber of the river bottoms of the South, but now the Ivory-billed Woodpecker is sought in vain through its old haunts. Perhaps it is extinct. At any rate, if you see a huge Woodpecker with a red crest, a flashing and magnificent bird, it will be the Pileated Woodpecker that happily still seems to be holding its own in the forests of the United States and Canada. You can't fail to identify it immediately if you have the luck to see one. It is our only Woodpecker of that size and the only Woodpecker of North America that has a crest.

The Pileated Woodpecker has a repeated cry much like that of the "wicker" of the Flicker, but the voice of the Pileated is more "throaty." It's difficult to describe the difference but where both birds are resident it soon is easy to distinguish one call from the other. When a Pileated goes to work on a tree to dig out grubs or adult bettles with its great bill, it certainly makes the chips fly. It whacks away with terrific force and from a distance it often sounds as though a man were chopping in the woods. An odd point is that sometimes a woodchopper at work will find that the blows of his axe have "called" a Pileated Woodpecker to the vicinity.

Though they are distinctly woodland birds, these big Woodpeckers swing out into the open when going from one place to another to feed. Sometimes they have favorite dead trees to which they resort regularly with no intention of hammering or hacking away at the glistening bare trunk or the ghostly gray branches. They merely loaf about the tree, edging slowly upward or backing slowly downward as they utter their loud calls at intervals. Where a ridge has been lumbered they will come frequently to inspect the old stumpage in search of grubs or grown beetles. If they find a stump that is a storehouse of these dainties, they will return at odd moments until they have picked it clean. In addition to their normal insect diet, they will eat some berries in season and they seem to have a real fondness for wild grapes in Autumn.

Almost any hole in any tree may be the work of a member of the Woodpecker family but where the Pileated has been at work the traces are unmistakable. This bird hews out rectangular hollows that look like topless boxes and it rips off heavy strips of bark that no other member of the family could begin to remove.

RUBY-THROATED HUMMINGBIRD

(About 3½ inches)

The simple facts about Hummingbirds are like the birds themselves, almost unbelievable. These are the smallest birds in the whole world. There are some 500 species and only one species is over 5 inches in length, long bill included. They are real all-America birds, found only from Patagonia to the Canadian woods, but most of the 500 species are tropical and only a dozen or so species are more or less common Summer residents of different sections of the United States. Only a single species is found regularly east of the Mississippi. That's the Ruby-throated Hummingbird that derives its name from the glittering gorget worn by the male and displayed at its brightest about the time that the female is building its marvelous little nest neatly balanced on an apple twig in an old orchard.

The Ruby-throated Hummingbird is "about as big as a minute" and weighs about as much as a copper cent. Like all Hummingbirds it has a tiny body, a long, thin, tube-like bill, iridescent plumage, and a wing motion so rapid that it is almost invisible to the eye. All we see is a blur where the wings are beating in the air as the bird hovers in front of some flower or flits about the garden with the humming sound that gives the bird its name. The hum comes from the rapid vibration of the wings. The voice of the Hummingbird is a sharp squeak or tiny buzz and usually is heard when males are quarreling over mates or territorial rights in the breeding season.

There are certain things that Hummingbirds like and certain conditions that please them. If these things are provided, Hummingbirds will visit you. They like water, though not necessarily in large quantities. But they like well watered meadows, especially where the brooks are lined with wild flowers. On the West Coast some of the abundant species will settle for bird baths and lawn sprinklers as all the water they need and will build their dainty downy nests in porch vines, but the Ruby-throated Hummingbird of the East is not quite that much domesticated. It will feed among the dooryard flowers and porch vines, but its tiny nest is hidden away on the limb of some shade tree or fruit tree around the yard, out in the orchard or down the road. A half-dollar would cover nest, eggs and all. There are 2 tiny eggs to a clutch and there may be one or two broods a year.

Hummingbirds are courageous little birds, often fighting among themselves or with other birds around the dooryard. They dart about with such speed that, with their needle-like bills, they look quite dangerous, but it's a rare thing for them to come to actual blows. They are such marvelous creatures on the wing that they can not only fly backward as well as forward but they can swing in the air from side to side as though they were riding on a pendulum.

PURPLE MARTIN

(About 8 inches)

This is the largest and darkest of our Swallows and it may be found as a Summer resident almost anywhere in North America. The male is a steely blue-black and, unlike our other Swallows, is practically the same color below as above. The female is duller above and grayish below. Because they are insect-eaters and sweep tirelessly through the air all day in pursuit of mosquitoes and other insect pests, Purple Martins have been cherished birds in this country since Indian days. The Indians used to hang out lines of dried gourds as nesting places for the birds in their villages. Early white settlers followed the custom and their descendants went on to make architectural improvements in the Martin dwellings. The Martins take naturally to community life and some of the elaborate structures now offered them as Summer homes look exactly like huge apartment houses for birds. English Sparrows and Starlings, by taking their nesting sites, have driven the Martins away from some sections of the country in which they were formerly abundant, notably New England, but efforts are being made to lure these feathered favorites back to their old homes again.

TREE SWALLOW

(About 6 inches)

The flashing Tree Swallow that sweeps in chattering flight over our Summer meadows is just as widespread over North America as its larger cousin, the Purple Martin. With bright sunlight on its plumage, the Tree Swallow is a metallic greenish-black above and clear white underneath. This contrast in color above and below makes it easy to distinguish from all our other native Swallows except the Violet-green Swallow of the West. But the Violet-green Swallow has two white patches that show clearly on its rump, whereas the Tree Swallow is a solid dark color above. In the wild state the Tree Swallow nests in holes in trees or crevices in rocks, but again like the Purple Martin, the bird has become half-domesticated to the extent that it will not only accept bird boxes put out as nesting places but will go looking for them and return year after year to nest in the same boxes. The Tree Swallow is the hardiest of the family and is usually the first to arrive in Spring and the last to leave in the Autumn. It gathers in great flocks for the Autumn migration to the Gulf Coast area where the birds spend the Winter.

LOGGERHEAD SHRIKE

(About 9 inches)

Shrikes are striking birds in color and habits. For their striking habits they are often called "Butcher Birds." If you see a dead grasshopper, mouse, or small bird hanging on a thorn in a bush or stuck on a barbed wire fence, that will be the work of the "Butcher Bird" or Shrike. There are two resident species in North America. The Northern Shrike is the larger and the more northerly in range. The Loggerhead Shrike is much more common and widespread over the United States, particularly in the southern half of the country. Otherwise the two Shrikes look much alike and act in the same murderous manner. They are generally grayish above and white below, with a heavy black line running back from the thickish black bill through the eye. They have black wings with white patches, and black tails fringed with white that shows best in flight. The Loggerhead Shrike is somewhat like the Mockingbird in color but not at all like it in voice or actions. The best the Loggerhead can do in song is a few gurgle-like notes and a buzz. The Mockingbird lacks the heavy black line through the eye that the Shrike wears.

HORNED LARK

(About 7½ inches)

This is a soft-colored, mild-mannered little bird of the open country, of wide plains, of barren territory almost bare of herbage, of the dunes by the seashore, of pasture land that has been closely cropped by cattle, of flat areas like the airports that now dot the country, and of those well-groomed gems of greenery, the golf courses of the United States and Canada. There probably is no golf course in North America that doesn't have, in the course of a year, more Horned Larks than members walking the fairways. These birds are a tan-brown above and grayish below. They have black on their foreheads, a black patch that starts back from the bill and drops below the eye, and a black band across the upper breast. There may be much or little yellow between the black patches on the bird's head and breast. The plumage varies in different parts of North America and at different seasons of the year. You have to move slowly and look carefully to find Horned Larks feeding because their color blends with the grass or ground. The birds crouch low when feeding and sometimes creep almost like mice through the short grass or over the bare ground. Do not look for the "horns" of the Horned Lark. They are usually invisible, if not imaginary.

HERRING GULL

(From 23 to 26 inches)

The Gulls of our lakes, rivers, harbors, and ocean shores are large birds—gigantic compared with our Sparrows and Warblers—and wonderful fliers. They are also noisy and numerous and there are so many different species that look much alike that it is a problem for the beginner to tell them apart. The best way to make a start is to get to know one Gull with certainty and use that as a standard. The Herring Gull is the best standard because it is the most abundant Gull of North America. It sits about on piers, buoys, rocks, beaches, and sand bars and is readily available for close inspection, which makes it an easy bird to know.

The first impression on looking at a group of Gulls, whether at rest or on the wing, is that there are "white ones" and "brown ones." The "white ones" are seldom completely white and the "brown ones" are really speckled or mottled, but the important distinction is that the "white ones" are the adult birds and the mottled ones are the younger ones. The young of all species of Gull are mottled and it takes them from two to four years—depending upon the species—to come of age in adult plumage and be one of the "white ones" in a Gull group. If the "white ones" are loked over carefully, it is seen that most of them have some gray or blue or black in their plumage. If the darker color is on the upper surface of the wings and across the back, it is known as a "mantle."

The adult Herring Gull may be known by its size, its blue-gray mantle with blackish wing tips and its *pale flesh-colored legs.* The color of the legs is most important because it sets the Herring Gull apart from such others as the Ring-billed Gull and the California Gull that, though smaller, are much like the Herring Gull in plumage. Once the adult Herring Gull is definitely identified, it is fairly simple to move ahead and identify other common species by the items in which they differ from the Herring Gull.

COMMON TERN

(From 13 to 16 inches)

Terns in flight over the ocean are certainly among the most beautiful and graceful birds in the world. They are often called Sea Swallows and it is a good name for them. They look like large black-capped white Swallows as they wheel and whirl in their ceaseless offshore patrol along our coast lines. They are, on the average, much smaller and thinner than Gulls and, as further marks of distinction ,the Terns have more or less deeply forked tails and sharp pointed bills. Even at a distance Terns can be known from Gulls by their lighter and more dashing flight and by their habit of plunging head-first into the ocean in pursuit of the small fish or other aquatic creatures on which they feed.

But Terns are like Gulls in one discouraging way: there are many different species and some of them look so much alike that only the field experts can tell them apart on the wing. Where there are four species that so closely resemble one another in size and plumage as the Common Tern, Roseate Tern, Forster's Tern and Arctic Tern, the expert tells them apart by their voices, a bit of light or dark shading on the back or the underside of the wings, the depth of the fork in the tail and the differences in the color of the bill.

The Common Tern and Forster's Tern are so much alike in general appearance, even to the orange-red color of the bill, that the beginner might give up hope of ever knowing one bird from the other, but there are small differences that are not too difficult to note if the birds are seen regularly at close range. From a top view the primaries (large outer flight feathers of the wing) of the Common Tern are dark compared to the remainder of the wing and in the Forster's Tern the primaries are lighter than the remainder of the wing. Also, the upper surface of the tail of the Common Tern is white whereas it is gray for the Forster's Tern. Still, it does take time and patience to learn these things.

COMMON LOON

(From 28 to 36 inches)

If Loons had lawyers they could sue persons who use the phrase "as crazy as a Loon." They are not crazy birds by any means. On the contrary, Loons are wise birds and it is difficult to get near them. The slanderous reference to their alleged lack of sanity grew out of the weird calls they utter on their breeding grounds and Summer haunts—repeated shrieks and chattering hoots that sound like hollow mockery or demoniac laughter echoing over a lonely lake or a melancholy marsh. Loons are among the most "watery" of our water birds and, indeed, are rarely seen out of water. Their feet are not placed or formed so they can walk comfortably on dry ground. The best they can do is an awkward waddle. In the water, however, they are altogether at home. Loons are large, dark-colored, sharp-billed diving birds that look like Geese at a distance on the water, but they may be known from Geese by their "flat heads," their sharp bills, and their habit of "sitting" much lower in the water.

The Common Loon in Summer plumage has a shining greenish-black head and neck, a white breast, and a general "body color" that from a distance looks all dark but on closer inspection is a delightful checkered pattern of little white squares and dots on a black background. On the side of the dark neck there is a horizontal white patch with vertical black lines running through it, but you have to be real close to see these lovely markings.

Loons are, for the most part, fresh-water birds through the Spring and Summer. They breed in the reeds around ponds and lakes, many of them in uninhabited areas, feeding themselves and their young on fish, shrimp, frogs, and even an occasional vegetable salad of marsh plants. In the Autumn migration they appear in great numbers along our coasts and they dive so deep for fish that they have been caught in nets 90 feet below the surface. They used their half-closed wings as well as their feet in swimming under water, and those who have seen it say that the birds seem to be actually flying through the water in pursuit of their prey.

SPOTTED SANDPIPER

(About 7½ inches)

Sandpipers are small birds with long thin bills and little legs and feet that seem to twinkle as they run rapidly along our ocean beaches, mud flats and lake shores in search of food at the fringe of the water. There are many kinds of Sandpiper but probably the best known and the most widespread of the family in North America is the Spotted Sandpiper, which may be found anywhere in the United States or Canada in the warmer months of the year. Whether it is an ocean beach or just the drinking hole for cattle on a farm, the Spotted Sandpiper will be there. It is greenish-brown above and white beneath, with a distinct white line through the eye and its white breast plentifully sprinkled with dark spots. It also shows a white line in the wing when flying and when it is standing still it has a curious "teetering" motion of the body. It seems to be trying a balancing act by lowering its head and raising the tail and rear part of the body. The young of the year have no spots and the parent birds lose the spots before going southward in the Autumn.

SOLITARY SANDPIPER

(About 8½ inches)

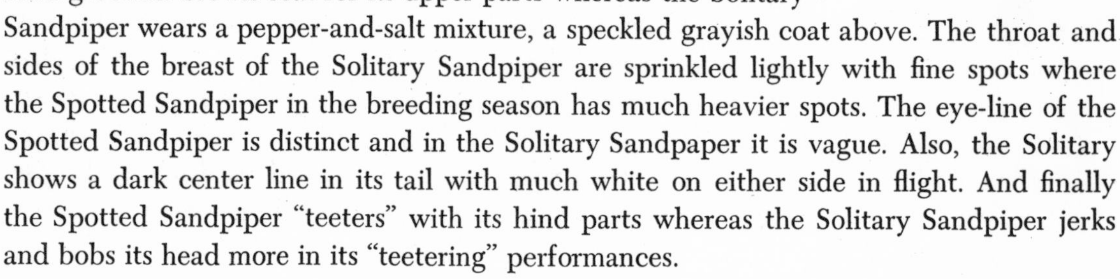

The Spotted Sandpiper is found on ocean beaches as well as around farm ponds, but the Solitary Sandpiper is a rare sight on an ocean beach. It takes to the inland swamps, the country ponds, and the lakes in the woods. It even nests in bushes or trees, like a Robin. In fact, it will use a Robin's nest after the real owners have abandoned it. The Solitary Sandpiper is a bit larger than the Spotted Sandpiper that is found as a Summer resident over the same territory and there are other differences that are easily noticed. The Spotted Sandpiper has a solid greenish-brown coat for its upper parts whereas the Solitary Sandpiper wears a pepper-and-salt mixture, a speckled grayish coat above. The throat and sides of the breast of the Solitary Sandpiper are sprinkled lightly with fine spots where the Spotted Sandpiper in the breeding season has much heavier spots. The eye-line of the Spotted Sandpiper is distinct and in the Solitary Sandpaper it is vague. Also, the Solitary shows a dark center line in its tail with much white on either side in flight. And finally the Spotted Sandpiper "teeters" with its hind parts whereas the Solitary Sandpiper jerks and bobs its head more in its "teetering" performances.

GREAT BLUE HERON

(From 42 to 52 inches)

This is probably the tallest native bird that you will see standing on two legs. There are a few others that may run taller—the Great White Heron, the Whooping Crane, the Sandhill Crane—but these are rare or, at least, uncommon sights around the country whereas the Great Blue Heron is a common permanent resident of most of the United States and a regular Summer resident of all of North America to the edge of the Arctic tundra. Where the Great Blue Heron and the Sandhill Crane or Little Brown Crane are found in the same regions, the birds can be identified in the air at considerable heights because, though Cranes and Herons alike fly with their long legs trailing out behind, the Cranes fly with their necks stretched to full length whereas Herons fly with their necks folded back in a flat "S" loop.

Herons belong to a group of birds that the scientists call "waders" because they walk about in the water or marshy places in search of food. For that purpose they are equipped with long legs, long necks, and long sharp bills. The Great Blue Heron stands about 4 feet tall and has a long sharp bill that can be a dangerous weapon when the bird is attacked. It feeds in swamps and marshes as well as along streams, rivers, and lakes. It will eat fish, frogs, shrimps, crayfish, salamanders, aquatic insects, and practically anything else it finds in the water. It will sometimes move to higher ground and dine on mice, grasshoppers, and beetles of various kinds. Fishermen say that it catches trout before they can get around to it themselves and for that reason they dislike the bird.

Great Blue Herons are lone hunters most of the time but in the breeding season they gather in colonies and nest together in trees or high bushes in swamp rookeries. When the young are growing up these rookeries are noisy and smelly places, filled with the grunts and squawks of old and young and the decaying remains of infertile eggs, lost food and other waste material from the nests. But once the young Herons are able to fend for themselves, the old birds part company and go on their lone hunting trips again. When ice forms on the lakes, ponds, and rivers of the northern part of the country, the Herons have to move southward to find food. Many of them move coastward at the same time and Great Blue Herons are numerous in our coastal marshes all through the colder months. Those that breed in the northern sectors will move in that direction as soon as the ice goes out in Spring.

PIED-BILLED GREBE

(From 12 to 15 inches)

Grebes are water birds that, from their size and general shape, might be mistaken for Ducks at a distance but they have pointed bills, sit much lower in the water than Ducks do and look as though they had no tails. Hunters often refer to them as "Hell-divers" because they dive so quickly and stay down so long. They have the ability to sink their bodies in the water and keep just their heads stuck up like periscopes. They do this when they are suspicious or frightened and wish to keep out of sight as much as possible. The Pied-billed Grebe is the smallest and most widespread of our common Grebes. It may be found as a Summer resident on almost any body of water, small or large, in North America. However, it does prefer the smaller ones and it breeds regularly in our inland swamps and marshes and in the reeds sorrounding our lakes and ponds. Seen on the water—and it is rarely seen out of the water—it is a small, dark, "roundish" bird with a somewhat snaky neck and head and a Chicken-like bill with a black band around it, the feature that gives the bird its name. Perhaps the only remarkable thing about the "Dabchick," as it is sometimes called, is its voice, a long loud call of "cow-cow-cow" repeated many times in the breeding season.

GREEN HERON

(From 16 to 22 inches)

In all of North America there is hardly a river, lake, marsh, swamp, pond, or water hole that isn't visited by a Green Heron at some time or other in warm weather. It is easily the best known, the most abundant and the most widespread of our Herons and has many different names given to it by farm boys. Its official name is the only confusing thing about this familiar bird. Why Green Heron? To most observers it shows more slate-blue or an even darker shade on most of its upper plumage. The crown is greenish-black and the feathers form something of a low raggedy crest at times. The neck is chestnut-reddish with a cream-colored streak running down the front and widening on the breast. When the Green Heron is flushed from its perch or from a feeding site in a bog it flaps away with a cry of "ske-ow!" if it makes any sound at all. Green Herons build crude nests in bushes or trees overhanging a pond, lake, marsh, or some other watery area. They eat the usual Heron diet and drift southward as soon as their Summer haunts are frozen over by cold weather.

BLACK-CROWNED NIGHT HERON

(From 23 to 28 inches)

The name Black-crowned Night Heron accurately describes the bird and gives a hint of its habits. It has a conspicuous blackish crown and it does a good deal of wandering about in the night when most other birds are asleep. It is a Heron that is easy to become acquainted with because of its large size, its abundance in North America and a notable but invisible feature, its voice. Henry Wadsworth Longfellow wrote in "Paul Revere's Ride" that to some of his alarmed countrymen of that era the patriotic silversmith on his immortal ride was

A voice in the darkness, a knock at the door,
And a word that shall echo forevermore!

The Black-crowned Night Heron is like Paul Revere to some extent. It doesn't go around knocking on doors but to many of our countrymen it is only a voice in the darkness, a strange sound in the night. As it flies silently through the dusk or dark from one feeding ground to another, the Night Heron now and then utters a loud "quawk!" that must startle any listener below, certainly the first time he hears it. Doubtless there are some dwellers in rural districts who know this bird only by ear and after dark; they never have seen it. It is, however, easy enough to find by daylight if there are any fair-sized marshy areas or bodies of water nearby. It is much more common near the coast than it is inland but it can be found almost anywhere in the United States where there is open water. It usually nests in trees in marshy or swampy areas, often in rookeries of considerable size.

The adult birds have greenish-black crowns and backs, blue-gray wings and white under-parts. There is a white patch on the forehead that can be seen if you are close to the bird. The bill is long, heavy, and dark and the legs of the bird are yellow. The young are grayish-brown with many light streaks and spots. There are only a few other marsh birds with which the young or adult Black-crowned Night Heron can be confused. There is a more southerly Yellow-crowned Night Heron that is about the same size but the head pattern is quite different. The young of the two Night Herons, however, are quite similar and hard to distinguish from one another in the field. There is also the American Bittern, which is a streaked bird of approximately the same pattern and size as young Night Herons, but the large Bittern is a rare sight compared to the common young Night Herons that wander about the country. The young Black-crowned Night Herons often are perched in trees. Bitterns are generally on the ground in a bog.

KILLDEER

(About 10 inches)

The Killdeer is a handsome, abundant, friendly, and most obliging bird. It stays out in the open where it can be seen and it announces itself by name quite clearly, calling "Kill-dee" at intervals in its flight. It is about the size of a Robin, a tannish-brown above, clear white below and it has two distinct black bands across its breast. It also shows a beautiful salmon-pink on its lower back and upper tail surface as it flies off. The Killdeer is a member of the Plover family and Plovers are classed as shore birds, but the Killdeer is only occasionally a bird of our ocean beaches or tidal mud flats. It is found inland all over North America through most of the year. It does play along the shores of rivers, lakes, and ponds but, on the whole, it prefers football fields, golf courses, the flat surfaces of airports, plowed ground—any place in the open where the grass is short or the ground is bare. It is an abundant bird on farm lands and likes to roam the close-cropped pastures with the cattle. When they are disturbed at night among the cattle they go flying around in the darkness uttering their plaintive cries of "Kill-dee, kill-dee, kill-dee," with an occasional purring note or skittering trill thrown in for added weird effect.

RUDDY TURNSTONE

(About 9 inches)

This shore bird on the wing looks like a flying marble cake. It displays a striking pattern of orange-red, jet black and pure white in a delightful way. There can be no chance of mistaking it for any other bird in flight but when the Ruddy Turnstone is feeding along our coasts it is often difficult to find on pebbled beaches or rocky headlands because there its mixture of colors may blend with the background. It is well named, because it turns over stones with its stout bill to get at the food it finds in such places. It looks like a small, squat, multi-colored Dove with bright orange legs and feet. Many of our shore birds are difficult to know, one from the other, because they are of a size and look so much alike, but the Ruddy Turnstone is a most satisfactory bird. There is no other shore bird anything like it except the Black Turnstone, which is easily distinguished because it is much darker, has a completely black head and lacks the orange-red upper parts of the Ruddy Turnstone. Also, the Black Turnstone is a West Coast bird whereas the Ruddy Turnstone is found along both coasts and on the Great Lakes.

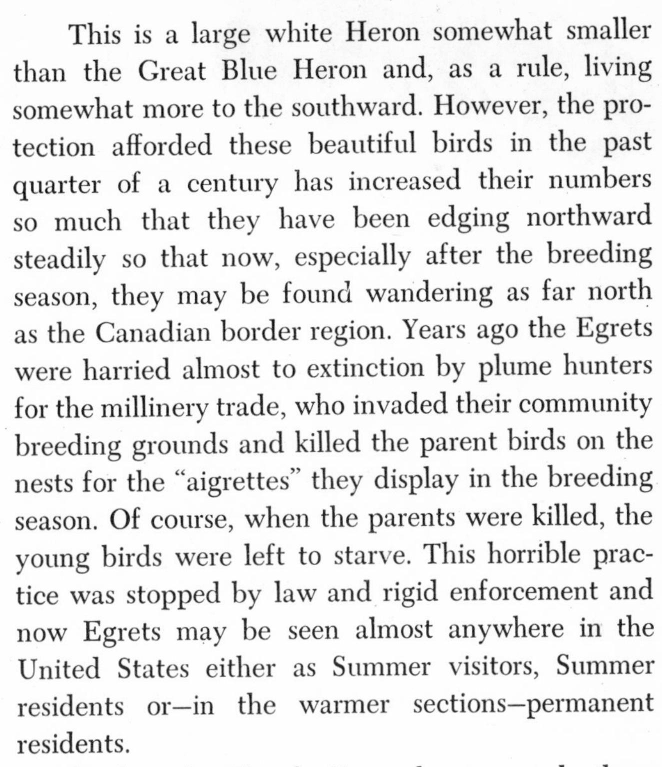

AMERICAN EGRET

(From 35 to 42 inches)

This is a large white Heron somewhat smaller than the Great Blue Heron and, as a rule, living somewhat more to the southward. However, the protection afforded these beautiful birds in the past quarter of a century has increased their numbers so much that they have been edging northward steadily so that now, especially after the breeding season, they may be found wandering as far north as the Canadian border region. Years ago the Egrets were harried almost to extinction by plume hunters for the millinery trade, who invaded their community breeding grounds and killed the parent birds on the nests for the "aigrettes" they display in the breeding season. Of course, when the parents were killed, the young birds were left to starve. This horrible practice was stopped by law and rigid enforcement and now Egrets may be seen almost anywhere in the United States either as Summer visitors, Summer residents or—in the warmer sections—permanent residents.

Since the Great White Heron is confined to the Florida Keys, there are only three large white birds of the Heron type that may be found over most of the United States. They are the American Egret, the Snowy Egret, and the immature Little Blue Heron that starts out with all-white plumage and doesn't reach the full blue stage until it is 3 years old. The American Egret is much larger than the Snowy Egret and the young Little Blue Heron, but unless the birds are seen together the difference in size may not be apparent at a distance. A difference that can be noted, however, is that the American Egret has a shining yellow bill whereas the Snowy Egret and the immature Little Blue Heron have decidedly dark bills. The American and the Snowy Egret have black legs but the Snowy Egret has yellow feet as an extra feature. This is a point that isn't always visible to the naked eye, however, because the birds are so often seen either on the wing or standing "knee-deep" in water. The Snowy Egret and the immature Little Blue Heron are white birds of approximately the same shape and size but, if you can get close to them, it is not difficult to know which is which. The Snowy Egret is much the daintier bird. Aside from the bright yellow feet of the Snowy Egret that may or may not be visible, the bill and legs are different. Except for a yellow patch at the base, the bill of the Snowy Egret is jet black to the tip. The bill of the Little Blue Heron is a dull lead color and it is thicker than the bill of the smaller Egret. The same comparison may be made of the legs of these two birds. The legs of the Snowy Egret are neat and really black. The legs of the immature Little Blue Heron are a trifle thicker and a rather sickly blue-gray in hue.

The easiest thing to remember is that the largest of these large white wading birds is the American Egret and it has a shining yellow bill as a sure indication of its identity.

WOOD DUCK

(From 17 to 20 inches)

The male Wood Duck is the most gloriously colored wild bird in North America. Not even the most gaudy of the little Wood Warblers can offer the striking pattern and iridescent hues that the male Wood Duck displays on the lakes, rivers, and woodland ponds of the United States and Canada where it makes its home. The female is a rather plain bird of darkish color with a white patch around the eye that gives it a frightened look at all times. The Wood Duck is quite different from most of our waterfowl. It likes the woods and will perch in trees like a Pigeon. It does not quack. It has a purring whistle for intimate conversation and a buzzing whine for an alarm note. There are a few other members of the Duck family that will nest in holes in trees but the Wood Duck makes a decided habit of it and often the holes are 30 to 40 feet above ground (or water). There are different accounts of how the newly-hatched youngsters get down from the nests to the ground or water below. Some say they flutter down safely and others say that the female carries them down one way or the other, but all agree that the little ones reach water safely within a day or two of hatching. They feed mostly on vegetable matter, with some occasional aquatic insect for dessert. The Wood Duck ranges all over the United States and Canada, going south in Winter only far enough to be sure of open water for feeding purposes. It is a trusting bird, very easily tamed and will return year after year to areas in which it is protected.

CANADA GOOSE

(From 34 to 43 inches)

This is the most abundant Goose of North America, the "honker" of the hunters, the bird that gathers with many others of its kind to migrate in V-formation with Autumn gunners banging away at it when it comes down to earth or water to feed or rest. Though the Canada Goose varies greatly in size, it can hardly be mistaken for any of its wild companions on the water except possibly the Brant, which, though it has the gray-brown body and the black neck and head of the Canada Goose, lacks the clear white "chin-strap" that marks the bigger and better known Canada Goose and its subspecies. These birds have powerful voices and often the great flocks of migrating Canada Geese are heard before they are seen far off in the sky. They spend all their lives in Canada and the United States, breeding in the northerly region and migrating to the more southerly sections when snow and ice cover their Summer homes.

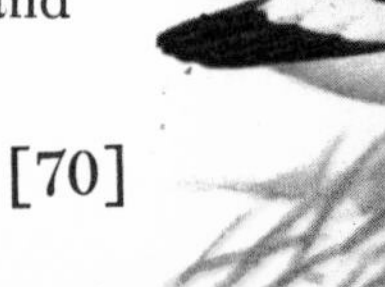

AMERICAN MERGANSER

(From 21 to 27 inches)

Mergansers are fish-eating members of the Duck family and have narrow saw-toothed bills with which they catch and hold their pray. There are three species of Merganser that are more or less common along our coasts and on the rivers, lakes, and ponds of North America. They are the American, the Red-breasted and the Hooded Merganser, the males of which are all strikingly handsome birds in their "nuptial" or breeding plumage. The females are much duller and much alike in color; grayish birds with reddish-brown heads and gray-white throats and breast. The Hooded Mergansers are much the smaller of the group and the female Hooded may be known by size alone from the similar but noticeably larger females of the American and Red-breasted species. Not only are these two larger females so much alike that only experts can be sure of the difference in the field, but the brilliant males take on that same plumage when the breeding season is over. So there can be plenty of confusion among the Mergansers until the males don their best suits again. But in full plumage, the American Merganser is easily known. It has a shining head of very dark iridescent green, a black back and an all-white body along the water line. The Red-breasted male in the same season is quite different. It is a much darker bird, showing only a white throat and a horizontal white patch in its wing, and wearing the brownish-red broad breast band that gives it the name it carries.

The American and the Hooded Mergansers are more widespread inland than the Red-breasted species, which seems to prefer the regions near the coast. All three Mergansers breed in fresh-water areas but the Red-breasted Mergansers seem to hurry back to salt water as soon as there is a touch of Autumn in the air. They definitely are the most abundant of the migrants and Winter residents in our coastal waters. The American and Hooded Mergansers are just so-so about salt water. They can take it or leave it alone. The Hooded Merganser in particular can leave it alone and, incidentally, the male Hooded Merganser does not go into a dull eclipse of plumage like its larger relatives. It keeps its striking pattern and its ability to raise and lower its handsome crest throughout the year, but it does turn a trifle browner in Autumn, though not enough to confuse anyone who sees it. The male Hooded Merganser is easy to recognize at any time of year.

FLORIDA GALLINULE

(From 12 to 15 inches)

Look in the marshes or around the reedy shores of lakes and ponds for the Florida Gallinule. The "Florida" part of the name is misleading. These birds may be found on or around water almost anywhere in the United States or southern Canada in Summer and anywhere below the ice and snow belt in the United States in Winter. They look strangely like misplaced barnyard fowl as they wander through the reeds or stalk across lily pads, picking at food as they go. Aside from the general dark plumage there is a white line along the lower edge of the wing and a white patch under the tail, but the mark that is as good as a name tag on this bird is the bright red bill with the extension running up the forehead. Unless they are harassed by boys throwing stones or older persons taking shots at them, they often become quite fearless in their Summer homes and go clucking through the reeds with their young like a hen leading a brood of chicks around a dooryard. Despite the fact that their feet are not webbed, they swim readily with a peculiar bobbing of the head.

COOT

(From 13 to 16 inches)

Practically everything that can be said about the Florida Gallinule is also true of the Coot—with one exception! The two birds are about of a size. They have approximately the same shape and general dark color. They live in the same places and have much the same actions and feeding habits. They even swim alike, with a similar bobbing of the head to balance each stroke of the foot. But there is one striking difference that makes it easy to know the Coot from the Florida Gallinule at any reasonable distance. As the mark of the Florida Gallinule is the bright red bill, the mark of the Coot is the "white nose," the shining white bill with the extension running up the forehead as the red runs up the forehead of the Florida Gallinule. There are other and less noticeable differences between the birds. The Coot is a trifle larger on the average, a little darker on the head, and lacks the white line that the Florida Gallinule displays along the lower edge of the folded wing.

OSPREY

(From 21 to 24 inches)

Osprey is the official name of this bird but more often it is called a "Fish Hawk," which is a good descriptive name for it because it lives almost exclusively on fish that it catches by plunging feet foremost into the water from a considerable height. It has talons like steel hooks to grasp and hold its prey and often its plunge is so swift that the Osprey disappears completely under the water. When it comes up with a fish—frequently a surprisingly large one—the Osprey shakes the water from its feathers, rests a moment on the surface and then flaps off toward its nest or toward a perch, always holding the fish so that its head is pointing directly in the line of flight.

This is really a magnificent bird. It has a wing-spread of 5 feet or more and is often mistaken for an Eagle because of its size and the fact that its head it largely white. However, the Osprey is clear white underneath, whereas both the Golden Eagle and the Bald Eagle are dark underneath. In fact, the Osprey is the only large bird of prey of North America that is clear white underneath. There really is no mistaking this bird, especially when it is seen in action along our coasts. It may be found over rivers and lakes anywhere in North America but it is much more numerous in the coastal regions where its huge nests atop dead trees, telegraph poles or platforms set out for it are objects that stand out against the skyline. They come back to the same nest year after year and are stubborn about retaining possession. If a nest is destroyed they will rebuild it time and again with sticks, seaweed, cornstalks, and whatever other odd material they can pick up.

There are usually 3 eggs in a clutch and the Ospreys are fond parents to the fledglings. Usually one of the parents stays on or near the nest to protect the young birds while the other is off fishing. Often these birds nest in small colonies and, in the breeding season, the air is full of the clamor of the young and the squealing whistles of the parents. Ospreys are migratory to the extent that they move southward along the coast in Winter, largely because the fish on which they prey head southward as the water becomes colder in the North. Of course, the Ospreys on inland waters have to go south when their northerly feeding range is frozen over. But wherever they may be found, Ospreys are wonderful to watch as they flap along some 50 to 100 feet over the water and then suddenly, sighting a fish below, plummet downward to hit the surface with a great splash, disappear for a few seconds and then come up and fly off with a dinner order of fish.

RED-TAILED HAWK

(From 19 to 25 inches)

Let's face it. There is no doubt that it is often difficult and sometimes impossible for an ordinary observer to know which particular member of the Hawk family is in view. Hawks come in many shapes and sizes and some of them look much alike. There are, however, a few points that may be helpful if kept in mind and there are a few members of the family that are easy to recognize. One of the easy ones is the Red-tailed Hawk, because it has the feature from which it derives its name. The upper surface of its tail is brick red. That might seem a foolish point to mention when the bird is usually seen high overhead, but the Red-tail belongs among the Buteo group of soaring Hawks with broad wings and short, rounded tails. As it soars in wide circles, scanning the ground underneath for sight or sign of prey, its tail is frequently tipped so that the upper surface is visible. It's remarkable how far off and how high overhead this identification mark of the Red-tailed Hawk can be seen, especially when the tail is turned at just the right angle on a sunny day.

Like others of the Buteo group, the Red-tailed Hawk is a much maligned bird. It is usually referred to as a "Chicken Hawk" or a "Hen Hawk" and farmers trap it or shoot it relentlessly. How often have you seen the sides of country barns covered with the carcasses of Hawks? Many of these birds are of the Buteo group and are testimony that the farmer has shot some very good friends, because these Hawks feed mostly on mice and other small mammals that are harmful on farm lands. The smaller Hawks of the Accipitrine group, which are bird catchers by profession, are the ones that do the most damage around the poultry yard. They dash in quickly and disappear with a chick or a broiler. The farmer hears or sees the excitement but the criminal has disappeared with the booty. Overhead is a Red-tail sailing around calmly, looking for mice. The farmer shakes his fist at the Red-tail, vows vengeance and takes it with a shotgun at the first chance. If the farmer knew one Hawk from another, he wouldn't slaughter his friends in that fashion. He would wait to catch the real criminal, which might be a Goshawk, a Cooper's Hawk or a Sharp-shinned Hawk.

The Red-tailed Hawk is a permanent resident over almost all of North America but some of the birds of the more northerly wilds move a bit southward in Winter to find better weather and a readier supply of food. As is the case with most birds of prey, the female is quite a bit larger than the male. The call is a loud husky squeal, something like escaping steam from a small valve. A bird much like the Red-tailed Hawk is its near relative, the Red-shouldered Hawk, which is almost as large as the Red-tail but lacks that "signboard" of the red tail, has a ruddy tinge on its under-parts and has a clear ringing "kee-you" cry as it soars in circles overhead.

COOPER'S HAWK

(From 14 to 20 inches)

Among the North American Hawks there are three close relatives that are winged terrors. They are the Goshawk, the Cooper's Hawk and the Sharp-shinned Hawk, members of the Accipitrine group, and they dine on wild birds or barnyard fowl with equal relish. They also eat mice, squirrels, and rabbits on occasion, but most of their food is feathered and includes song birds, game birds and farm poultry. The Accipitrine Hawks have short, rounded wings and long tails and they fly by alternately flapping rapidly and sailing. The Goshawk, much the largest of the three, is a grayish bird, northerly in distribution, never common, and seen mostly in Winter in the United States. The Cooper s Hawk and the Sharp-shinned Hawk, common throughout the United States and Canada, are blue-gray above and whitish below with red-brown cross barring. They are almost identical in everything except size and the shape of the ends of their tails. The Cooper's Hawk is the larger and has a rounded tail. The "Sharpy" has a square tail.

SPARROW HAWK

(From 9 to 12 inches)

This lovely little representative of the famous Falcon family is not, on the average, much larger than a Robin but it is a typical Falcon in flight, wheeling and turning sharply and darting swiftly through the air, often uttering the high-pitched "killy-killy-killy" cry that gives it the name of "Killy Hawk" in some localities. It lives largely on insects, worms and mice but it may occasionally catch a few small birds in Winter when other food is difficult to find. The general body color of the Sparrow Hawk is a rich pinkish-brown above and lighter below, with a plentiful sprinkling of dark cross-bars, streaks and spots. The smaller male is easily known by its blue-gray wings. From other small Hawks the Sparrow Hawks are distinguished by the two black vertical stripes on the whitish sides of their heads. A larger relative of this delightful and handsome little Hawk is the Peregrine Falcon or Duck Hawk, a noble bird and the fastest feathered flier in North America.

BOB-WHITE

(About 10 inches)

The Bob-white, which keeps calling its name clearly over and over again so that there will be no mistake about it, is a Quail and the best known of that family over the central and eastern sections of North America. Quail are small round birds like plump, short-legged Chickens and they have much the same feeding habits as Chickens. In general the Bob-white is reddish-brown with many dark bars and spots. The male has a clear white throat and a clear white line over the eye. In the female the throat and line over the eye are buffy. Except in the breeding season, Bob-whites go about in small groups called bevies and in the bevy they have a remarkable sleeping arrangement. They sit in a tight circle on the ground, all tails together in the center and their heads making the outer rim of the circle. They are placed like spokes in a wheel. If they are attacked in the darkness by a fox, raccoon, skunk, or prowling house cat, they immediately fly off the way they are headed, which means in all directions. That's the reason for this odd way of gathering for sleep. It's a safety device.

CALIFORNIA QUAIL

(About 10 inches)

There is no difficulty in identifying the friendly little California Quail with its quaint nodding plume dangling over its forehead as it feeds in the fields, orchards, and kitchen gardens of the Far West. The only bird with which it might be confused is the Gambel's Quail, quite similar in color and general pattern and wearing practically the same picturesque plume. But the Gambel's Quail has a bright chestnut-reddish crown and, in the middle of its lighter lower breast, it has a distinct black patch like a large inkspot. Not only are these differences easily noted but the Gambel's Quail is largely a bird of the desert regions of the Southwest, whereas the California Quail is much more widespread over the Rocky Mountain and Pacific Coast region and is so familiar a bird around inhabited areas that it is often seen in public parks and even vacant lots in California towns.

RUFFED GROUSE

(From 16 to 19 inches)

If you go walking in the woods and a big brownish bird starts up almost underfoot with an explosive whirr of wings that scares the wits out of you, that will be the Ruffed Grouse, the finest upland game bird of North America. It has a decided preference for the woods or brush-covered country and rarely ventures into the open where there is no thick cover in which it can quickly disappear. If you happen to see it walking on the floor of the forest it will look like a short-legged, plump, dark brown barnyard hen with mottled plumage. There are many kinds of Grouse in different parts of the world and we have seven or eight species in the United States and Canada. Of these the best known and most widely distributed is the Ruffed Grouse that gets its name from the "ruff" of greenish-black feathers sprouting from the base of the neck and draped over the shoulders of the bird. The male wears the larger and shinier ruff and it can be fluffed out in courtship or when challenging some rival male. It's the male, too, that does the famous drumming, an odd sound often heard where these birds are plentiful. It is done partly to allure the female and partly to challenge male rivals. The performances are more numerous in the Spring, but it has been heard at all times of the year and at all hours of the day and night. The male Ruffed Grouse picks out a stump or log for a regular drumming platform and then begins the performance, which is all done with its wings. The drumming starts like a series of slow, heavy thumps and gradually increases in rapidity until it is a hollow roll at the finish. Sometimes a bird will drum every five minutes or so for an hour at a time and often the drumming of one male will be answered by the drumming of another at a distance.

The female lays from 7 to 15 eggs in a depression on the ground in the woods and the young follow the mother off the nest as soon as they are hatched. It isn't long before the little ones sprout enough flight feathers to be able to flutter to low branches for safety if the brood is attacked by a fox, a lynx or a hunting house-cat. If you come upon a mother with young, the mother will often attempt to frighten you off by rushing at you with all her feathers raised. If that fails, she will flop away as if her wing were broken, trying to lure you away from the place in which the young are crouched motionless and invisible on the ground.

The Ruffed Grouse is a hardy bird that is able to get along in rugged country through the coldest weather and the deepest snows of Winter. A curious feature is that in the snowy season its toes sprout little hair-like fringes that help it to walk over soft snow. The delicate tracks of these fringes may be seen in the snow under haw bushes and other such spots where the Ruffed Grouse gather to feed in the Winter.

TURKEY VULTURE

(From 26 to 32 inches)

The Turkey Vulture must be the champion non-stop glider of the feathered world. It soars the skies ceaselessly, a huge blackish bird that looks as big as an Eagle and often circles over the same area for an hour without once flapping its wings. The Golden Eagle and the immature Bald Eagle—before it has developed the white head and tail—also look like huge blackish birds at any distance in flight but there is no need to mistake a Turkey Vulture for an Eagle on that account. The Eagles are uniformly dark on the under side of their wings but there is a two-tone pattern to the wings of the Turkey Vulture that is an easy mark of identification when the bird is circling overhead. The forward half of the wing is the same blackish color as the rest of the bird's plumage but the rear half is a tan-brown that stands out by contrast. The dividing line is sharp and the distinct two-tone pattern usually is quite clear when the bird makes a favorable turn in the air. Since the Turkey Vulture circles much of the time, it usually isn't long before it makes a turn that provides a good glimpse of the under side of the wings.

Because of the bare red skin of its upper neck and head and its custom of feeding on dead animals, garbage, and other such tidbits, the Turkey Vulture sometimes is looked upon as a repulsive bird. It is not a thing of beauty nor is it a singer to be compared with the Mockingbird. About all it utters is an occasional croak or sharp hiss when disturbed. But it is valuable as a scavenger. It is an unpaid but very willing worker in any clean-up campaign around the country. In fact, it is in such good repute as a feathered "street cleaner" that it is protected by law in many sections. If there is a dead horse in a field or a dead fox in the woods, the Vultures will find it quickly and gather to dispose of the remains in their own way. Sometimes they feast so strenuously that they take on too much weight and can't lift themselves from the ground when they try to take off in flight. In that case they readily disgorge some of the banquet, a habit that gives them another black mark for horrible table manners. They often gather around the city dumps by the dozens in the southern part of the United States, the region in which they are most abundant. They may be found as residents over much of the country, though they prefer the southern half. They are hardy individuals, however, that push as far north as the Canadian border region all the way from Maine to the Pacific Coast.

The first cousin of the Turkey Vulture is the somewhat smaller Black Vulture that doesn't range as widely as its larger relative. It keeps mostly to the southeastern and south central part of the United States. The bare skin of its upper neck and head is not red but a grubby pearl-gray or even darker color. Its tail is noticeably shorter than that of the Turkey Vulture, which is much the more graceful bird in the air.

BALD EAGLE

(From 30 to 34 inches)

Everybody knows the Bald Eagle, the national bird of the United States that is famous in song and story, but not everybody realizes that many Bald Eagles in the air show no signs of "baldness" and are often mistaken for Golden Eagles, which never grow "bald" or white-headed. The mistake occurs because it takes young Bald Eagles from three to four years to acquire the white head and tail by which the species is so well known and easily recognized. Through their junior years Bald Eagles wear a complete costume of mottled dark brown that makes them look black at a distance and, since young Golden Eagles are much the same color and only slightly larger in size, except for experts in the field there is much confusion in identifying immature Eagles. But when the Bald Eagle comes of age and dons the white head and white tail of its tribe, all confusion ends.

Benjamin Franklin bitterly opposed the selection of the Bald Eagle as the emblem of the United States. He insisted it was a disreputable bird that made a living as a robber, taking from other and weaker birds the food they had garnered for themselves. Franklin favored the Wild Turkey as our national bird. He contended that the Turkey had none of the vices of the Bald Eagle, was a self-supporting bird and, in addition, was good to eat. Others have spoken worse of the Bald Eagle than Benjamin Franklin did. It is accused of having carried off and devoured little children, but such stories are regarded as fairy tales.

It's true that Bald Eagles will engage in armed robbery, threatening lesser birds with their terrific talons and making them yield up the food they are carrying. Ospreys are frequent victims of such air raids because they catch fish and Eagles dote on fish. The Bald Eagle haunts lakes, rivers, and ocean shores, feeding eagerly on fish of any kind, large or small, dead or alive, honestly earned or boldly stolen. It will also roam the hills and eat small mammals, frogs, snakes, lizards and anything else that it can catch. It has some faults but it is a majestic bird of great dignity, noble bearing and wonderful powers of flight. Of such a bird it was well written by Alfred Tennyson:

He clasps the crag with crooked hands;
Close to the sun in lonely lands,
Ring'd with the azure world, he stands.
The wrinkled sea beneath him crawls;
He watches from his mountain walls,
And like a thunderbolt he falls.

Such is the way of Eagles.

An Introduction to Nature

PART 2

WILD FLOWERS

ILLUSTRATED BY TABEA HOFMANN

SKUNK CABBAGE

(*Symplocarpus foetidus*)

The lowly Skunk Cabbage deserves honorable mention if for no other reason than that in the swamps, low meadows, and wet woods, it is the herald of Spring over a large section of North America, the first wild flowering plant to thrust itself above the ground and burst into bloom. It's true that its flowers are not spectacular in size or color. In fact, you have to get down on your hands and knees to see the flowers at all. If you lower yourself to that extent and peer inside the heavy, twisting, purple-streaked helmet or hood by which we all recognize the plant, you will see a thick stalk on which there is something like an egg-shaped, brownish-yellow pincushion. The many and somewhat raggedy "eruptions" on that pincushion are the true flowers of the Skunk Cabbage.

Botanists call the helmet or hood a "spathe" and the flowering stalk a "spadix" in the Skunk Cabbage, the Jack-in-the-pulpit, and other plants that flower in the same fashion. The "skunk" part of the name comes from the disagreeable odor given off by the Skunk Cabbage when crushed, and the "cabbage" part is a tribute to the large cabbage-like leaves that come after the flowering period and flourish mightily in moist places throughout the Summer. The helmets of the early Spring rarely exceed 6 inches in height but the broad leaves may stretch up 2 feet or more. The Skunk Cabbage is found from Nova Scotia to Georgia and as far west as Minnesota and Iowa. The Western Skunk Cabbage, common along the Pacific Coast, differs from this species in having a bright yellow, shell-like spathe.

Don't look down upon the Skunk Cabbage because of its low estate, its soggy surroundings, and its lack of bright colors. Much can be learned from this sturdy plant that shoulders its way up through frosted ground and often blooms defiantly in the snow when "Winter, lingering, chills the lap of Spring." From the Skunk Cabbage we can learn that some plants flower before they produce leaves, and that flowers may be small, comparatively colorless, and located in odd places on a plant. We could learn many other things from the Skunk Cabbage, but perhaps the first lesson is best closed with a few words from the diary of Henry David Thoreau, whose keen eye noticed that the Skunk Cabbages in a swamp near his Concord home never completely surrendered to oncoming Winter. Even as the broad leaves withered and fell under the impact of Autumn he noticed the hoods beginning to form for the Spring push. And so he wrote of them: "They see over the brow of Winter's hill. They see another Summer ahead."

COLTSFOOT

(*Tussilago farfara*)

This low-growing, bright yellow flower of the early Spring is common only in the northeastern section of the United States, and even there it often goes unnoticed because, at a casual glance, it is easily mistaken for a Dandelion. A closer look will show that the Coltsfoot bloom is smaller and the flower stalk—the "scape" of the botanist—is not smooth and hollow as in the Dandelion but quite hairy and made up of overlapping segments. The leaves, coming after the flowers have gone to seed, are supposed to be about the size and shape of a colt's foot—hence the name—but the outline is jagged all the way around. The plant was brought from Europe by early colonists on the theory that its juices would cure colds, and for generations many country stores in New England sold Coltsfoot candy sticks that children liked well enough because there was more sugar in them than Coltsfoot flavor. The plant grows on sterile, gravelly, or muddy slopes, roadside embankments and such places. It has lost standing as a cold cure but is gaining ground steadily as the wind carries its plumed seeds to new locations.

DANDELION

(*Taraxacum officinale*)

This must be the best-known flower in the world, and one of the most unappreciated. It is found in all inhabited regions of the earth. Where men can live the Dandelion will lift its golden head through most months of the year, but, because it is so widespread and so abundant, its beauty is overlooked. The plant has another good point. Dandelion salad is a regular part of the food supply of families in many countries. The narrow leaves with the jagged edges gave the plant the French name of "*Dent-de-lion,*" or "lion's tooth," centuries ago, and we have taken over the name in slightly changed form. Owners of well-kept lawns usually look upon Dandelions as impudent intruders and go after them with vigor and indignation, but children still view the bright yellow flower head with high favor. It catches their youthful eyes and they are allowed to pick it unhindered. And what fun at a later stage when the flower head has become a feathery sphere and they blow on it in a childish attempt to know "what o'clock" it may be! There is much to be said for the humble, abundant, and beautiful Dandelion.

HEPATICA

(*Hepatica americana*)

Over a large section of North America—from Florida to Nova Scotia, from Missouri to Manitoba—the first flower of Spring to appear in the upland woods is the Hepatica, called Liverleaf or Liverwort in some regions because its 3-lobed leaves are somewhat liver-shaped in general outline. Indeed, the name Hepatica is derived from the Greek "*hepar,*" meaning liver, there being an ancient belief that the plant could cure diseases of this organ. From among the dead leaves of the forest floor the fuzzy flower stalks—"scapes" technically—push up to a height of 3 to 6 inches, each bearing a single flower about ½-inch in diameter and usually pale blue, but it may be light purple, pink, or even white. There may be from 6 to 12 or more "petals" that are really sepals but we need not get excited about the difference. There are many flowers whose sepals look like petals to the ordinary eye. Of these the botanists write: "Sepals, petaloid." At the time of flowering, only last year's Hepatica leaves—thick, fleshy, and rusty green—are found at the base of the flowering stalks. The new leaves come later and lie along or hang just above the litter of the forest floor.

DUTCHMAN'S-BREECHES

(*Dicentra cucullaria*)

The name, the shape, and the general appearance of this flower combine to make it a favorite with children wherever it grows, and it is found over most of North America east of the Rockies and also in the Pacific Northwest. It seems like something that might be produced in a toy shop or sold at a candy counter. The flower stalks with their 4 to 12 "little breeches" hanging from them are from 5 to 10 inches tall. The lacy leaves, cut into innumerable feathery green ribbons, are almost as attractive as the flowers. The leaves come up first in the Spring. Look for patches of them on slopes and in glens in rich woods as the snow disappears. A little later these green patches of feathery foliage will produce Dutchman's-breeches in abundance and give children the chance to pick their first real bouquets of upland flowers of the season.

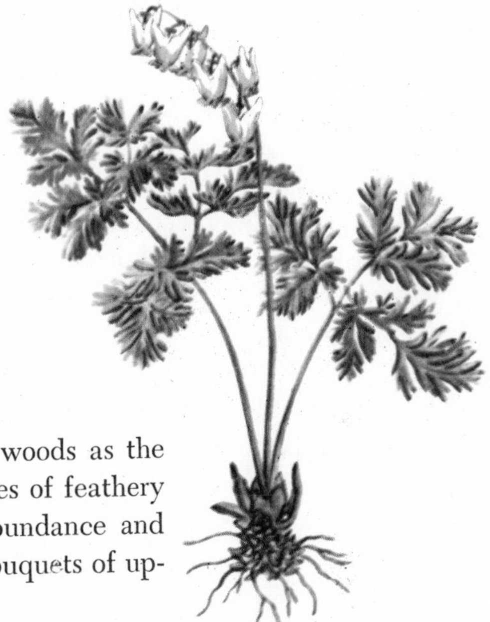

BLOODROOT

(*Sanguinaria canadensis*)

There is no more beautiful or delicate flower in the wildwood than the angelic-looking Bloodroot that is found in early Spring in rich woods over most of North America east of the Rocky Mountains. This plant likes moist banks and shelves in rocky woods. The flowers are found in clumps, groups, and patches, springing up from rootstocks that run under the forest floor. Despite the fact that the flower is pure white, strikingly lovely, and fairly common over such a wide territory, it is not always easy to find. For one thing, it doesn't grow just everywhere in the woods but only in favorable locations to which it is faithful. Another thing is that leaf and flower come up quickly together and a thick, fleshy, and deeply lobed leaf usually curves in cylinder fashion around the rising flower stem—"scape" to the botanist—as though to protect the bud from the bitter winds or the cold rains of the early season. When you find the Bloodroot you will notice that the leaf and flower stalks part company where they come out of the ground but, nevertheless, they grow up in close contact to a height of 8 to 16 inches, and the bud generally overtops the leaf at the last.

But even when the buds burst open and the 6 to 16 petals of each flower form themselves into a wonderful white chalice, you have to be alert to find them because they come and go so fast. If you want to see Bloodroot at its peak, you have to be as regular as a watchman making his rounds. If you miss even a few days of patrol, the glory may have departed from the Bloodroot of your territory. The best way to find the flower is to look for the leaves curved protectively around the flower stalk as they come up from the ground. These leaves are so thick and tender to the touch that they seem to be made out of something like gray-green rubber. But their size and odd appearance catch the eye, and it is easy to find them if you patrol suitable locations faithfully at the right time—which varies from late March to May, depending upon where you live. When the flower bud rises above the leaf the time of blooming is at hand and will pass quickly. Be vigilant!

The unlovely name—Bloodroot—for such a lovely flower is due to the crimson juice that comes from any break in the plant, particularly the rootstock. The scientific name *Sanguinaria* is a reference to the same peculiarity, being derived from the Latin word for blood. It is said that the American Indians used a dye made from the red juice of this plant not only in coloring their garments and handiwork but also as a war paint when occasion called for such decoration.

MARSH MARIGOLD

(*Caltha palustris*)

These are the bright golden flowers of the wet meadows, brooksides, and swamplands that country folk often call "Cowslips" and which some of them use as the first "greens" or "pot-herbs" of the season, eating buds, young leaves, stems, and all. They gather it, treat it, cook it, and eat it much as they do spinach. The plant stem is thick, fleshy, and hollow, and the leaves are large and round. The flower-bearing stalks may carry the blooms to a height of 1 or 2 feet above the ground. Here again the glowing yellow "petals"—there may be from 5 to 9 of them—are really sepals. If you look underneath these golden offerings you will see that they do not have the usual green sepals that are found under the colored petals of many flowers. In this case—as in some other flower families—the petals are missing and the sepals, turning to a glistening gold color, look just as bright as any petals could be in the Spring sunlight.

This is a plant that loves to "keep its feet wet" without going overboard. It is found from Newfoundland to Alaska and as far south as Nebraska and the Carolinas. It comes into bloom in late March in the southerly part of its range and may be found in flower in June in its northerly homelands. It looks something like a stout Buttercup and, indeed, is a member of the large Crowfoot Family along with the Buttercup, Hepatica, Anemone, Columbine, and Pasque Flower. The explanation of its scientific name, *Caltha palustris*, is that "*caltha*" is the Latin name for Marigold and "*palustris*" is Latin for "swampy," referring to the fact that the Marsh Marigold prefers wet ground generally and flourishes abundantly in swamps.

There are days in Spring before the Alders, Dogwoods, Viburnums, Willows, and Red Maples have spread their greenery when such swamps seem to be floored with gold, so thickly spread and so sturdily displayed are the bright yellow flowers of this plant. Later the same area will be the "haunt of coot and hern," the home of the Red-winged Blackbird, the lurking place of the Yellowthroat, the feeding ground of the Bittern, the concert stage of the Veery—or the Willow Thrush of the Northwest. It is a good thing to keep such matters in mind, because it is impossible to go looking for flowers without finding birds, just as it is impossible to go looking for birds without finding flowers—and shrubs and trees and insects and other things, too. One thing leads to another outdoors. Nothing stands alone or lives alone. And nowhere better than in a swamp is this community of interests so well established and so easily observed. Most persons look on swamps as waste territory but to lovers of wildlife they are happy hunting grounds.

SPRING BEAUTY

(*Claytonia virginica*)

To be specific, this is the Narrow-leaved Spring Beauty that carpets the Spring woods from Quebec to Georgia and from Minnesota to Texas. It's a plant from 4 to 7 inches in height with grasslike leaves and anywhere from 2 to 40 flowering stems that carry loose clusters—"racemes," the botanists call these clusters—of white flowers with pink veins or pinkish flowers with darker veins. The flowers are 5-petaled and when fully open may measure 1 inch across, but they close up tight in cold snaps or even when the sky is overcast on cool days. You may find the woodland floor almost white with them one day, and the next day, if it has turned cold, you will have to look close to find any trace of the whiteness so conspicuous the previous day. There are close relatives of the Narrow-leaved Spring Beauty in other parts of the country, all differing a bit in leaf and flower, but if you know this one—and it is easy to find and identify—you will recognize the others as relatives. The Latin name of the group, *Claytonia,* is a memorial to Dr. John Clayton, a colonial botanist who was born in England but spent most of his life—he died in 1773—in Virginia.

TRAILING ARBUTUS

(*Epigaea repens*)

There is no difficulty in recognizing the lowly, lovely, and fragrant Trailing Arbutus; the trick is to find it. Though it ranges all the way from Newfoundland to Saskatchewan and south to Florida and Mississippi, it is rarely abundant in any locality. It likes shady places and most often is found in clumps and patches in the woods, particularly where there are evergreens. But it may be found in shaded nooks in old pastures too. It is called the Mayflower in many regions—particularly New England—but so many other flowers are also called Mayflowers that it is better to call this one the Trailing Arbutus. It really does trail along the ground on hairy stems and twigs, bearing its thick, oval, green and often rusty leaves and, in April or May, its clusters of little tubed pinkish flowers whose 5-lobed "faces" are about ½-inch in diameter. The flowers are waxy but sturdy and stand up well through late frosts and cold rains of unsettled Spring weather. When you come upon a clump of Trailing Arbutus, get on your hands and knees and inhale the wonderful perfume for which the flower is famed. But do not pick the flowers. They are too lovely; they are too scarce; they are too valuable. This is so well recognized that in many regions it is unlawful to pick them. But it is not against the law to look for them, find them, and enjoy their fragrance.

PASQUE FLOWER

(Anemone patens)

This is the hairy-stemmed, golden-centered, pale purple or pinkish-blue flower that covers the open hillsides, the great plains, and the wide prairies from Illinois to Texas and north to British Columbia in early Spring. In addition to Pasque Flower, it is called Prairie Smoke, Wild Crocus, Rock Lily, Hartshorn Plant, Headache Plant, and probably many other things in different sections in which it flourishes. The leaves that branch off from the base of the stem are cut and slashed into numerous ribbon-like segments, and the woolly stem may carry its single flower to a height of from 1 to 1½ feet. The color of the flower varies from purple to almost pure white, and the blooming period extends from March in the southerly part of its range to May in the northerly area. Though it will make no difference to beginners in the field—meaning the readers of this book—the 5 to 7 "petals" around the golden center of the Pasque Flower are not petals but colorful sepals. It's a trait of the Anemones to display sepals instead of petals and the Latin name of the Pasque Flower shows that it is one of the Anemones.

However, there is no other native Anemone that puts on such a magnificent display over such a wide area. It is so popular in South Dakota that it has been named the State flower there, and it is a prime favorite with children all over its range. There are more or less good reasons for some of the names by which this flower is known. It is called Pasque Flower because it blooms about Easter time over much of its range and Easter is the Pasque or Paschal Feast on the church calendar. It is called Wild Crocus because it pushes up quickly from the bare ground in early Spring like the cultivated Crocus and also bears some resemblance to the Crocus in shape and color. It is called Prairie Smoke in parts of its range because, after the blooming period, the golden center of the flower becomes a globular mass of silky hairs like the Dandelion head in the "five o'clock" stage—the ripening seeds with feathery attachments—and when the wind blows these feathery masses about, the effect is that of low waves of smoke moving across the prairies. The feathery appendages, of course, help in the distribution of the seeds by the wind. Many plants use that method of seed distribution, but there are some that use running water, flying birds, or ambling animals to spread their seeds around. Some even shoot their seeds out as from spring-guns! The variety and ingenuity of these methods are amazing. You can learn more by watching flowers go to seed than by looking at them in bloom.

WINDFLOWER

(*Anemone quinquefolia*)

With thin stems and light leaves that tremble at every whisper of the wind, these dainty little white flowers are well-named. In fact, the scientific name traces back to "*anemos*," the Greek word for "wind." There are in North America about 20 species of Anemone, differing in size and color as well as shape of leaves. The Windflower, also called the Wood Anemone, is found in open woods, thickets, and clearings from Quebec to Manitoba and Minnesota, and southward as far as North Carolina and Kentucky. It grows to a height of from 4 to 9 inches with 3 leaves, each divided into 5 parts with rather pointed ends, at a wide angle on the stem several inches or more below the single flower with 4 to 10 white "petaloid sepals" that look like petals to the ordinary eye. Much of what is said about the Windflower is also true of the Rue Anemone, a near relative and a fellow member of the great Crowfoot Family. The Rue Anemone is about the same size and color as the Windflower and grows in the same places over much of the Windflower range, but the Rue Anemone leaves are gently lobed or "scalloped," there are two or more flowers at the top of the stem and usually a "collarette" of leaflets just beneath the flowers.

BLUETS; QUAKER LADIES; HOUSTONIA

(*Houstonia caerulea*)

This dainty little light blue flower is found underfoot in open grassy places as soon as Spring really warms to its work. It is common in New England and as far south as Georgia, but it thins out to the westward and a traveler would be hard put to find a goodly clump of it in most of the country west of the Mississippi. It is a little plant quite grasslike in appearance that grows to a height of from 3 to 7 inches with the small pale blue flowers with lighter centers—usually white with a touch of yellow—trembling shyly at the touch of every passing breeze. The petals are joined in a tube that opens into 4 divisions in a flower "face" that is about ⅜-inch across. Sometimes they are numerous enough to seem like a blue haze running through the grass in all directions. They love pasture lands. In addition to Bluets, Quaker Ladies, and Houstonia, they are also called Innocence, Eyebright, Nuns, Little Washerwomen, and Quaker Bonnets. If you are in doubt about the local name, ask the neighbors.

VIRGINIA BLUEBELL, VIRGINIA COWSLIP

(*Mertensia virginica*)

This plant—the Mertensia of the cultivated gardens—has crossed the Canadian Border in a few favored places, but mostly it is found in wet meadows, around the edges of marshes, and along the banks of streams across the United States from the Atlantic Coast region to the Rocky Mountains. It's smooth and fleshy in leaf and stalk, with oval leaves from 2 to 5 inches long, the upper ones smaller and "sessile" or "sitting on the main stem" that rises to a height of 1 to 2 feet or possibly a little higher. The numerous flowers are carried at the top in what are called "terminal" clusters. Occasionally the main stem has branches and in such cases there are flower clusters at the ends of these, too. The flowers are narrowly bell-shaped, or perhaps you might call them trumpet-shaped, about 1 inch long, with the flaring open ends rather gently 5-sided. The buds are pink, but the color of the open flowers varies from pinkish-purple to lavender-blue. Sometimes the flowers are almost white, but in general they display the hue that justifies the name "Bluebells" by which they are known over much of their range.

Another name for this plant is Lungwort, derived from an ancient belief that some part of it—whether leaf, flower, stalk, or root is not stated—would cure diseases of the lungs. The ending "wort" is frequently found in flower names such as Liverwort (Hepatica), St. John's-wort, Miterwort, Ragwort, Spiderwort, the Figworts, and many more. The "wort" part comes from the old Anglo-Saxon "wyrt," which simply means "plant." Thus Liverwort is supposed to be good for diseases of the liver, Lungwort is credited with being helpful in cases of lung trouble, and Frances Theodora Parsons wrote of St. John's-wort that "it was formerly gathered on St. John's Eve and was hung at the doors and windows as a safeguard against thunder and evil spirits." In olden days the magical properties of plants were taken quite seriously by many of the populace but now they survive only as quaint legend.

One way in which botanists may do honor to their friends is to name plants after them. Thus the scientific name of the Virginia Bluebell is *Mertensia virginica,* the second part of which does honor to Virginia where presumably the species was first found and the first part is in memory of Franz Karl Mertens, a German botanist who lived from 1764 to 1831 and will never be completely forgotten as long as the *Mertensia* comes into bloom.

TROUT LILY; DOG'S-TOOTH VIOLET

(*Erythronium americanum*)

In moist woods and thickets and the more solid parts of shady bogs you will find the mottled leaves of this beautiful low-growing flower carpeting the ground soon after the snow has departed. The smooth flower stem rises to a height of 6 to 10 inches from between the two narrow mottled leaves that point in opposite directions. The single nodding yellow flower has 6 segments that curl back at the tips when in full bloom. This species—there are more than a dozen close relatives in different parts of the country—is found from Nova Scotia across Canada to western Ontario and in the United States from Maine to Florida and as far west as Minnesota and Oklahoma. Dog's-tooth Violet is a poor name for this flower. It is not a member of the Violet family and doesn't look like a dog's tooth. Some call it Adder's-tongue because of a fancied resemblance of the stamens to a snake's tongue. But John Burroughs, the famous naturalist, gave it the name Trout Lily because it is a member of the Lily Family and comes into bloom at the start of the trout season. Fawn Lily is another name, appropriate because of its dappled leaves.

LARGE-FLOWERED BELLWORT; GREAT MERRYBELLS

(*Uvularia grandiflora*)

The pale yellow Bellworts or Merrybells flourish in close company in rich woods, and the plants hang their heads as though they had done something of which they were all ashamed. They are from 10 to 20 inches in height, and, with narrow drooping leaves partially concealing the downcast flowers, they look like miniature patches of sowed corn in the woodlands. They are found from Nova Scotia to Georgia and from Ontario to Kansas. There are two species that look much alike and inhabit much the same territory, this one and its first cousin, the Perfoliate Bellwort. To the ordinary eye the main difference is that the Large-flowered Bellwort earns its name with flowers that are from 1 to 1½ inches in length. Since the 6 narrow yellow segments hang close together the width is not worth mentioning. The Perfoliate Bellwort has smaller flowers and smoother leaves as well as other differences of which the botanists take official note. But the Large-flowered Bellwort is just as "perfoliate" as its cousin. If you look closely, you will see that the stem of the plant grows through the bases of the leaves.

RED TRILLIUM

(*Trillium erectum*)

There is a difficulty with the Trilliums because there are so many different kinds about the country with so many overlapping names. There are a dozen or so species that may be found in the Spring woods or along shaded roadsides of almost any section of temperate North America. The plants are much alike in general appearance and growing habits, but some are larger than others, some hold their flower faces up, some let them droop, and the color differences often are striking. Any one of these many different species may be locally called a "Wake-Robin," and, indeed, there is some dispute as to just which species John Burroughs had in mind when he wrote his famous book, *Wake-Robin*. The Burroughs family tradition is that the author meant the Large White Trillium (*Trillium grandiflorum*), but the Red Trillium also is commonly called the Wake-Robin in many localities. It is sometimes called the Ill-scented Wake-Robin, for an obvious reason if you sniff the flower, and it is further known as the Purple Trillium, Wet-dog Trillium, Nosebleed, Red Benjamin, Squaw-flower, Birthroot—and Stinking Willie!

It is a fleshy plant growing from about 1 to 1½ feet in height, with 3 large somewhat heart-shaped leaves held out at wide angles from the stem at the same level and 1 flower carried on a slender stalk—or a "peduncle" if there is a botanist in the party. The 3 red or purplish petals are backed by 3 narrower bronze-tinted sepals that fill in the spaces between the petals and sometimes make it look like a "6-petaled" flower. The head of the flower tends to droop over shortly after it comes into bloom, which is about the time that the Robins come back in Spring to carol in our dooryards; hence the name of Wake-Robins for all of the Trilliums. The confusion that often exists with a number of different English names for a single flower is the reason why the botanists use Latin names for each species. It is not to show off their knowledge but to make sure of the identity of the species under discussion. The Red Trillium—if that's what you want to call it—has half a dozen other more or less accepted common names in different sections, but it has only one scientific name, *Trillium erectum,* and that is in a dead language not subject to change. The name Trillium comes from the Latin word "*tres,*" meaning "three," and refers to the fact that most of the flowers of this name have three leaves, three petals, and three sepals. The added "erectum" for this species indicates that it holds its flower face skyward at blooming time—though not always! You may pass many Red Trilliums without noticing them because they are modestly hanging their heads. Be on the watch for that when you see the leaves in the Spring woods.

JACK-IN-THE-PULPIT

(*Arisaema triphyllum*)

Here we have a childhood favorite, the familiar and picturesque Jack-in-the-pulpit. It is a member of the same family as the Skunk Cabbage (the Arum Family), but it makes its appearance a little later in the season than its hardy cousin. It grows to a height of 2 or even 3 feet amid the early greenery of the moist woods all the way from Nova Scotia to Minnesota and points north, and as far south and west as South Carolina and Kansas. Its curious construction and its quaint common name combine to make it a childhood attraction. Like the Skunk Cabbage, the flowering part has a protective hood or "spathe," with a flower-bearing stalk or "spadix" within. In this case the hood forms the famous "pulpit" and the pencil-shaped, flower-bearing stalk inside the "pulpit" is the Reverend Jack at his silent preaching.

The 1 or 2 leaves, each divided into 3 large leaflets, are taller than the flowering part of the plant and often hide the Reverend Jack and his pulpit from view. The pulpit may be more or less heavily striped on the inside. Some of these plants bear only male flowers and others only female flowers, but in general the tiny and usually unnoticed flowers are clustered around the pencil-shaped "Jack" himself, the staminate flowers above the pistillate. If you keep an alert eye on the floor of damp woods in Summer, you will often find clusters of red berries on the tops of fleshy stalks. These are the remains of the Reverend Jack, the product of the fertilized pistillate flowers. The leaves wither. The pulpit droops and falls away. The clusters of red berries frequently go unrecognized in the Summer by the children who eagerly search for the Jack-in-the-pulpit of the Spring woods.

The plant is sometimes called Indian Turnip. That's because it has a turnip-shaped root that, after much boiling, was eaten by the American Indians. Do not sample it without boiling it severely or the pulp may cause a burning of the tongue and lips that will last for hours—even a day or more. The Indians also boiled and ate the red berries, which are much easier on the tongue than the root. The North American Indians were a hardy race and ate many plants and roots that the white invaders of this continent were unable to relish or digest. That's one reason why we call this plant Jack-in-the-pulpit instead of Indian Turnip. Another name for it is Starch-plant. It is a relative of the Cuckoo-pint of England from which starch was made to stiffen Elizabethan ruffs.

WOOLLY BLUE VIOLET

(*Viola sororia*)

There are blue Violets, white Violets, yellow Violets. There are Violets of the dooryard, Violets of the wet meadows, Violets of the deep woods. There are the Violas and the Pansies of the cultivated gardens, members of the same widespread family that inhabits not only most of North America but most of the temperate regions of the world. The leaves differ in many species and the flowers vary in size, shape and color, but they are all Violets and as such dearly prized wherever they are found. Poets have sung of them in many languages. They are hardy, lovely, and fragrant. Some come with the return of the birds in Spring and some linger with us on the high hills until the heat of Summer beats them down. We find them in the swamps and on mountain peaks. Some of them dare to sprout a few adventurous blooms in September or even October. It is enough for the ordinary person to distinguish the white or yellow Violet from the blue, but to go much further than that is not so much the desire of the flower lover as it is the business of the botanist who has the task of identifying all the species of a particular region. The Woolly Blue Violet is found from Quebec to Minnesota and south to North Carolina and Oklahoma.

GAY-WINGS; FLOWERING WINTERGREEN

(*Polygala paucifolia*)

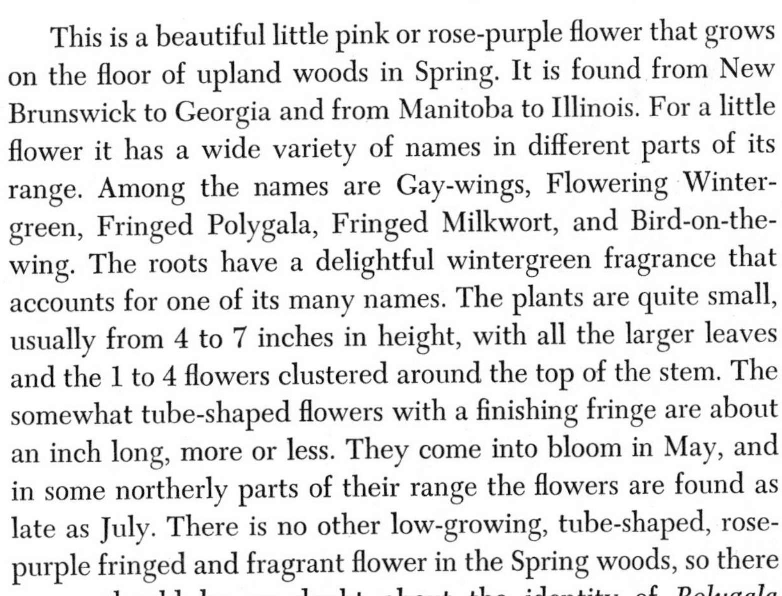

This is a beautiful little pink or rose-purple flower that grows on the floor of upland woods in Spring. It is found from New Brunswick to Georgia and from Manitoba to Illinois. For a little flower it has a wide variety of names in different parts of its range. Among the names are Gay-wings, Flowering Wintergreen, Fringed Polygala, Fringed Milkwort, and Bird-on-the-wing. The roots have a delightful wintergreen fragrance that accounts for one of its many names. The plants are quite small, usually from 4 to 7 inches in height, with all the larger leaves and the 1 to 4 flowers clustered around the top of the stem. The somewhat tube-shaped flowers with a finishing fringe are about an inch long, more or less. They come into bloom in May, and in some northerly parts of their range the flowers are found as late as July. There is no other low-growing, tube-shaped, rose-purple fringed and fragrant flower in the Spring woods, so there should be no doubt about the identity of *Polygala paucifolia* if you come upon it. The only doubt will be the common name applied to it in that locality.

WILD (or FALSE) LILY-OF-THE-VALLEY

(*Maianthemum canadense*)

This abundant little Spring flower, which is a relative of the familiar Lily-of-the-valley of city florist shops and suburban gardens, grows in widespread patches on the forest floors and other shaded places all the way across the North American continent from Newfoundland to the Canadian Rockies and as far south as Georgia, Tennessee, and Iowa. It is called Wild (or False) Lily-of-the-valley because it is a small white flower growing amid much larger rich green leaves close to the ground in large patches and perhaps from a distance and at a casual glance it does bear a general resemblance to its cultivated cousin, but any close inspection will show the difference. This plant grows from 3 to 7 inches in height, and the stem, which is often zigzag, has from 1 to 3 (generally 2) lance-shaped to oval leaves that are heart-shaped at the base. Along the upper part of the stem the many little flowers jut out sidewise in what the botanists call a "terminal raceme." So if you take a good look at the arrangement of these flowers along the stem, you will have a clear idea of what a "terminal raceme" is. If you have a good eye—or a handy magnifying glass—you will see that the "face" of each tiny flower is 4-parted. They bloom in May and June, and even into July at the northern fringe of their range.

CINQUEFOIL; FIVE-FINGER

(*Potentilla simplex*)

There are so many species and varieties of Cinquefoil or Five-finger in North America that only a botanist can deal with them. The Old-field Cinquefoil pictured here is one of the more common species and may be found in fields and open woods from Nova Scotia to Ontario and Minnesota and south to North Carolina and Oklahoma. It has the 5-fingered leaves—the leaflets extended like an open hand—that are the mark of most of the clan, along with a small, 5-petaled, yellow flower. Some farm folk refer to this species as well as to the low-growing Common Five-finger (*Potentilla canadensis*) as the "Yellow Strawberry," but the Wild Strawberry has a white flower and 3-section leaves instead of the "five-finger" leaves and the yellow flowers of its close neighbors of the open fields. The Old-field Cinquefoil lifts its roving stem higher than the Common Five-finger—sometimes to a height of 18 inches—and it may reach out a yard or more with its rooting tip. You can't go far afield in Spring or Summer without finding one or other of the Cinquefoils in bloom. They are really quite pretty little flowers but they are so small that few persons notice them.

WILD COLUMBINE
(*Aquilegia canadensis*)

One of the most delicate, beautiful, and odd-shaped of our native wild flowers is the common Wild Columbine that generally grows around rocks in shaded ground and may be found in such places almost anywhere in temperate North America. The only excuse for using the word "common" in describing such a lovely flower is to distinguish it from the other native Columbines that are not so numerous nor so widespread over the country. The curious and beautiful flowers are the delightful terminal decorations of a branching plant that grows to a height of 1 to 2 feet or more. The foliage is feathery to the eye, much divided, and has somewhat mitten-shaped leaflets that are rather sharply scalloped or lobed. The odd shape of the flowers that —most of them, anyway—hang "face downward" is due to the fact that the 5 petals grow backward in tubular spurs that are highly spectacular. All the Columbines have flowers of that shape, though the different species and varieties differ in size and color as well as in haunts and habits. The species pictured here is the best known and most abundant from Nova Scotia to the Northwest Territory and south to Florida and Texas.

Rocks are not essential as a growing ground for the Wild Columbine, but it flourishes so often around or amid rocks and boulders on shady banks and wooded slopes that it is called Rock Bells in some localities. Depending upon the latitude, it flowers from April to July. The usual color combination is bright or deep red running into a cream yellow or white, but this may vary somewhat over its full range. Because of its attractiveness it is everywhere cherished and even protected by law in some areas. It belongs to the Crowfoot Family, which includes the Buttercups, Anemones, and Hepaticas with many less-known wild flowers. There is some dispute among botanists as to the meaning or derivation of the scientific name of the Columbines, *Aquilegia*. Some say it comes from the Latin word for eagle, "*aquila,*" because of the fancied resemblance of the spurred petals to the claws or talons of an eagle. Others assert that it traces from "*aqua,*" the Latin word for "water" and "*legere,*" meaning "to collect," in reference to the little drops of sweet fluid—nectar—found at the bottom of the spurs of the Columbine petals. The lovely Long-spurred Blue Columbine (*Aquilegia caerulea*) found on shaded high ground from New Mexico to Montana is the State flower of Colorado.

WILD GERANIUM; SPOTTED CRANE'S-BILL

(*Geranium maculatum*)

When the Oaks and Elms and Maples and Ashes are beginning to hang out their first leaves of Spring and "the time of the singing of birds has come," the Wild Geranium or Spotted Crane's-bill abounds in open woods and shady places from Maine to Manitoba and as far south as Georgia, Alabama, and Kansas. The delicate, 5-petaled, rose-purple flowers are from 1 to 1½ inches in diameter, and the deeply cut leaves are 5-parted, like a palm-upward hand with the fingers spread wide. The plants reach a height of from 1 to 2 feet and are most numerous in light woods and on moist rocky hillsides. They are not fond of either the thick woods or sunlit open ground. The name Geranium comes from the Greek word for the bird we know as the crane, and the reference, which also explains the other common name of the flower, is to the shape of the ripening fruit when the petals drop away from the flower head. What is left is the long, pointed pistil projecting from the little overlapping sepals at the base of the flower, and the combination is shaped somewhat like the small head and long thin bill of a crane. Or at least it must have looked that way to the man who first gave the name Crane's-bill to the flower. There are several other species of Wild Geranium in North America but this is the most abundant over a great part of the continent east of the Rocky Mountains.

Sometimes there is as much enjoyment in reading about flowers as there is in finding them in the woods and fields. For instance, there is in *Leaves from Gerard's Herball*, by Marcus Woodward, an account of the virtues of the Crane's-bill plant as set down by the quaint old English surgeon and gardener John Gerard, when he published his famous *Herball* in 1597. Though he was weighing the good points of a different species, doubtless he considered them family virtues and, as such, would have said or written the same things of our own Spotted Crane's-bill or Wild Geranium. Of his Crane's-bill, a cousin to our own, he wrote in part:

"The herbe and roots dried, beaten into a most fine pouder, and given halfe a spoonfull fasting, and the like quantitie to bedwards in red wine or old claret for the space of one and twenty daies together, cure miraculously ruptures and burstings, as my selfe have often proved, whereby I have gotten crownes and credit: if the ruptures be in aged persons, it shall be needfull to adde thereto the powder of red snailes (those without shels) dried in an oven. . . ."

However, such treatment is not recommended in medical books of today.

COMMON WILD MUSTARD

(*Brassica nigra*)

This is a common plant of waste places, wild fields, and roadsides all over the United States and southern Canada. It grows from 2 to 7 feet in height, is often much branched, and bears clusters ("racemes") of small yellow flowers at the ends of the branches. Like all members of the great Mustard Family, it has 4 petals. The Latin name for the family is *Cruciferae,* meaning "cross-bearing," because the 4 petals are arranged somewhat in the shape of a Maltese Cross. There may be a dozen or more flowers in each cluster but the individual flowers are only ½-inch or less in diameter. The leaves are larger at the base of the plant and grow smaller upward along the stem and branches. They are saw-toothed along the edges and usually deeply lobed or cut, many of them having the "bow-tie" or even double "bow-tie" effect along the lower part of the mid-vein. This and several other species of Wild Mustard are not native but invaders from Europe. The best-known and most useful members of the Mustard Family are such "kitchen garden" reliables as Cabbage, Broccoli, Kale, Brussels Sprouts, and Cauliflower, all of which, if they are allowed to flower, will produce clusters of yellow or whitish-yellow 4-petaled flowers much the size and general shape of those of the Common Wild Mustard shown in this picture.

PHILADELPHIA FLEABANE

(*Erigeron philadelphicus*)

The Fleabanes—and there are many of them—look like delicate downy Daisies of different pale colors and, as a matter of fact, they belong to the same great Composite Family that includes all the Asters of our fields and woods, the common White or Field Daisy, the Black-eyed Susan, and many other wild flowers. There are more than a dozen species of Fleabane that are fairly common in different parts of Canada and the United States. Though it may be locally rare or absent, the Philadelphia Fleabane is to be found from Newfoundland to British Columbia and from Florida to Texas. It grows from 1 to 3 feet high, and the "ray flowers" or silky "fringe" of the flower head may be light rose-purple, pink, or whitish. The hue is variable in the "rays," but the "disk flowers" (center circle) are always yellow. The expanded flower may be as much as an inch in diameter, but more often is something less than that. The leaves at the base of the stem may be 3 inches long and narrowish. The leaves sparsely scattered along the stem are smaller and "sessile," meaning that the base of the leaf is right on the stem. This species has a long blooming period and may be found in flower any time from April through August.

SWAMP or MARSH BUTTERCUP

(*Ranunculus septentrionalis*)

If there are two flowers that everybody knows, they are Daisies and Buttercups. There are some three dozen species of Buttercup spread over North America and the Swamp or Marsh Buttercup is just one of the many, but it is the common species found in swamps, wet meadows, and low ground over most of the United States and southern Canada from the Atlantic Coast to the Ozarks. It grows from 1 to 3 feet high, with considerable branching. Each leaf has 3 large divisions and many smaller divisions ending in rather sharp points. The spread of the 5-petaled shining yellow "cup" is about 1 inch across, and it may be found in bloom—depending upon the location—from April through July. The differences among the many native species of Buttercup concern the botanist more than they do any reader of a book like this. To the ordinary person, a Buttercup is a Buttercup wherever it is found. For centuries to come—as for centuries in the past—children will be holding the golden chalices close under the chins of their companions to tell by the yellow reflection "whether or not they like butter." The test always brings the same answer. Apparently all children like butter!

FORGET-ME-NOT

(*Myosotis scorpioides*)

The lovely little Forget-me-not has been introduced from its native Europe to the banks of ponds, brooks, and streams in the northeastern part of the United States where it may be found creeping in tangled and matted masses from which the stems reach up feebly to show their terminal clusters of tiny blue flowers with yellow centers. Tennyson wrote in his lovely poem *The Brook* (with the brook itself speaking):

> *I steal by lawns and grassy plots:*
> *I slide by hazel covers;*
> *I move the sweet Forget-me-nots*
> *That grow for happy lovers.*

The American Brooklime or Speedwell (*Veronica americana*), which grows in similar places over most of the United States, might be mistaken for the Forget-me-not at a quick glance, but it can be noted that the flower face of the Forget-me-not is 5-lobed, whereas the Speedwell's is 4-lobed. Also the leaves of the Speedwell are shorter and wider and grow in pairs on opposite sides of the stem.

CLIMBING (or BITTERSWEET) NIGHTSHADE

(*Solanum dulcamara*)

This is a vine that grows from 2 to 8 feet in length, creeping along stone walls, rail fences, or almost any kind of support. It was introduced into New England long ago from Europe and has been spreading westward and southward steadily with such success that it has been reported as far from its New England landing place as Kansas. It is a member of a remarkable family that includes the Potato, the Tomato, and other plants with fruits that are not so tasty. In fact, some are poisonous. If you ever have seen a Potato or Tomato plant in bloom, you may have noted the handsome little flower, 5-pointed, with the stamens jutting out in a bunch like a narrow cone. That's the way it is with the Climbing Nightshade, and the contrasting colors of the golden stamens and the deep violet or purple 5-pointed flower face form a striking combination that catches the eye. The leaves are what the botanist calls "hastate," meaning that near the base they have 2 little divisions, one on each side, as though somebody had made a bow tie on the "neck" of the leaf. The flowers grow in somewhat drooping sprays called "cymes" from May to September, and the fruit is a shining, red (and rather watery), poisonous berry produced in clusters. In Midsummer flowers and fruit are found in profusion together on the vines. Many birds seem to be immune to Nightshade poisoning and suffer no harm from eating the berries.

SHOWY ORCHIS

(*Orchis spectabilis*)

This beautiful and fragrant member of the Orchid Family is easily overlooked because —though it is common to abundant on many wooded hillsides from New Brunswick to Ontario and south to Georgia and Arkansas—it is a low-growing plant that may be obscured by taller neighbors. The flowering stalk rarely reaches a height of 8 inches. The easiest way to find the flower is to look for the 2 shining leaves—about 6 to 8 inches long, slightly wider toward the outer end—that stretch upward and outward on opposite sides of the base of the stem. It is easier to spot these rich green leaves on the forest floor than it is to catch sight of the lovely purple and white flowers that, in many areas, are the first of our native Orchids to come into bloom. Depending upon where you live, look for them from late April to early June in rich woods and shaded rocky hillsides that are spillways for Spring seepage.

MOCCASIN FLOWER; PINK LADY'S-SLIPPER

(*Cypripedium acaule*)

Look for the Moccasin Flower—also known as the Moccasin Orchid, Stemless Lady's-slipper, and Pink Lady's-slipper—in sandy or rocky woods "when April melts in Maytime," though the average time of blooming might be mid-May over its full range, which extends from Newfoundland out to Manitoba and southward to Georgia and Alabama. It is a member of the Orchid Family. It sometimes surprises our citizens to know that we have many wild Orchids growing in North America, some of them rare and beautiful and some of them quite common and plain in appearance. The Moccasin Flower is among a group that is cherished for its elegance and dignity. The stalk or "scape" on which the single flower is carried grows to a height of 6 to 15 inches, and the lovely "slipper" may be 2 inches in length. There are 2 oval leaves, 6 to 8 inches in length, at the base of the flower stalk or "scape." Because lumbering operations have cut into the woods in which it used to grow and ruthless picking has lessened its numbers, the Moccasin Flower is protected in many areas either by State law, local option, or honored tradition.

YELLOW LADY'S-SLIPPER

(*Cypripedium pubescens*)

The Yellow Lady's-slipper—some persons prefer to call it the Yellow Slipper Orchid—usually is found on a lower level than the Moccasin Flower, its pink cousin of the Orchid Family. Where it moves up wooded slopes or climbs mountain ranges, it follows the water courses. The plant has a fondness for keeping its feet wet. It grows in moist woods and thickets nearly throughout the United States—except California and Florida—and well up into Canada. It blooms a little later and grows much taller than the Moccasin Flower. It differs, too, in having a few oval leaves growing along the stem that may reach a height of 2 feet or more. Look for the Yellow Lady's-slipper in May and June but do not pick it when you find it. Leave it for others to enjoy. There are other kinds of Lady's-slippers across the country, all of them beautiful and all of them needing protection. The lovely Showy Lady's-slipper—white, with pink stripes—has been almost exterminated by ruthless picking over much of its natural range. If you know where any are to be found, don't spread the news too widely.

WILD LUPINE

(*Lupinus perennis*)

From Maine to Ontario and Minnesota and as far south as Florida the blue spikes of the Wild Lupine are held aloft in April, May, and June to a height of 1 to 2 feet in dry sandy soil. The plant likes the sun. It will move in where the ground is left bare and take over dry banks where the soil has been exposed. The Wild Lupine is a member of the Pulse or Pea Family and is related to the Alfalfas, Clovers, Vetches, the Wistaria Vine, the Locust Trees, the cultivated Sweet Pea, and the common garden product that is so often served with lamb chops and mashed potatoes. There are countless species of Lupine in North America; dozens in California alone. In this widespread species the leaf is composed of 7 to 11 leaflets 1 to 1½ inches long growing outward like spokes of a wheel from a common center. A near relative of the Wild Lupine is the beautiful little Texas Bluebonnet, the official flower of the Lone Star State. Unfortunately, it is not hardy north of Texas and, in fact, is found wild only in a comparatively small section of that vast territory. But there are other Bluebonnets and Lupines to be seen in season in almost any part of the country—all with a general resemblance—so be on the watch for them.

GOLDEN (WILD or CALIFORNIA) POPPY

(*Eschscholtzia californica*)

Only tourists or new settlers on the West Coast need to be told the name of this flower, because it is the State flower of California and its common name is California Poppy. To see it is to know it when the California hillsides are yellow with the blooms in Spring. It grows by hundreds of thousands in wide patches in uncultivated areas and is so highly prized that it has been taken into cultivation and may be found in different shades and a number of varieties in western and even eastern gardens. It grows to a height of 2 feet, and the individual flowers are carried aloft on their own little stems or "peduncles." The leaves are deeply cut and narrowly "many-fingered" like those of the Dutchman's-breeches, of which it is a not too distant relative. It's wonderful to walk along a California hillside bright with these flowers in Spring. What Wordsworth wrote of England's famous Daffodils well fits a golden horde of California Poppies in bloom:

A poet could not but be gay
In such a jocund company.

COMMON DAISY; OX-EYE DAISY; WHITE DAISY

(*Chrysanthemum leucanthemum*)

There is no need to describe the Common or White Daisy, also called the Ox-eye or Field Daisy. It is known to everybody and grows abundantly in fields and along roadsides over most of temperate North America, though it is more common in the northern and eastern sections than in southern and western areas. As common, widespread, and well-known as it is to the inhabitants of North America, it is not native to this continent. It comes from southeast Europe and Asia, but it has been here from colonial days and has become one of our most beloved wild flowers. It grows in abundance and is easily picked for a handsome bouquet. It does not fade quickly after plucking as so many wild flowers do if gathered and put in a vase. It is used to make school and college "daisy chains," and, for childhood's happy hours, it still serves its legendary purpose in telling—as little fingers pluck it apart—whether he or she "loves me" or "loves me not." It is in high favor with everyone except the farmers, who look upon it as a weed in their hayfields, occupying space and stealing sustenance from the soil that could be put to better use in providing just that many more stalks of tasty timothy hay for horses and cows. The farmers are justified in their complaint, but to the rest of us there is no more gay sight of a sunny June morning than a field of Daisies in full bloom.

Since everybody knows the Daisy, it can be used as a help in identifying lesser known wild flowers and learning more about them. For instance, the Daisy is a member of the great Composite Family, the term "composite" meaning "placed together" and referring to the fact that what we might think to be a single flower—a single Daisy in this case—is really a grouping of many small flowers of two kinds: ray flowers and disk flowers. The disk flowers, individually too small to notice without a magnifying glass and too many to count in a hurry, form the yellow center of the Daisy. The ray flowers are the white strap-shaped or ribbon-like "rays" that grow outward in a circle around the yellow center and ordinarily are called the "petals" by all but botanists and their students. The Composite Family is the largest of all flower families and there are many differences in the family circle. The ray and disk flowers may be the same color or of contrasting colors. In some members of the family the blooms consist only of ray flowers and in others only of disk flowers.

Whether the ray or the disk flowers or both are fertile or not is another detail for the botanist. It is enough for the ordinary person to know that the common Daisy, with its delightfully attractive and easily observed arrangement of two sorts of flowers, can stand as a good representative of the Composite Family.

HAIRY SOLOMON'S-SEAL

(*Polygonatum pubescens*)

There is a smoother and larger species of Solomon's-seal than this one, but the Hairy Solomon's seal, whose lovely leaves are pale and covered with very fine hairs on the underside, is the more abundant over a wider area in North America. It is found in woods, thickets, and shaded ground from Nova Scotia to Manitoba and as far south as South Carolina. The stem grows on an arching slant from a rootstock, and the broadly lance-shaped leaves of fine texture alternate on opposite sides of the stem the length of the plant, which may reach a height of 1 to 3 feet. The tiny flower stems ("peduncles" to the botanist) grow out from the points where the leaves are joined to the stem. Such places are called "axils" and flowers that arise there are "axillary." Usually there are 2 little narrowly bell-shaped or tubular green flowers hanging beneath the stem at each leaf-joint, but there may be just 1 or even 3 or 4. The name Solomon's-seal comes from the "scars" on the rootstock left by growths of previous years. If you dig up the rootstock, you will note these marks that resemble ancient seals. King Solomon's name was borrowed—probably without permission—to add majesty to poetic fancy.

FALSE SOLOMON'S-SEAL; SOLOMON'S-PLUME

(*Smilacina racemosa*)

This is a stouter, larger, taller, more abundant, and even more widespread plant than the true Solomon's-seals to which it is a second cousin and which it does resemble in growing habit and leaf shape. But there the general resemblance ends, because the flowers of this plant are carried in a cone-shaped spray at the end of the stem (a "terminal raceme" or "panicle" to the botanist), whereas the flowers of the true Solomon's-seals are hung like wash on a line from the undersides of the stems. The False Solomon's-seal or Solomon's-plume (sometimes called Wild Spikenard) grows in wet woods, along shaded roadsides, or in moist shaded ground almost everywhere in temperate North America. The flower spray appears in May or June over most of its range but it may bloom as early as April in the South and as late as July at its northern limits. The sturdy stem, springing from a rootstock, usually grows on a slant to a height of from 1 to 3 feet, and the flower spray eventually turns into a cluster of red berries. The tiny individual white flowers are like 6-pointed stars and well worth a closer inspection than most persons ever give them.

YELLOW STAR-GRASS; GOLDSTAR-GRASS

(*Hypoxis hirsuta*)

This attractive little flower practically identifies itself. It is bright yellow or golden in color and is shaped like a 6-pointed star. It flourishes over most of the United States east of the Rocky Mountains and may be found in bloom almost any time between May and October. The plant is grasslike in appearance and grows among grasses of many kinds. Perhaps the bright little flower would be better known if it were not overtopped by so many of the tall grasses among which it modestly hides. These plants like the sun. They will grow in open woods but they prefer sunlit meadows and roadsides of dry soil. The leaves of the Yellow Star-grass look just like leaves of grass a foot or more in length, often drooping at the tips. The flowers are carried on stalks ("scapes" to the botanist) that look something like the leaves but are shorter. There may be from 1 to 6 flowers on a stalk, all springing from one terminal point, but the average number is 3 and ordinarily only one flower of each cluster is in bloom at a time. Look for them from early Summer to the beginning of Fall among the taller grasses of old fields and open roadsides, and remember that the bright flower face is only about ¾-inch in diameter and rarely reaches up more than 6 inches or so from the ground.

BLUE FLAG; WILD IRIS

(*Iris versicolor*)

There is no great need to describe this flower in detail since it is so well known in general through the cultivated members of its family that bloom in so many bewildering varieties in our gardens. There are numerous species of wild Iris in North America. They vary in color and size and other minor details, but most of them are largely blue in main color with dark streaks on the lighter touches of yellow or white in the center part of the flower segments. This species—sometimes called Larger Blue Flag—is the most abundant and the most widespread of our wild Irises and may be found in wet meadows, in marshes, along the edges of ponds and meandering streams, and in open wet places in general from Newfoundland to Manitoba and down to Virginia. The leaves are like the blade of a sword, long and narrow and slightly curved. The stem, atop which there may be one or more flowers, is circular, almost rodlike, and grows to a height of 2 or 3 feet. It comes into bloom in late Spring or early Summer.

SPIDERWORT; SPIDER-LILY

(*Tradescantia virginiana*)

This is a 3-petaled deep violet-blue flower from 1 to 2 inches in diameter carried on a plant that grows to a height of 1 to 3 feet in rich moist ground from Maine to Wisconsin and southward to Georgia and Missouri. Depending upon the location, it may be found in bloom from May to August. There are numerous buds in a group, but only one or two come to full flower at a time and the individual flowers wither quickly—often by noon of the day they open. Look for these flowers in the morning. The plant prefers shade to bright sunlight and is found most frequently in wet woods and along the shady fringes of lakes, slow streams, swamps, and ponds. The leaves are long and narrow, like small Cattails. The *Tradescantia* of its scientific name is in honor of John Tradescant, head gardener for Charles I of England, of whom it was written by Isaac D'Israeli in *Curiosities of Literature* that in 1620 he "entered himself aboard of a privateer, armed against Morocco, solely with a view of finding an opportunity of stealing apricots into Britain; and it appears that he succeeded in his design."

GOLDEN RAGWORT

(*Senecio aureus*)

This flower—also called Squaw-weed and Golden Groundsel—looks something like a small yellow Daisy and grows in ditches, swamps, and open wet places from Newfoundland and northern Quebec as far south and west as Florida and Missouri. It might be confused with some of the yellow Asters, but the Golden Ragwort blooms in May or June, which is early for any of the yellow Asters, and there are other differences, including the shape of the leaves and the size of the "disk" or central part of the flower head, which is smaller in the Ragworts. The basal leaves of the Golden Ragwort are from 1 to 6 inches long, heart-shaped and long-stalked. The upper leaves growing closely along the stem are narrower and much cut up or "indented." There may be from 5 to 15 or so flower heads in a loose cluster—called a "corymb" by the botanist—at the top of the stem, and from 8 to 18 yellow rays to each head. The flower "face" is somewhat less than 1 inch in diameter. Roughly speaking, if you see anything like a "yellow Daisy" in moist ground in May or June, it's probably the Golden Ragwort or some related species.

PINK AZALEA; PINKSTER FLOWER

(*Rhododendron nudiflorum*)

One of the spectacular glories of the Spring woods is the flowering of the Pink Azalea, Pinkster Flower, Mayflower, Wild Honeysuckle, or whatever else it may be called over its range that extends from New England to Ohio and south to South Carolina and Tennessee. The branching shrub grows from 2 to 6 feet or more in height, and the flowers that come just ahead of the leaves are tubed or funnel-form (like the Honeysuckle) with a spreading outer end that flares into a 5-pointed star that may be 2 inches across. The narrow leaves, 2 to 4 inches long, are pointed at both ends. There are about a dozen species of Azalea in the United States, including the Rhododendron that has been brought into common cultivation and the lovely and now rare rose-purple Rhodora, of which Emerson wrote:

Rhodora! if the sages ask thee why
This charm is wasted on the earth and sky,
Tell them, dear, that if eyes were made for seeing,
Then Beauty is its own excuse for being.

MOUNTAIN LAUREL

(*Kalmia latifolia*)

The beautiful Mountain Laurel, much cherished throughout its range that extends from New England to Indiana and down to the Gulf of Mexico, is a shrub that varies from 2 to 20 feet in height and flourishes best in the woods and shady places, though it does venture into the open here and there. It has rather narrow, shiny leaves from 1 to 5 inches long and, blooming in May or June, bears a wealth of half-round clusters of lovely pink or pinkish-white flowers shaped like curiously dented and ribbed little bowls. Even before the flowers open they are a delight to the eye. In the bud they are a deeper pink with radiating lines that make them look like candy stars, good enough to eat. As food, however, the plant has a poor reputation; both this species and its smaller and darker-tinted relative, the Sheep Laurel or Lambkill, are known to make cattle ill. The scientific name *Kalmia* is in honor of Peter Kalm, a Swedish botanist who traveled eastern North America in colonial days and sent back botanical specimens to be classified and named by the great Linnaeus.

WILD PINK; DEPTFORD PINK

(*Dianthus armeria*)

There is an air of mild mystery about this modest but persistent little deep pink flower. It is very common, fairly widespread, and quite pretty in a small way, yet it is rather generally overlooked. Brought here by choice or by chance from Europe many years ago, it has been gaining ground steadily and has spread from Quebec, New England, and Georgia as far west as Ontario and Missouri. It's curious that it is not better known over this territory, because it grows readily in old fields and along roadsides and even pops up on lawns, where it will bloom between cuttings unless the lawn mower is kept busy. It has no great claim to fame itself, but it comes of a famous family—the Pink Family—and has some notable relatives. It is a cousin of the cultivated Carnation, of the Sweet William of the flower garden, and of the Bladder Campion and Bouncing Bet of waste places and roadsides across this country.

Another curious thing about this flower is its preferred English name of Deptford Pink. Here is a flower that is native to much of temperate Europe and it is named for a busy borough—Deptford—in England, a part of metropolitan London, a section filled with iron works, railroad shops, and shipyards on its Thames waterfront. The only claim to botanical distinction that Deptford can offer is that John Evelyn, keeper of a famous diary and author of a great work on English trees, lived at Sayes Court in Deptford from 1652 to 1694 and did considerable experimenting on trees and flowers in his gardens there.

The plant itself is grasslike in appearance. The stem, which may have 1 or 2 branches near the top, grows to a height of 6 to 18 inches with some grasslike leaves along it and a group of flower buds at the top—or at the top of each branch if it is branched. Though there may be numerous buds in a cluster, only one or two in each cluster will be in bloom at one time. The flowering season is from June through the Summer, and the rich pink 5-petaled flower is approximately ½-inch in diameter. If you look closely—better use a magnifying glass—you will see that each tiny petal is notched or "toothed" at the tip. It should be added that a small and inexpensive magnifying glass is not only a big help in trying to learn something about flowers but it also reveals strange and wonderful details of stamen and pistil construction that would be missed by the naked eye. The original cost is low, the upkeep is nothing, and it will last a lifetime. There are few things to be purchased today that will give as much pleasure and profit for the money expended as an ordinary pocket magnifying glass. When you have one, use it often. You will be pleasantly surprised at what you see—and how much you learn!

SLENDER BLUE-EYED GRASS

(*Sisyrinchium mucronatum*)

Though you might not suspect it to look at it, this is a member of the Iris Family. There are many species of Blue-eyed Grass in the United States and Canada, some of them so much alike that even the botanist has to look closely to distinguish one from the other. The one pictured here—the Slender Blue-eyed Grass—will serve as a good representative of the group. It grows in meadows, fields, and open woods from Maine to Wisconsin and south to North Carolina. The plant is grasslike in appearance—hence the name—and grows among ordinary grasses to a height of from 6 to 18 inches, but if you finger the stems or long narrow leaves, you will note a decided difference from the ordinary grasses at once. The stems and leaves of the Blue-eyed Grasses are quite stiff and flattened so as to be sharply double-edged in a small way. In this species the 6-parted violet-blue flower with a yellow center is about ½-inch in diameter and it can be found in bloom in different parts of its range in May or June. If you look at the flower under a magnifying glass, you will see that each of the 6 segments has a tiny bristle and a double notch at the tip.

DWARF WILD ROSE

(*Rosa carolina*)

There are about two dozen species of Wild Rose in North America, and most of them look much alike to the ordinary observer. The Dwarf Wild Rose, also called Low or Pasture Rose, is probably the most common of the group over the eastern half of the United States. It is found in dry rocky ground—often in upland pastures—and grows from 6 inches to a couple of feet in height, frequently much branched. The lovely flowers have a most delightful odor and one flowering bush of this species is enough to fill the vicinity with a delicate perfume. Like all of its clan, the plant is armed with sharp thorns but, for the most part, they are only at the places where the leaves branch from the stem. The beautiful 5-petaled flower is about 2 inches in diameter, and the compound leaf usually is composed of from 5 to 7 leaflets, the odd one being "terminal," meaning placed at the outer end. Note the general resemblance of the leaves and leaflets to those of the Strawberry, Blackberry, and Cinquefoil. They all belong to the Rose Family.

PITCHER PLANT

(*Sarracenia purpurea*)

This curious plant is found only in bogs, swamps, marshes, and wet soil generally. It flourishes over most of temperate North America east of the Rockies but is very choosy of its ground. You may search ten bogs of a region and find never a sign of a Pitcher Plant, and the whole floor of the eleventh bog may be covered with it. The name comes from the strange shape of the fleshy leaves that grow in a low rosette that may be 12 to 18 inches in diameter around the base of the plant. These leaves are hollowed like narrow, curving pitchers with a large pouring lip and a projecting "wing" or "flange" that might easily serve as a handle. The stiff and rather dull-colored nodding flower that rises a foot or two on a bare stalk—"scape" to the botanist—has 5 sepals and 5 petals that are purplish-brown. The Pitcher Plants are meat-eaters like the Venus Fly-trap. The insects that crawl into the hollow leaves are unable to push their way out again because of the backward-pointing stiff hairs that line the inside of the leaves. The insects eventually perish, fall into the water held by the leaves, and are absorbed as food for the Pitcher Plant. The full diet is a varied one, however. The roots find other food in the ground.

RED CLOVER

(*Trifolium pratense*)

Hail to the Red Clover! It is both useful and beautiful. It is loved by man and beast. Introduced from Europe, it now grows everywhere in North America and blooms through all the warmer months. When other flowers fail, a handsome bouquet of Red Clover can be gathered in any region free of charge. It is a sturdy member of a great family—the Pulse or Pea Family—that contributes mightily to the food supply of the world, and it may stand as a handsome and worthy representative of all the Clovers whose rooted habit it is to enrich the soil in which they grow through the slave labor of the countless millions of nitrogen-fixing bacteria they hold captive in subterranean nodules. There may be some persons who look on the Red Clover as fodder and not as a flower, but that seems snobbish at the very least. If you haven't considered it among the flowers of the field before, take a good look at the next Red Clover that you see in bloom. It is a lovely flower. In fact, each globular head of Red Clover is a collection of lovely little flowers, but it's the "ensemble" that strikes the eye and sticks in mind. Most of the Clovers are sweet and all of them are good, but the Red Clover is the "cream of the crop."

WILD CARROT; QUEEN ANNE'S LACE

(*Daucus carota*)

Wild Carrot or Queen Anne's Lace, though not a native, flourishes all across the United States and Canada throughout the warmer months of the year and is attractive to the eye, but whether it is a beautiful flower or a detestable pest is a matter of opinion. Or of profession. An artist can look on it as a lovely flower with leaves of a delightful design, but farmers view it as a weed in their hayfields and dairymen despise it because it adds an unwanted faint flavor or aroma to the milk produced by the cows that graze on it—something like the odor of the crushed leaves of the plant, which is on the strong side. But like it or not, the Wild Carrot is with us in abundance from the first real touch of steady warm weather until the nipping frosts of Autumn lay it low. It grows to a height of from 1 to 3 feet and the flat-topped clusters of white tiny 5-petaled flowers may be from 2 to 4 inches in diameter. The leaves are feathery, much divided and subdivided to the extent that they have a fernlike appearance. If you give the flower clusters more than a passing glance, you will notice that there is often a dark spot near the center of the white circle of tiny flowers. Perhaps you have noticed such spots and thought they were insects on the flower cluster, an understandable mistake. But they are tiny dark purple flowers—one or more—and the curious thing is that they only appear, if at all, near the center of the circular cluster of their white brethren. How or why this happens is a mystery even to the botanists.

Sometimes the Wild Carrot is called Bird's-nest Plant, because, when the flowers begin to fade, the outer edge of the cluster curls upward to form a cuplike enclosure something like a bird's nest. The common or garden variety of yellow Carrot that goes into the soup or the stew is a lineal descendant of the Wild Carrot, and both are members of a famous family that includes such tasty or nutritious representatives as Caraway, Anise, Parsley, Parsnip, and Celery. The scientific name of the family is *Umbelliferae,* meaning "umbel-bearing," and refers to the family custom of producing flowers in "umbels" or "compound umbels" of which the Wild Carrot is a prime example. You will notice that the outspread supports of the flower cluster have a common starting point. Botanists call that arrangement an "umbel." If there is a further division of the same type along each one of these supports—as in the Wild Carrot—the resultant flower display is a "compound umbel."

BLADDER CAMPION

(*Silene cucubalus*)

This is a common flower of the roadsides and waste places and is a favorite with many children because of the sound effect that they get from it. Everybody knows how to blow up a paper bag and make a loud noise with it by suddenly crushing it in a way to make it "explode" under the pressure. On a small scale, children can do something like that with this flower because of the cuplike calyx behind the white petals. They pick the flower, pinch the top of the calyx closed with the thumb and forefinger of one hand, and then "explode" it by tapping it smartly against the outstretched palm of the other hand. If they have the top of the calyx pinched tightly, the resultant "pop" is considered well worth the effort. There are many other species of Campion and close relatives in North America—they are all members of the Pink Family and some are quite beautiful in color—but none equals the Bladder Campion in producing a fine "pop" under expert youthful handling.

This species is a hardy branching plant that grows to 3 feet or more in height and bears its white flowers in numerous loose clusters at the top and the ends of the branches. The flower has 5 petals but each of them is so deeply divided that it looks like 2 petals at a quick glance. Some of our Campions are natives and some have been introduced from other continents. The Bladder Campion, a native of Europe and Asia, was brought over here by early New England settlers, and, after getting well-rooted in that region, it began to spread south and west in slow but steady fashion. It may turn up almost anywhere in the United States now. It has even been reported from California. The rather narrow leaves are 3 to 4 inches long, rounded at the base, pointed toward the tip, and grow opposite one another along the stem. A handsome relative of the Bladder Campion is the Starry Campion or Widow's-frill that grows in open woods and shaded places from Massachusetts to Minnesota and south to Georgia and eastern Texas. The white flowers of the Starry Campion have their petal margins cut like a fancy fringe that is most attractive, and the leaves grow in 4's set like spokes of a wheel—"whorled" says the botanist—around the stem. There will be no doubt about this species when you find it, because the dainty fringes of the petals will catch your eye as soon as you come near them.

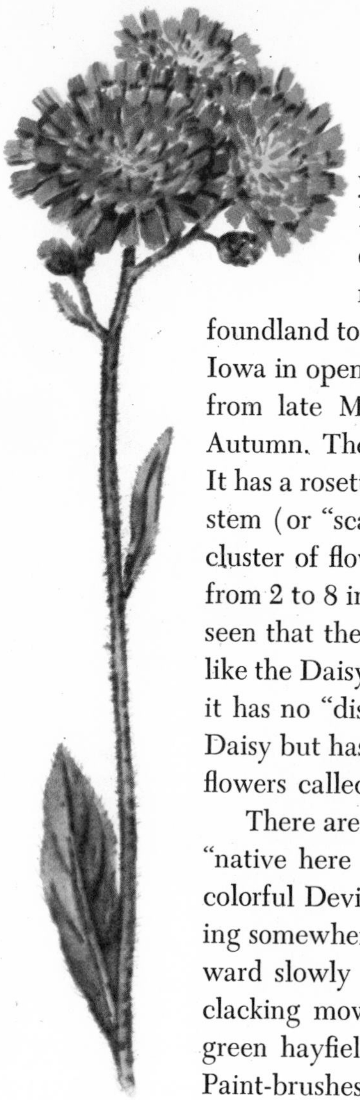

DEVIL'S PAINT-BRUSH; ORANGE HAWKWEED

(*Hieracium aurantiacum*)

A stranger could easily lose his way among the many yellow-flowered Hawkweeds, but the Orange Hawkweed or Devil's Paint-brush is a relief in this group because it stands out clearly with its flowers that display a mixture of yellow, red, and burnt orange. It is found in abundance from Newfoundland to Minnesota and south to Virginia, Ohio, Indiana, Illinois, and Iowa in open sunny places such as hayfields and roadsides, and it flowers from late May or early June all through the Summer or even early Autumn. The whole plant is quite "downy" or covered with tiny hairs. It has a rosette of narrowly oval-shaped leaves at the base of the flowering stem (or "scape") that rises to a height of from 1 to 2 feet or so with a cluster of flower heads at the top. The leaves in the low rosette may be from 2 to 8 inches long and are green on both sides. At a glance it can be seen that the Devil's Paint-brush belongs in the great Composite Family like the Daisy and the Dandelion, but it is more like the Dandelion in that it has no "disk flowers" like the yellow center of the Common or White Daisy but has a flower head composed entirely of individual strap-shaped flowers called "ray flowers." This is true of the Hawkweeds as a group.

There are many species of Hawkweed in North America, most of them "native here and to the manner born," but some of them, including the colorful Devil's Paint-brush, are invaders from Europe that, after a landing somewhere in the Northeast, have been pushing southward and westward slowly but relentlessly. Through June and July—at least until the clacking mowing machine comes along to cut down the hay crop—the green hayfields of New England are brightened by myriads of Devil's Paint-brushes in bloom, to the delight of the tourist or Summer boarder and the utter despair of the farmer. They take up the room and absorb the plant food that would otherwise produce good hay, which the Devil's Paint-brush is not. The hay crop is spoiled, and the farmer and his cows mourn together. In another field overrun by Devil's Paint-brushes it may be, as John Milton put it, that "the hungry sheep look up and are not fed." But who can deny the beauty of the flower?

Among the Hawkweeds with yellow flowers there are three species that botanists tell apart but ordinary country folk lump together under the common name of King Devil. To the average eye they look much like the Devil's Paint-brush except in color. The group characteristics of the Hawkweeds are not hard to recognize, but when it comes to pinning down the species the botanical battle begins. The scientific name for the group or "genus," *Hieracium,* comes from the Greek word "*hierax*" meaning "hawk," the reference being to an ancient belief that hawks ate the plant to sharpen their eyesight. When European botanists began to separate the Hawkweeds into thousands of species, subspecies, varieties, and forms, an American botanist mourned in print that "with eyesight stimulated beyond that of ancient hawks" they had brought matters to a hopelessly fine point.

RATTLESNAKE-WEED; VEIN-LEAF HAWKWEED

(*Hieracium venosum*)

This is one of the yellow-flowered Hawkweeds, but it is a native of North America and a respected inhabitant over a large area—Maine to Ontario and south to Missouri and Florida. It is quite different in appearance and habit from the yellow King Devils and the orange Devil's Paint-brush. For one thing, the Rattlesnake-weed stays modestly out of the way in dry woods. Furthermore, its famous and somewhat dreaded cousins have leaves and stalks that are covered with fine hairs that give them a fuzzy look. This is a smooth plant from its large purple-veined leaves in a rosette at the base to the dainty, yellow Dandelion-like flowers something over ½-inch in diameter that are carried on the much-branched stalk to a height of from 1 to 3 feet amid the undergrowth of dry woods from May to October. The name of Rattlesnake-weed is supposed to have originated from some fancied likeness of the purple-veined leaves to a rattlesnake's skin. It is also alleged that in old days a juice made from the leaves of this plant was used to cure the ill effects of rattlesnake bites. This lifesaving record is viewed with more than a little suspicion by the teachers in our modern medical schools.

COMMON ST. JOHN'S-WORT

(*Hypericum perforatum*)

Ancient authorities credited this plant with various marvelous properties such as the power to keep off witches or the ability to foretell marriage for maidens provided it was gathered on June 24, St. John's Day (hence its name). It was also said that the dew gathered from its flowers was good for sore eyes. We have more than two dozen native species of St. John's-wort in North America, but this introduced species from Europe is more abundant and widespread than any of the others. It grows plentifully in waste places and along roadsides and is almost a pest to the farmers in some areas. Cattle dislike it, which is one reason why it flourishes. The plant grows to 2 feet or more in height and the 5-petaled yellow flowers, roughly star-shaped and an inch or less in diameter, are clustered at the top in a loose spray (or "cyme"). If you look closely you will see that the yellow petals are much sprinkled with black dots. The little oval leaves are "sessile," or "sitting" on the stems or branches, and the plant flowers from June throughout the Summer.

ASIATIC DAYFLOWER

(*Commelina communis*)

We have native Dayflowers, but this species, introduced from Asia, is now the common one over much of New England, New York, Pennsylvania and southward and westward to Alabama and Kansas. It blooms in great abundance in late Spring and through most of the Summer in moist ground around dooryards and along the fringes of pools, ponds, brooks, and rivers. It is a low-growing plant with stems that may be 1 to 3 feet long but often grow slantwise and rarely lift themselves more than a foot or so above ground. The leaves are long and narrow, and the blue flowers appear to have only 2 petals. There is a third much smaller petal that only botanists note, but it plays a part in the story of how these flowers came by the scientific name of *Commelina*. The tale is that the great Linnaeus, who had his lighter moments when naming flowers, saw in the two fine petals and the one much less attractive petal a resemblance to a Dutch family group named Commelin. There were three Commelin brothers, of whom two were notable botanists and the other "died before he accomplished anything in botany." The common name Dayflower refers to the short life of the individual flowers that bloom only for a day and then fade away. But that's no great loss because numerous fresh flowers are coming along all Summer.

YELLOW POND-LILY; SPATTERDOCK

(*Nuphar advena*)

This is a common, widespread, and beautiful flower that should be easy to find and recognize. It is abundant in ponds and slow streams in all but the coldest parts of North America east of the Rocky Mountains and may be found in bloom from April to September in different parts of its range. It's true that Marsh Marigolds are good-sized golden-yellow flowers that grow in swamps and along the fringes of ponds and slow streams, but where the two plants might be growing together in the same general area, the Marsh Marigold flowers will have gone to seed before the Yellow Pond-lily comes into bloom. There are other differences easily noted. The Yellow Pond-lily flower is much larger—from 2 to 3½ inches in diameter—and has a large "core" or raised center composed of pistils, stamens, and petals. What look like the petals to the ordinary observer are the 6 sepals that are, like the pistils, stamens, and petals, a glowing golden-yellow. The thick stems, large rounded leaves, and seeds of the plant are food for deer, muskrat, beaver, ducks, and other forms of wildlife.

WILD YELLOW LILY; CANADA or NODDING LILY

(*Lilium canadense*)

We walk in the ways of the gospel (according to St. Matthew) when we consider the Lilies of the field, how they grow. "They toil not, neither do they spin; yet Solomon in all his glory was not arrayed as one of these." It may be, as some botanists insist, that the Lilies of the Bible were not the flowers that we call Lilies today, but that seems a minor matter. To look on any beautiful flower is good for the soul. There are wild Lilies of many species and different colors in North America. The Wild Yellow Lily—also called Canada Lily or Nodding Lily—ranges from Nova Scotia to Indiana and southward to Alabama, and its preferred haunts are swamps, wet meadows, and well-watered fields. The stiff stem reaches a height of from 2 to 5 feet with narrow and pointed leaves, 2 to 6 inches long, growing in circles or "whorls" along it at intervals. The yellow nodding flowers—there may be any number from 1 to 16—are carried on long stalks ("peduncles" to the botanist) and hang like a "carillon" or set of bells shedding silent music on the ground below, as if to lend flowery authority to the lines of John Keats:

Heard melodies are sweet, but those
unheard
Are sweeter;

Look for the cluster of yellow, bell-shaped nodding flowers of this species in June or July, and keep an eye out for some of the other members of the family, too, for this is the time that the Lilies spread their glories abroad over a wide area in North America. Look especially for the lovely Wood Lily (*Lilium philadelphicum*) that is found from Maine and southern Quebec to Ontario and south to North Carolina and Kentucky. The Wood Lily grows in dry thickets, open woods, and clearings, reaches a height of from 8 inches to 3 feet or more, and usually holds its 1 to 5 deeply cut flowers toward the sky like cups that certainly would not hold water. The 6 segments that form the slashed cup vary somewhat in color, but usually they are a deep orange-red much spotted with purple. When these flowers grow in the open the stem is not so tall. On the moors of Nantucket they average only about a foot in height and usually carry only one flower at the top of the stem. Look also for the Turk's-cap Lily that grows taller, blooms later, and has orange-red and much spotted flowers with segments that curve sharply backward at the tips.

WHORLED LOOSESTRIFE

(*Lysimachia quadrifolia*)

This flower may be found in bloom from late June into August in open woods or along somewhat shaded roadsides from Maine to Ontario and south to Georgia and Alabama. The stem comes straight up to a height of from 1 to 3 feet and around it there are "whorls" or circles of leaves at intervals, usually 4 leaves to a "whorl," though the number may vary. Near the upper part of the stem the little yellow flowers that look like 5-pointed stars are carried outward on thin stalks from the upper sides of the leaf-joints or "axils," so that the flowers, too, are "whorled." There are many different kinds of Loosestrife in North America but none easier to identify than this species. It is abundant in many places and, though the flowers are only about ¾-inch in diameter, the whorls of leaves—and of flowers when they are in bloom—form a striking pattern. The name comes from an ancient belief that creatures that fed on these plants would "lose strife" and become peaceful, for which reason Loosestrife was fed to yokes of oxen to make the partners work in harmony. It was supposed to have a pacifying effect on humans, too, but from the record of wars down the ages and the continued madness of modern times, either the report is completely false or the human race never has eaten enough Loosestrife.

BUTTER-AND-EGGS; RAMSTEAD; TOADFLAX

(*Linaria vulgaris*)

The farmer's daughter hath soft brown hair;
(Butter and eggs and a pound of cheese)
And I met with a ballad, I can't say where,
Which wholly consisted of lines like these.

C. S. CALVERLY

Call it what you will—Butter-and-eggs, Ramstead, Toadflax, Jacob's-ladder, Dead-men's-bones, Brideweed, Eggs-and-bacon—this bright "sunny-side-up" Summer flower, an importation from Europe, is common almost everywhere in waste places and along roadsides all up and down and across temperate North America. It grows from 1 to 3 feet high, usually in thick patches. As you can tell by looking at the "spurred" flowers, it is a close but poor relation of the aristocratic Snapdragon that blooms haughtily in so many cultivated gardens. The color scheme of the flowers that appear in spikes at the top of the stem explains the common name of Butter-and-eggs. Notice that the leaves are grasslike and the flower is tightly 2-lipped, with the "eggs" on the lower lip.

COMMON YARROW; MILFOIL

(*Achillea millefolium*)

We have some native Yarrows in North America, but the Common Yarrow or Milfoil that blooms in waste places and along roadsides across the country from June to November was brought here from Europe. It grows from 1 to 2 feet high, holding up a rather flat and seemingly white spray of innumerable small flowers that on closer inspection look like Daisies on a tiny scale. The individual flower heads with their yellow centers and 4 to 6 white rays are only about ¼-inch in diameter, but the floral spray (a "corymb" to the botanist) may be from 3 to 6 inches or more in width. The leaves, fern-like and very finely cut, give off a strong but not unpleasant odor when crushed. There are many tales of the virtues of this plant. Its scientific name *Achillea* comes from the legend that it was used to heal the wounds of the soldiers of Achilles in the Trojan War. In Merrie England of old it was believed that chewing the leaves of this plant would cure the toothache. Old wives of the Orkney Islands made tea from the leaves, and in Sweden the plant was used in the brewing of beer. And some gentlemen of bygone days dried and powdered the leaves and used them for snuff.

BOUNCING BET; SOAPWORT

(*Saponaria officinalis*)

Anyone who rambles along railroad tracks through the Summer months will find the Bouncing Bet growing in profusion along the cindery right of way. It is an importation from Europe that now flourishes mightily on railroad embankments, along roadsides, and in waste ground generally over most of the eastern and central sections of North America, and it is pushing westward steadily, infiltrating all the way out to the Pacific coast. It grows to a height of 2 feet or so on a thick stem with leaves that are rather narrow, 2 to 3 inches long, and grow opposite one another on the stem. The many 5-petaled pinkish-white flowers grow in a flattish or somewhat round cluster (another of those "corymbs") at the top of the plant, each flower being about 1 inch in diameter. The plant is a member of the Pink Family and is thus related to the Deptford Pink and the Bladder Campion as well as all the cultivated Pinks of the aristocratic gardens. The name Soapwort sometimes applied to it comes from the fact that a lather can be worked up by crushing the leaves in water, and it is said that the plant was so used for washing purposes in rural England in olden times.

MOTH MULLEIN

(*Verbascum blattaria*)

There are those who say that the Moth Mullein came by its name because moths are attracted by its flowers, but a more logical explanation in the eyes of most observers is that the flowers themselves look much like pretty moths. Take a look and decide for yourself. The plant is an importation from Europe that has made itself very much at home on this continent and may be found in old fields and waste places, on dry banks, and along roadsides all across temperate North America. It has a round stem that comes up as straight and as stiff as a lance to a height of from 2 to 6 feet, with a rosette of large oval leaves at the base and smaller leaves lessening in size and number upward along the stem toward the flowering spike—a "loose terminal raceme" to the botanist—at the top. When fully open the flowers are about 1 inch in diameter and may vary in color from a rich yellow to a pale white. What gives them the mothlike appearance is the purplish fuzz that grows along the stamens. The blooming period is from June through the Summer.

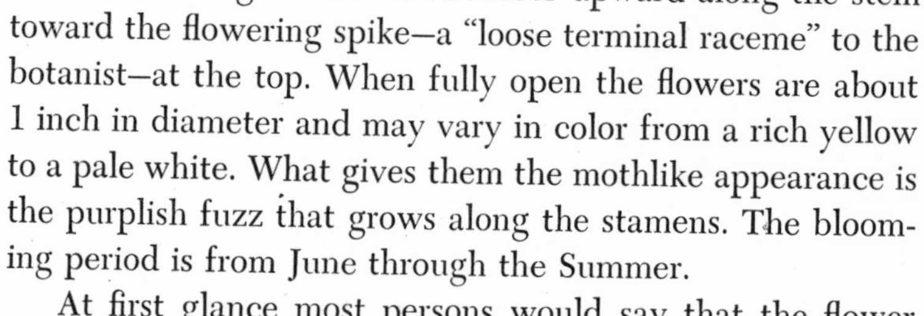

At first glance most persons would say that the flower has 5 petals, but a botanist would not agree and anyone who has gone this far in a book about flowers may be interested in knowing why not. What look like 5 separate petals in the flower of the Moth Mullein are merely the deeply lobed or divided parts of one general corolla or petal surface around the center section of the flower. You can see this for yourself if you examine it closely. There are many flowers—like the Wild Rose or the Common Wild Mustard—that have a number of separate petals while others have the petal section united into a cup as in the Mountain Laurel or into a tube as in the Morning Glory. There are still others—including the Moth Mullein—that seem to have separate petals that turn out to be, on closer examination, the more or less deeply divided segments of what the botanist terms a "corolla." The sooner the beginner in the field learns to take note of such details the sooner he or she will be able to track down and recognize strange flowers found in walks in "fresh woods and pastures new."

Another thing that can be learned from the Moth Mullein is that the seed pods of flowers are worth looking at for several reasons. Flowers produce seed in an astonishing variety of ways and in all sorts of containers. The Moth Mullein flower produces a little round capsule that eventually splits in two and lets the tiny seeds inside fall to the ground. The Moth Mullein is a member of the Figwort Family, of which all produce seeds in much the same fashion. The empty seed pods cling to the tall stem long after flowers and leaves have gone and thus help to identify the plant.

COMMON MULLEIN

(*Verbascum thapsus*)

Here is a plant with dozens of names including High-taper, Velvet Plant, Flannel Leaf, Aaron's-rod, and, the one by which it is best known, Common Mullein. It sends up a stem that grows just as straight but even taller and thicker than that of its first cousin, the Moth Mullein, and it bears its flowers in a long cylindrical spike at the top. It grows from 2 to 7 feet in height and the leaves and stalk are covered with tiny branching hairs that give a flannel-like appearance to the large oblong leaves that often reach a length of a foot in the rosette at the base of the stem but grow smaller upward along the stem. The flower buds in the terminal spike are arranged somewhat like kernels in an ear of corn, but all the kernels in an ear of corn become ripe at about the same time whereas the individual flowers in the Common Mullein spike blossom out at intervals. What happens is that the spike keeps growing and the upper flowers follow the lower ones in bloom. The yellow 5-segmented flowers are about 1 inch in diameter, and usually three of the stamens are "furred" with tiny yellow or whitish hairs. The resemblance to the flowers of the Moth Mullein is apparent, but the distinctive purple color of the fuzz along the Moth Mullein stamens stands out to catch the eye.

All our Mulleins are importations from the Old World. They are also all "biennials," meaning that it takes two years for them to grow to maturity and produce flower and seed. The first year the Common Mullein spreads its big jumbled rosette of large flannel leaves just above the ground, and the next season it sends up the stiff flowering stalk that country boys often use as a dueling sword or knightly lance in mimic battle. The plant likes high and dry ground and seems to be particularly fond of cow pastures. They may be found in bloom from June through the Summer months. In ancient times the dried stalks were dipped in oil or covered with tallow and used as torches in funeral processions. There was also an ancient belief that the Mulleins, properly applied, could cure diseases of the lung in man or beast and, indeed, one of the old English names for this plant is Bullock's Lungwort. But the physicians and veterinarians of today use other methods in treating any lung trouble that may afflict men, women and children or assorted farm animals.

PURPLE MILKWEED

(*Asclepias purpurascens*)

There are dozens of species of Milkweed in North America, all with the same general type of flower cluster and fruit pod and all with the family trait of oozing a sticky milky sap where there is a cut or break in flower, leaf or stem. The Purple Milkweed shown here has clusters of bright reddish-purple flowers and the midribs of the fleshy leaves are tinged with the same color. This species is found in woods, thickets, and openings from New Hampshire to Ontario and North Dakota and south to North Carolina, Mississippi, and Oklahoma. It has a rather slender stem, grows to a height of 2 or 3 feet and has somewhat tapering oval leaves that grow opposite one another in pairs or are "whorled" in 3's around the stem.

There are some Milkweeds with leaves almost as narrow as pine needles and seed pods no thicker than a fountain pen, but the Common Milkweed (*Asclepias syriaca*) found in open places from New Brunswick to Saskatchewan and south to Georgia and Kansas is noted for its stout stem, its large rubbery oval leaves, its clusters of pale purple or greenish-purple flowers, and its conical pods 3 to 5 inches long that contain the exquisitely arranged array of rich brown seeds with the silky white "milkweed down" attached to carry them off on the Autumn winds. The individual flowers are wonderful to behold. Please look at them under a magnifying glass. They are shaped like a tiny eggcup divided into 5 segments top and bottom, with 5 little caves or tunnels at the base of the top section of the cup.

The young shoots and leaves of the Common Milkweed are frequently used as pot-herbs in country kitchens, and during World War I, when the foreign fiber stuffing for life preservers on ships—kapok—was unobtainable, "milkweed down" was used as a substitute and children were paid a penny each for pods of the Common Milkweed. One of the most attractive of the Milkweeds is the Butterfly-weed or Pleurisy-root (*Asclepias tuberosa*) that grows from 1 to 2 feet high in fields and along roadsides over the eastern half of the United States and nearby Canada. The narrow, hairy leaves, 2 to 6 inches long, are not opposite but alternate along the stem, and the flower cluster at the top is a rich orange-red or orange-yellow and much favored by butterflies. Hence the name, Butterfly-weed.

FIREWEED; GREAT SPIKED WILLOW HERB

(*Epilobium angustifolium*)

Where there has been a fire in the woods or fields the Fireweed springs up to justify its name. Aside from this decided preference for burnt-over areas, it is a tall plant of waste places and roadsides all across the northern half of the United States and up to the sub-Arctic regions of Canada as well as in the cooler parts of Europe and Asia. The stout stem grows to a height of from 2 to 8 feet with many pinkish-purple or magenta 4-petaled flowers at the top in a "terminal spike" or "raceme." The lower flowers appear first, the result of which is that while the upper flowers of the spike are in bloom or coming into bloom the long narrow pods (2 to 3 inches long) left by the lower flowers that already have gone to seed are a real help in distinguishing this plant immediately from others that also display purplish flower spikes. The blooming period of the Fireweed is from July to September, and the opened flowers are about 1 inch in diameter. The plant is sometimes called the Great Spiked Willow Herb because its leaves—2 to 6 inches long—are shaped like those of the Willow Family. When the seed pods open you will notice the fine white hairs attached to the seeds and this will be a further identification mark of the plant.

WAND LOOSESTRIFE

(*Lythrum alatum*)

This is another pinkish-purple flower that appears in Summer in terminal spikes like the Fireweed, but the Wand Loosestrife is a smaller plant—only 2 to 3 feet tall—and grows in swamps or wet meadows, whereas the Fireweed is found on dry ground. Furthermore, the Fireweed flower is about 1 inch in diameter and its 4 petals are broadest at the outer ends, whereas the Wand Loosestrife flower is less than ½-inch in diameter with usually 5 or 6—though sometimes 4—narrow pointed petals. It's easy to know the Wand Loosestrife from the Fireweed, but a real problem is to distinguish the Wand Loosestrife from the Purple or Willow Loosestrife (*Lythrum salicaria*), an invader from Europe quite similar in flower and leaf. The intruder is a slightly larger and coarser plant, more or less downy, with a showier flower spike. The Wand Loosestrife is found all over the United States except in the extreme Northeast where—especially along the rivers and streams of New York and New England—the Purple Loosestrife chiefly holds sway. But the resemblance is such that, where the species overlap, it is best for the beginner to let a botanist decide which is the Purple and which the Wand Loosestrife.

BLACK COHOSH; BUGBANE; BLACK SNAKEROOT

(*Cimicifuga racemosa*)

This is a tall white flower of the Summer woodlands that is fairly common from Massachusetts to Georgia and as far west as Ontario, Wisconsin, and Missouri. It is easy to recognize, but confusion may start when you try to give it an English name because it lives and flourishes under so many different names in various sections of its range. Exercising local option, men, women, and children may call it Black Cohosh, Bugbane, Black Snakeroot, Rich-weed, Rattletop, Fairy Candles or anything else that comes to mind at the moment. The Latin name, of course, remains comfortably constant wherever the flower is found. The *Cimicifuga* refers to the old belief that bugs ("*cimices*" in Latin) dislike the offensive odor of the flowers so much that they hasten to fly away—in other words, become "fugitives"—when they smell it, and the *racemosa* merely means that the flowering spikes of the plants are "racemes" to the botanist. By this account the English name Bugbane would seem to have a reasonable foundation and so would the English name Black Snakeroot, because the American Indians believed that the plant would cure the ill effects of bites by poisonous snakes, but such beliefs are more legendary than factual. No doctor today would prescribe any part of the plant to cure snakebite, and certainly there are some insects that fly to it and not away from it when it is in bloom.

You can't miss this plant if it grows in your neighborhood because it reaches up above all other undergrowth in rich woods—sometimes to a height of 8 feet—and the white flower spikes are from 1 to 3 feet long and easily catch the eye "in the dim green place of the trees." The name Fairy Candles—favored in one of the present-day Wild Flower Guides—is a good indication of the general appearance of these long white spikes that are held up above the general level of the green undergrowth among which it flourishes. The tiny individual flowers look like dainty white pompons as they come into bloom not all at once but beginning at the lower part of the spike and working upward. The botanist will tell you that the tiny narrow petals are transformed stamens, but stamens and petals probably will look alike to you and they join in giving each individual flower its pompon appearance. The plant is a member of the Crowfoot Family and has the compound, saw-toothed foliage of many members of that group. It blooms from June to September, and if you miss the flowers, you may find the tall stalks later carrying the oval seed pods that, when hard and dry, make a rattling noise when the stalks are shaken. That's why the plant is known as Rattletop in some regions. Forest fires or lumbering operations may leave the Black Cohosh temporarily "without a roof over its head," so watch for it in such newly exposed areas.

BLACK-EYED SUSAN

(*Rudbeckia serotina*)

The lovely and sturdy Black-eyed Susan that grows to a height of from 1 to 3 feet along our Summer roadsides and—to the rising indignation of farmers—in our hayfields is native to North America and common from the Atlantic Coast to the Rocky Mountains. There are a number of species and varieties of *Rudbeckia,* but this is the most abundant and the best known over a wide range. It is, like the Common White Daisy, a member of the Composite Family, which means that each Black-eyed Susan is really a cluster of "ray flowers" and "disk flowers," the "ray flowers" being the circular fringe of yellow or orange-yellow strap-shaped parts that look like petals to the ordinary observer and the "disk flowers" being the tightly packed, brownish-black central part of the Black-eyed Susan. The dark central "disk flowers" are the fertile ones, and if you watch closely during the blooming period, you easily can see the tiny flowers opening and the pollen forming and ripening from the outer edge toward the center or apex of the dark cone.

The scientific name *Rudbeckia* for this attractive group of wild flowers traces back to the student days of the great Linnaeus at Upsala University in Sweden. Olaf Rudbeck the Elder was Professor of Botany at Upsala to the time of his death in 1702 and he was succeeded by Olaf Rudbeck the Younger, who held office when Linnaeus arrived as a student, by which time Olaf the Younger was quite elderly himself. Linnaeus was poor. His clothes were shabby and he was often hungry. But he was a fine student and he wrote a paper on botany that came under the eyes of Professor Rudbeck. When the professor discovered that Linnaeus was very poor, he took the young man into his home, helped him to earn money by tutoring, and eventually launched him on a Lapland collecting expedition and a remarkable career. Those who think that Nature Study is dull or "sissified" should read the story of the stirring adventures of the young Linnaeus in Lapland. But his great work in science, however, was in devising the modern system for the classifying and naming of all living plants and animals found on earth. When Linnaeus gave the name *Rudbeckia* to the genus that includes our Black-eyed Susan, he conferred immortality on his old professor. "So shines a good deed in a naughty world" and thus is the memory of a kindly act kept green down the ages of botanical history.

HEDGE BINDWEED; GREAT BINDWEED

(*Convolvulus sepium*)

This is, as can be seen at a glance, a member of the Morning Glory (or Convolvulus) Family and many persons call it simply a Wild Morning Glory, which is not only legal but reasonably sound botanically. But the Hedge or Great Bindweed, though probably the most common and most conspicuous of the family over most of temperate North America, is only one of the dozens of species to be found in this country. The different species vary not only in the color and size of the flower but also in the size and shape of the leaves. The common flower shown here grows in fields and waste places and rambles along roadsides and hedgerows. It climbs stone walls and rail fences. The length of the blade of the leaf that is shaped like a broad arrowhead is from 3 to 5 inches, and the funnel-form flowers grow singly on long stalks ("peduncles") that come off the stem at the "axils" or leaf-joints. The main stem, which may climb straight up or run off diagonally or horizontally, may be from 3 to 10 feet long, twining around anything that will give it support. It begins to bloom in late Spring and is in flower as late as August over much of its wide range. It is a delightful decoration in waste places, but it can become something of a nuisance when it invades cultivated ground, as gardeners know.

AMERICAN WILD MINT

(*Mentha arvensis*)

Unless you search for it carefully, you probably will smell the American Wild Mint before you see it. The plant is highly and pleasantly odorous when crushed by stepping on it where it grows lushly to a height of from 6 inches to 2 feet or more along the fringes of brooks or almost anywhere in wet soil over most of temperate North America north of the Carolinas. The small pale blue flowers appear in groups just above the places where the narrow leaves, 2 to 3 inches long, spring from opposite sides of the stem, and sometimes the flower clusters surround the stem like a ruff or with a pincushion effect. If you feel the stem with your fingers, you will notice that it is square instead of cylindrical as in most plants, and if you look closely at the tiny flowers, you will see the "two-lipped" effect of the funnel-form flower that is 5-parted at the rim, with 2 parts forming the upper lip and 3 parts the lower. These things are family traits that will help you to recognize some of the many other Mints we have in this country.

CHICORY

(*Cichorium intybus*)

This is a real roadside flower that blooms persistently but irregularly throughout the Summer along the highways and byways of this country. It is a native of Europe and the Near East that was brought here by the early colonists, who considered it a useful plant, and now it is completely at home over most of temperate North America. It grows in a somewhat staggering style to a height of about 3 feet with a stem that zigzags at awkward angles and a sparse display of raggedy leaves of no particular size or shape that clasp the stem and branches at the joints in forlorn fashion. The leaves at the base of the stem are longer and larger and somewhat on the order of Dandelion leaves, though not so numerous nor so firmly settled in place and in pattern. Cut almost any part of the plant and a milky juice will ooze out. To see these flowers is to know them because we have nothing else quite like them. Some persons call them Blue Daisies or Blue Dandelions because of the general shape and appearance of the flower heads that are, of course, a gathering of individual strap-shaped "ray flowers" as in the case of the familiar Dandelion. The expanded flower heads, light blue to whitish in color, may be as much as 1½ inches across and the plants bloom intermittently from July to October, mostly in the open and on dry ground. The flower heads spread themselves in the morning but fade rapidly as the sun climbs the sky and are usually closed by noon.

The root of this plant, dried and ground up, is the chicory of commerce that is used as a filler or flavoring agent in coffee mixtures. There is some difference of opinion as to whether or not the addition of chicory to coffee is desirable. In the northern section of the United States most coffee drinkers like their coffee "pure and unadulterated," but majority vote in the South favors the inclusion of some chicory and most European coffee drinkers like it that way, too. The leaves of the plant are used for salad in some countries and long ago it was recorded that the Egyptians boiled and ate the root as a vegetable. In England this plant is called Succory, and in different parts of this country the blue flower heads may be called Wild Succory, Blue Sailors, Bunk, or even—to add to the confusion—Bachelor's Buttons. There seems to be no end to the confusion over the accepted English names for flowers but, to most persons, the "real" Bachelor's Buttons are the *Centaurea cyanus* of our cultivated gardens.

SEGO LILY; MARIPOSA LILY; BUTTERFLY TULIP

(*Calochortus nuttallii*)

These lovely western flowers come in three colors—white, yellow, and lavender—with regional variations in the Dakotas, Nebraska, Colorado, Utah, Arizona, and California. The citizens of Utah have chosen it their State flower under the name of Sego Lily, and they prefer it wearing white when it comes into bloom in June and July. The early Spanish explorers of the Southwest called these flowers and their close relatives "Mariposas" because "*mariposa*" is the Spanish word for "butterfly" and, when a breeze was blowing across the great grasslands of the West, these flowers looked to them like myriads of butterflies clinging to the tops of grass stems and swaying with the wind. Like the cultivated Tulips they resemble in shape, they are members of the Lily Family and grow from bulbs. The stem, which usually has only a single grasslike leaf, may reach a height of 2 feet and carry from 1 to 5 of the delicately chaliced flowers that are about 1 inch across and about 1½ inches deep. Tradition has it that the Mormon settlers of Utah, in their early days of hardship, ate the bulbs of the Sego Lily when they ran short of better rations. Thus the plant may be useful, but, when you see the Sego Lily in bloom, you will agree that it could have won the election as State flower of Utah on beauty alone. There are many closely related species in assorted colors in our Rocky Mountain and Pacific Slope territory.

BEE BALM; SCARLET WILD BERGAMOT

(*Monarda didyma*)

This is the most flamboyant member of the Mint Family and such a special favorite that it is often cultivated in gardens not only because of its flaming color but also because it has the virtue of attracting Hummingbirds to probe the long floral tubes with their needle-like bills. It grows from 2 to 3 feet high in moist soil and may be found blooming from July to September over the eastern part of North America from Georgia northward. It has relatives of more conservative hues that may be found here or there all the way out to British Columbia and Southern California. The stem is "square" like that of a true Mint, and the toothed leaves, 3 to 6 inches long, grow opposite one another along the more or less hairy stem. The scarlet-hued, long-tubed flowers grow in a top ("terminal") cluster and are the crowning glory of this attractive plant. It is sometimes called Oswego Tea because the Oswego Indians are said to have made tea from its leaves.

COMMON EVENING PRIMROSE

(*Oenothera biennis*)

This is a common flower of the Summer roadsides and waste places over most of temperate North America. It prefers dry ground, including highway and railroad embankments, and is easily recognized by its stiff stem 1 to 5 or 6 feet tall, its narrow, pointed leaves growing alternately along the stem, and the terminal spike of yellow 4-petaled flowers, 1 to 2 inches across, that usually open in the evening and give their fragrance to the night air. Despite its color and its "last name," this is not the flower Wordsworth had in mind when he wrote:

A primrose by a river's brim
A yellow primrose was to him,
And it was nothing more.

This is an Evening Primrose, quite a different family. The individual flowers appear, like theatrical stars on tour, "for one night only," but new buds open further along the spike on succeeding evenings, leaving the stiff, narrow seed capsules of previous blooms below them. There are many species showing variation in size of stem, leaf, and flower in different parts of the country and some may bloom in broad daylight.

SPOTTED TOUCH-ME-NOT; SNAPWEED; JEWEL-WEED

(*Impatiens capensis*)

This hollow-stemmed and much branched plant grows to a height of 2 to 5 feet or more in wet woods and along the (preferably shady) sides of streams, lakes, and brooks over most of temperate North America. The numerous orange-red flowers, shaped somewhat like tiny broad-rimmed dunce caps and held at odd angles, are hung out on slender stalks (peduncles) that grow out of the "axils" or angles where the leaves appear along the stem or branches. In this species the inside of the flower is much spotted with reddish-brown. There is another much similar species, the Pale Touch-me-not (*Impatiens pallida*) with yellow flowers only sparingly spotted within. They are called Touch-me-nots in English and *Impatiens* (meaning in effect "impatient") in Latin because, when the bean-shaped seed pods ripen, the slightest touch will cause them to "explode" with a quick spiraling motion that throws the seed some distance away. Show children how to pinch the tips of the seed pods and they will have a lot of fun.

TALL MEADOW-RUE

(*Thalictrum polygamum*)

The high, white, and feathery flower clusters of the Tall Meadow-rue practically command attention when they are in bloom from June through August in moist or wet ground over most of the eastern half of temperate North America. The plant rears itself to a height of from 3 to 11 feet—averaging 5 to 6 feet—and is common in wet meadows, along the borders of swamps, and in moist ditches along roadsides over its range. It often follows the winding ways of brooks through low meadows. It flourishes in sun or shade but prefers rather open locations, where, in Summer bloom, it stands "divinely tall, and most divinely fair." You can't miss it in season, whether you are afoot, in an auto, or speeding across the countryside by train.

The leaves, light green above and paler below, are much divided and subdivided into gracefully scalloped or lovely lobed leaflets that are as tender in texture as they are attractive in appearance. The peculiar thing about the cream-white or pure white flower clusters —they may be "racemes" or "panicles" to the botanist, depending upon the arrangement of the particular clusters—is that the color is not provided by petals but by the white filaments or "shafts" of the stamens of the little individual flowers, which have no petals at all. By this time the reader will have realized that petals are not essential to all flowers either for beauty or utility, that other parts of a flower may be as attractive as petals, and that what look like petals to the ordinary eye may be something quite different to the botanist.

A close relative of the Tall Meadow-rue is the Early Meadow-rue (*Thalictrum dioicum*) that grows to a height of from 1 to 2½ feet in rich woods and damp ravines from Quebec to Ontario and Minnesota and south to Georgia and Alabama. It is often a neighbor to the Red Trillium and comes into bloom at about the same time —April and May—but its sprays of greenish or greenish-yellow flowers, with drooping stamen filaments, do not catch the eye as easily as the white sprays of its taller cousin that blooms much later in the season and out in the open. But the foliage of the two species is of the same general design—compounded in series of 3's with leaflets that have scalloped outlines or graceful lobes—and the final proof of relationship will be the individual flowers that, with their drooping green or greenish-yellow filaments, look like little silk tassels. The Meadow-rues are a widespread group and our many species in North America have close relatives in such far places as the hill country of India and the plains of South Africa.

PICKERELWEED

(*Pontederia cordata*)

This is a blue flower that often appears in wide patches in swamps, bogs, and slow water courses all the way from Nova Scotia to Ontario and Minnesota and south to Florida and Oklahoma. It grows in abundance in shallow ponds and along the banks "of weedy lake, or marge of river wide," and blooms through the Summer months until the cold nights of approaching Autumn cut it down. It usually shows just a single large, shiny heart-shaped leaf above water and, reaching well above it, the stout stem may carry the spike of blue flowers to a height of 4 feet, though about half that would be nearer the average. The individual tubular flowers, which are numerous on the spike, are 2-lipped at the outer end and each lip is divided into 3 narrow segments. You may need boots or a boat to inspect the flower closely. The common name of Pickerelweed refers to the fact that the plant and pickerel frequently are found in the same shallow waters. The *Pontederia* of its scientific name is a tribute to an Italian botanist, Giulio Pontedera (1688–1757), who taught at the University of Padua, and the *cordata*, meaning "heart-shaped," refers to the leaf. It is said that only muskrats find the plant edible, but the spikes of blue flowers are a joy to everyone who sees them.

FRAGRANT WHITE WATER-LILY

(*Nymphaea odorata*)

There are two common—and very beautiful—species of white Water-lily found in lakes, ponds, and still or slow-moving waters over much of the United States and nearby Canada but the Fragrant or Sweet-scented is the more abundant and the more widespread of the two. The other is the Tuberous White Water-lily (*Nymphaea tuberosa*) and, where they occur in the same waters, it is sometimes difficult to know them apart. The Fragrant White Water-lily has a delightful odor, whereas its rival has hardly any perceptible scent, and the fragrant species may be either white or pink or white with a pinkish tinge, whereas the Tuberous White Water-lily is always pure white. But it really doesn't matter (except to the botanist) which is which; the flowers are lovely decorations on our inland waters and their large circular leaves give aid and comfort to the frogs that sit on them to survey the watery world around them with a placid air of complete and well-fed contentment.

FRINGED LOOSESTRIFE

(*Lysimachia ciliata*)

This is another and one of the most widespread of the many Loosestrifes found abundantly in North America, but it grows in places that are somewhat off the beaten paths and thus avoids public notice to some extent. The Fringed Loosestrife likes moist ground and a little shade. It grows by preference in damp thickets and the drier parts of swamps to a height of from 1 to 4 feet or more, and it ranges over almost the entire United States and southern Canada. Depending upon latitude and altitude, it may be found in bloom from early June through August and its handsome 5-parted yellow flowers may be as much as 1 inch across. Notice that the ovate leaves (2 to 6 inches long) grow in pairs opposite one another along the stem and that the flower stalks ("peduncles") spring from the "axils" or leaf-joints at these points. Under a magnifying glass you can see that the leaf stalk or "petiole" is fringed with fine hairs that account for the English name of "Fringed" Loosestrife for the plant and also for the *ciliata* in its scientific name, "cilia" being fine hairs such as eyelashes or the threadlike appendages that fringe many microscopic creatures and furnish motive power for them in water. Another detail to observe is that each of the yellow segments of the flower is finely toothed at the outer edge and there is a tiny tip that sticks out like a bristle. There may be up to half a dozen buds in a flower cluster, but usually only one or two of the cluster are in bloom at a time.

The shape and size of the leaf, the "fringed" or hairy petioles, the size of the flower, and the bristle tip to each petal segment will help to distinguish the Fringed Loosestrife from any of its close relatives that may be blooming in the same area. One of its relatives with which there is no danger of confusion is the low-growing Moneywort (*Lysimachia nummularia*) that hugs the ground on a creeping stem 1 to 2 feet in length and has roundish leaves about 1 inch in length growing opposite one another in pairs at short intervals along the stem. The yellow flowers are about the size of those of the Fringed Loosestrife, but the petal segments lack the outer teeth and bristle tip. The Moneywort is an invader from Europe that is now found from Newfoundland to Ontario and south to Georgia and Kansas. In swamps you will find the Swamp-candles (*Lysimachia terrestris*) with their conical terminal sprays of little star-shaped yellow flowers.

YUCCA; SPANISH BAYONET; OUR-LORD'S-CANDLE

(*Yucca filamentosa*)

This is probably the most familiar of the Yucca group that runs to about a dozen striking species in Central America and the warmer sections of North America. In general they are all called Spanish Bayonets (or Spanish Daggers) because of the long, narrow, sharp-pointed leaves that do look much like bayonets or sword blades and often are formidable objects with which to collide or even touch. The narrow leaves and the tall flowering spikes that raise themselves aloft are common to all the group. The leaf arrangement and the flower colors vary in the different species, and the time of blooming depends on the species and the area in which the plants are found. This species is often found in cultivation or as an escape from cultivation over much of the United States, but in the wild it flourishes in sandy soil, dunes, old fields, and pinelands from the Gulf Coast northward to southern New Jersey. Wherever it grows it is sure to catch the eye with its alarming rosette of leaves around the base and the sturdy flower-bearing spike ("peduncle") that may reach a height of 10 feet or more bearing a great "plume" of cream-white, 6-parted, pendulous, bell-shaped flowers innumerable in quantity.

Aside from the bayonet-shaped leaves and the spectacular sprays of flowers, there is another notable feature of the Yucca group. The flowers of the Yuccas are in their most expansive mood from dusk to dawn and, being mostly white in color, they are easily found by night-flying insects. There is a curious bond between the Yuccas and a small group of night-flying insects, moths of the genus *Pronuba*. Just as Bumblebees are needed to fertilize Red Clover blossoms, Pronuba Moths are needed to fertilize the Yucca flowers and no substitutes in the insect world are acceptable. Not only that, but it has been discovered that different species of Yuccas may have their own particular species of Pronuba Moth to carry the pollen from stamen to pistil. It's the female moth that does the good work and it also lays its eggs in the flowers. The larvae—the moths in the caterpillar stage—feed on the Yucca seeds, but enough seeds escape eating to carry on the species. It's an odd cycle—the flowers providing food and lodging for the moths and the moths being the necessary agents in the continued production of Yucca flowers.

CORN COCKLE

(*Agrostemma githago*)

Farmers and gardeners often have very definite ideas of the difference between "flowers" and "weeds," but botanists pay little heed to such fine distinctions. An old definition had it that "a weed is a flower out of place." A more modern definition, in a fair-sized dictionary, runs as follows:

"Weed, noun. 1. Any unsightly or troublesome plant that is at the same time useless; especially, a plant that is noxious or injurious to crops."

But who is to say which plants are "sightly" and which ones are "unsightly"? And what does the term "useless" imply in the definition? Useless to whom? A plant that is of no direct use to a farmer may be very useful to birds or insects that, in turn, may be useful in the production or the protection of farm crops. The Corn Cockle is often called a weed and certainly looked upon as a weed by farmers when they come upon it in their growing grain fields or "hand in hand with Plenty in the maize," to borrow a poetical sheaf from Tennyson. But who can deny the beauty of this pink or rose-purple flower? It is another of the European invaders that have found this country to their liking, and it has spread rapidly in all directions. It is found not only as a trespasser in grain fields and where the tall corn grows, but as a wanderer along the roads and a camper in waste places over most of temperate North America. It belongs to the Pink Family, along with the Bladder Campion, the Bouncing Bet or Soapwort, the Deptford Pink, and many others of our common wild flowers.

This plant grows from 1 to 3 feet in height with narrow grasslike leaves paired off on opposite sides of the stem like other members of its family. Almost all parts of the plant except the petals are covered with fine hairs. The 5-petaled flowers are 1 to 3 inches across when fully open, and they are carried on stiff stalks (or "peduncles") that emerge from the stem at the leaf-joints, which means that they are "axillary." An easily noted feature of this flower is that the sharp-pointed calyx lobes—5 in number—jut out far beyond the petal circle. The plant may be found in bloom from June into September. As for the question of whether or not it is an unwelcome "weed," let each farmer or property owner decide that for himself. Here it can be looked upon as a beautiful flower of our fields and roadsides.

STEEPLEBUSH; HARDHACK

(*Spiraea tomentosa*)

Those who know the Spiraeas of the cultivated flower gardens will have no trouble recognizing their many relatives in the wild. There are more than a dozen species native in North America, and, of the group, the Steeplebush or Hardhack is probably the most widespread east of the Rockies and the easiest to recognize because of its abundance, its sturdy stem, its upright character, and its rich wine-purple color. It grows to a height of 1 to 4 feet from July to September in old fields and unused pastures. It likes the open sky above it but otherwise is not particular and will flourish from low wet ground up across high, dry, and rocky territory. The toothed leaves, 1 to 2 inches long, circle the stem closely up to the terminal cluster of many tiny flowers. The Meadowsweet or Quaker Lady (*Spiraea latifolia*) is found over much of the same area but its leaves are a little broader, its flowering cluster is not so pointed or steeple-shaped, and its color is usually white or pinkish. If there is any doubt in your mind, look at the underside of the leaf. The Meadowsweet leaf is smooth beneath, whereas the underside of the Steeplebush leaf is covered with what looks like brownish-pink wool.

WILD SUNFLOWER

(*Helianthus giganteus*)

Leave to the botanist the task of sorting out the many different species of native Sunflowers that burst into bloom all across the country in late Summer or early Autumn. This particular species flourishes from Quebec to Florida and roams westward as far as Saskatchewan and Colorado. It grows in swamps, wet meadows, and moist ground generally and may be any height between 3 and 12 feet. The flower head, which is a collection of central "disk flowers" and a fringe of bright yellow "ray flowers," may be 2½ to 3 inches across. The leaves are 2 to 6 inches long, narrow and toothed along the edge. The name Sunflower comes from two Greek words, "*helios,*" "the sun," and "*anthus,*" "flower." The garden or dooryard Sunflower that furnishes most of the seed so much appreciated by certain birds is the *Helianthus annuus* of the botanist or nurseryman. It originally came from Peru and is now cultivated all over the world. Sunflowers do like sunlight and naturally the flower heads turn toward the source of light but Thomas Moore let his poetic fancy roam a bit in the lines:

As the Sunflower turns on her god, when he sets,
The same look which she turned when he rose.

BROAD-LEAVED ARROWHEAD

(*Sagittaria latifolia*)

There are more than three dozen species of Arrowhead or *Sagittaria* to be found growing in shallow waters across North America, but this is the most abundant, the most widespread, and, to most eyes, the prettiest of the lot. Where you find the Pickerelweed, there you will find the Broad-leaved Arrowhead, a plant well deserving the name it bears because the shape of the leaves that show above water—very decidedly in this species though not at all in some others—is that of an exaggerated arrow head. This same plant, however, has underwater leaves that are long and narrow like blades of grass. The leafless stem or "scape" on which the flowers are carried may project above water from a few inches to 4 feet or more and the flowers appear in little circles or "whorls" of 3's at intervals along the scape. The conspicuous male flowers, probably the only ones you will notice, have 3 white petals and are about 1 inch across when fully spread. The female flowers are smaller and duller and usually grow below the male flowers on the scape, though there may be plants that produce only flowers of one kind, male or female. For the most part, the female flowers usually go unnoticed except by botanists or the insects that carry the pollen from the stamens of the male flowers to the pistils of the female flowers, a most important function. The dainty white male flowers—and the dull female flowers, too—begin to appear in July and may be found in bloom through August and September.

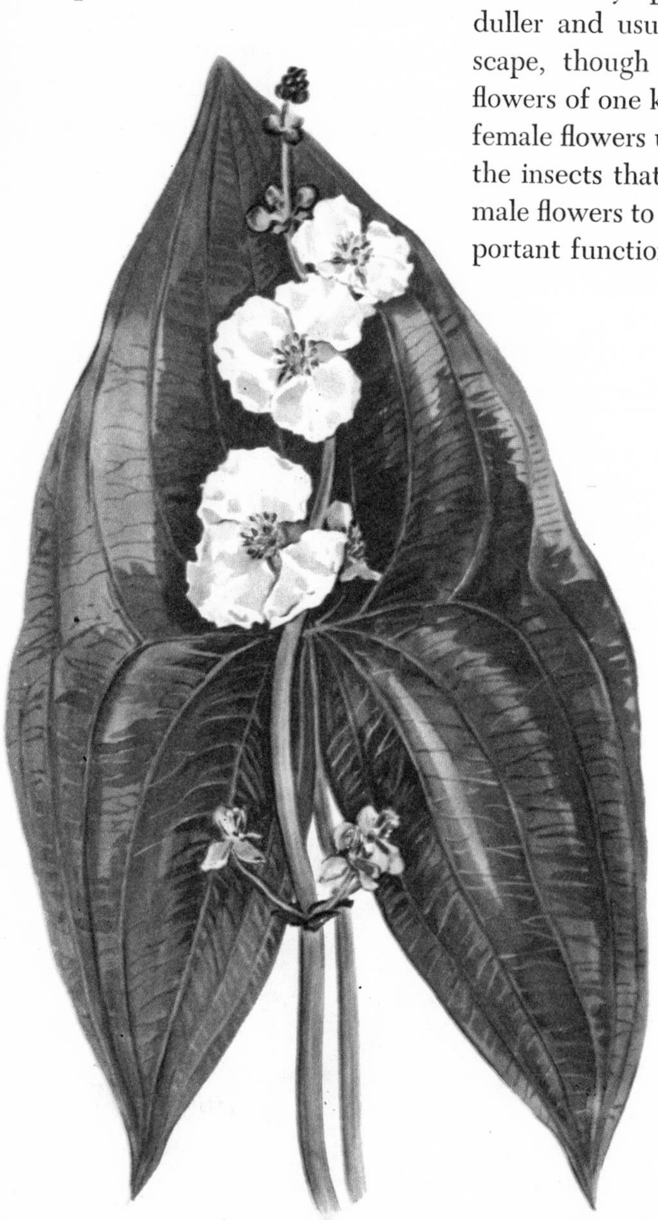

This plant is sometimes called Swamp Potato or Duck Potato because of the potato-like tubers produced along its submerged root system. Ducks, geese, and swan feed with gusto on these tubers, though sometimes they are buried so deep in the mud that only the larger and stronger waterfowl can dig them up. But the lovely Wood Duck, the most colorful bird in North America, feeds on them, and, among the diving ducks, the Canvasback rates them just behind Wild Celery as a delicate article of diet. Indeed, the American Indians boiled and ate the tubers, and history has it that the early colonists, when they were hard pressed for food, took a tip from the Indians and did likewise. But it must be admitted that the colonists abandoned such food when their own crops yielded them tastier table dishes.

GREAT BLUE LOBELIA

(*Lobelia siphilitica*)

The distaste most persons have for getting their feet wet—at least when they are wearing shoes—is probably the reason why the Great Blue Lobelia is not a more familiar flower to all of us. This sturdy member of the Lobelia group is found over most of the United States east of the Rocky Mountains, but it grows most frequently in moist soil or wet places, often along brooks and streams or around the edges of ponds and lakes. Furthermore, though it sends up a stiff stem to a height of from 1 to 3 feet or more, it is inclined to hide away among other plants of approximately similar height and, in lush growths in shaded or half-shaded places, it may be easily overlooked despite the terminal spikes of inch-long tubular blue flowers. Not only is the flowering spike often semi-obscured by surrounding greenery but each flower of the spike is buttressed by a green leaflike "bract" that helps to conceal it. Another point is that blue as a color does not stand out like red, orange, yellow, or white against a green background. All of which helps to explain why so many Great Blue Lobelias are born to blush unseen in rural regions where they have long flourished and where they flower regularly each August or September.

The Lobelias are world-wide in distribution, and there are more than two dozen species in North America. They were named after a Flemish botanist, Matthias de L'Obel (1538–1616). Among the common features of the group are a milky juice that is very bitter and indeed poisonous, leaves that grow alternately—that is, not opposite one another—along the stem, and tubular flowers that are, for the most part, 2-lipped with the upper lip split into 2 segments and the lower lip into 3. The flowers of the Mint Family are 2-lipped also, but the lip segments of the Mints are gently rounded like lobes whereas those of the Lobelias are sharp like teeth. Other differences are that the Mint leaves grow opposite one another along their stems and practically all Mints are strongly aromatic when crushed, which Lobelias are not.

A first cousin to the Great Blue Lobelia is the Indian Tobacco (*Lobelia inflata*) commonly found along the roadsides of North America from Nova Scotia to Saskatchewan and south to Georgia and Arkansas and just as commonly overlooked because its pale blue flowers, shaped like those of its distinguished relative, are small and inconspicuous. In fact, the inflated seed pods later are more often noticed than the flowers. The Indians are said to have smoked the dried leaves, hence the name.

CARDINAL FLOWER; RED LOBELIA

(*Lobelia cardinalis*)

This spectacular flower—the most brilliant in hue of the many Lobelias that flourish in North America—is easy to recognize when you see it, but the difficulty is to find it and come upon it close at hand. Like most of the Lobelia group, it prefers to keep its feet wet and usually is found growing along water courses or in fairly moist ground. Often it is sighted just out of reach along the fringes of rivers, lakes, and streams. If you have luck, you may find it growing in flaming patches in the gravelly shallows of some farm brook meandering around and about the open meadows. In such places you can get close to the flowers dry-shod and notice that, though the color is in striking contrast to that of the Great Blue Lobelia, the general shape of the two flowers is much the same. As a matter of fact, the two plants are much alike in stem, leaf, and general habits of growth. The Cardinal Flower ordinarily is the taller, growing from 2 to 5 feet high, and the individual flowers are not only usually larger but much more deeply "slashed" than those of the Great Blue Lobelia. Another difference is the Great Blue Lobelia is more modest than its brilliant cousin. For the most part, it keeps in the shade if possible. But the flaunting Cardinal Flower is not one to hide its beauties. It lifts its flaming clusters of 2-lipped scarlet flowers in sunny places and seems to clamor for attention. The added touch of sun may be one reason why it comes into bloom in July, whereas the Great Blue Lobelia usually waits until August to spread its first floral display of the season. Both species bloom through August and into September.

Scientists tell us that birds prefer red as a color and insects—especially bees—prefer blue. There is more in that than meets the eye, but, not to go into it too deeply, the Great Blue Lobelia is constructed so that it is fertilized by the bees that push their way into it for food and eventually carry the pollen from stamen to pistil as they journey from one blossom to the other. But the pistil and stamens of the Cardinal Flower are so placed that it's no trouble at all for Hummingbirds to perform that same useful purpose. Hummingbirds are particularly attracted to red flowers and, with their long thin bills, are admirably fitted for sipping nectar from tubular blossoms like those of the Cardinal Flower. Furthermore, they love to forage up and down sunny brooks, where these flowers often grow. If there are Cardinal Flowers in bloom, the Hummingbirds will find them. It's a mutual benefit association. These brilliant flowers range widely in North America and may be found from Quebec to Ontario and Minnesota and south to Florida and east Texas.

PEARLY EVERLASTING

(*Anaphalis margaritacea*)

This is one of the most dainty and satisfactory of the wild flowers because it is easy to find, easy to know, and easy to gather in a bouquet that will keep if not everlastingly, at least for many a long day. It grows in upland pastures and on dry open hillsides all across the northern half of North America almost up to the Arctic snow line. The stem, topped by the spray of pale flowers that look so delicate and persist so sturdily, grows from 1 to 3 feet in height with longish, narrow, grasslike leaves of somewhat silky texture appearing at intervals along it. It blooms through the late Summer, and Thoreau referred to it as "the artificial flower of the September pastures." The flowering arrangement is doubly compound. The whole spray is made up of numerous flower heads, and the flower heads, in turn, are groups of tiny individual flowers. The Pearly Everlasting is a member of the Composite Family, the great group that includes the Goldenrods, the Daisies, the Joe-Pye Weed, the Ironweed, the Sunflowers, the Asters, and many other common flowers.

PURPLE MILKWORT; PURPLE CANDYROOT

(*Polygala sanguinea*)

This is a modest little flower that is easily overlooked, even though it blooms all through the Summer in fields and meadows and along roadsides from Nova Scotia to Ontario and Minnesota and as far south as the broad belt extending from South Carolina to Louisiana and Oklahoma. It grows only to a height of from 6 to 15 inches on a slender stem that often forks near the top so that 2 or more flower heads are carried on one main stem. The flower heads, of course, are clusters of many tiny individual flowers, as you will note if you bend over and look closely. The short grasslike leaves, the pale purple (sometimes greenish) flower spike, and its lowly estate combine to keep the Purple Milkwort or Purple Candyroot from general recognition and a hearty welcome each year. It has somewhat the appearance of a thimble-shaped, pale purple Clover head, but the grasslike leaves prove immediately that it is not a member of the Clover group. It has a delicate bearing, but it stands sturdily through the heat of Summer and blooms well into September in favorable locations. It forces itself on nobody's attention, but it is a lovely, soft-hued, friendly little flower that is well worth your acquaintance. It is called Purple Candyroot by many persons because of the wintergreen flavor of the crushed root.

PASTURE THISTLE

(*Cirsium pumilum*)

As the Rose is traditionally the national flower of England, so the Thistle is the badge of Scotland. But Thistles of several hundred species are found scattered all over the Northern Hemisphere, and there are some 60-odd species native to North America. They are notable, of course, for the sharp prickles that stick out from the leaves and other parts of the growing plant and also for the "thistledown" that appears at the end of the blooming season of the truly beautiful flower heads. Here we have another member of the great Composite Family in which many individual flowers are clustered closely to give a striking mass effect. Most Thistles have purple flowers, but there are some species that come in pink, yellow, cream, and white. Thistles are hardy plants, and their prickles protect them from grazing cattle that cut down unarmed flowers in pasture lands. It is useless for a beginner to try to sort out the Thistles in any area. That's a task for the botanist, or at least a student in botany. But even a beginner will notice that there are different kinds of Thistles here and there.

INDIAN PIPE

(*Monotropa uniflora*)

The walker in the woods may come upon a little colony of Indian Pipe almost anywhere in North America. It is a "saprophytic" plant, meaning that it feeds on decayed organic matter, and, lacking the green coloring matter (chlorophyll) of most other plants, it has a fragile, pale, ghostlike appearance. There is a real flower at the top of the stalk or "scape," but usually it hangs like a bowed head and you will have to turn it up to see that it is narrowly cup-shaped and there may be 4 or 5 petals, or even 6. The only touch of color about the plant is the yellow of the pollen in its brief period of ripening. Except for that, flower and scape and buried roots are a fleshy, sickly grayish-white. It rarely reaches a foot in height and the stem looks something like a pale, emaciated asparagus stalk. You may find these odd flowers pushing up from the forest floor in little groups almost any time from June through September. False Beech-drops, a near relative, grow a little taller, are tawny or brownish-yellow, much thicker in stalk, and sometimes venture so far out of the woods that they may be found in shady spots on lawns.

TURTLE-HEAD; SNAKE-HEAD

(*Chelone glabra*)

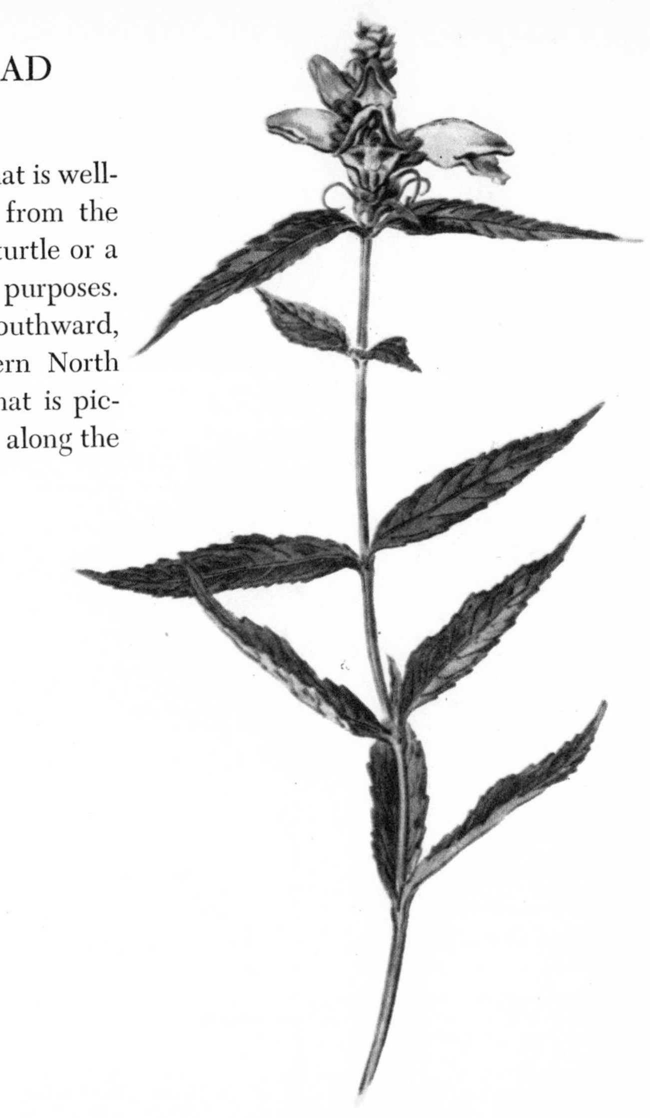

Here we have another common flower that is well-named. The individual blossoms, viewed from the side, do look something like the head of a turtle or a snake with its mouth open for business purposes. There is a pink species (*Chelone obliqua*) southward, but the common one over most of eastern North America is the cream-white Turtle-head that is pictured here. It's a sturdy plant that flourishes along the fringes of streams, swamps, wet meadows, and roadside ditches and grows to a height of 2 to 5 or even 6 feet on a stiff stem with the flowers closely bunched in a blunt spike at the top. The flower buds may be numerous, but they do not all open at the same time. In keeping with the usual procedure when flowers are carried in such spikes, the lower flowers open first and the order of blooming is upward. The long narrow leaves, shaped like a lance head, grow opposite one another, are toothed all around, and are so short-stalked (or "petioled") that they seem to be growing right out of the stem. The time to look for Turtle-head in bloom is from late July until the first hard frost.

Turtle-head is a member of the Figwort Family and, as such, a relative of the common Butter-and-eggs or Wild Snapdragon. You may notice something of a family resemblance in the shape of the flowers. Another member of the same family is the Smooth White Penstemon or Foxglove Beard-tongue (*Penstemon digitalis*) with a pale lavender or nearly white flower that might possibly be confused with the Turtle-head by beginners. This is only one of the dozens of Penstemons in North America, but it seems to be gaining ground in all directions. A native of the Mississippi Basin, it has spread to South Dakota and Texas on the west, has reached Virginia on the east, and has been pushing boldly into New England in recent years. It grows to a height of 5 feet or so in groups and patches in open woods, thickets, and fields, but its tubular flowers, though somewhat like those of the Turtle-head in size and general shape, are more open at the outer edge and definitely 5-parted. But the big difference is that, where the Turtle-head flowers sit close along a blunt terminal spike, the Smooth White Penstemon flowers are carried well apart in a loose spray (a "thyrsus" to the botanist) with each flower on a stalk or "pedicel" 1 to 3 inches long. Also, the Turtle-head flower is a solid cream-white, whereas the Smooth White Penstemon flowers look as though they might be made of waxed paper or frosted glass.

WOODLAND GERARDIA

(*Gerardia tenuifolia*)

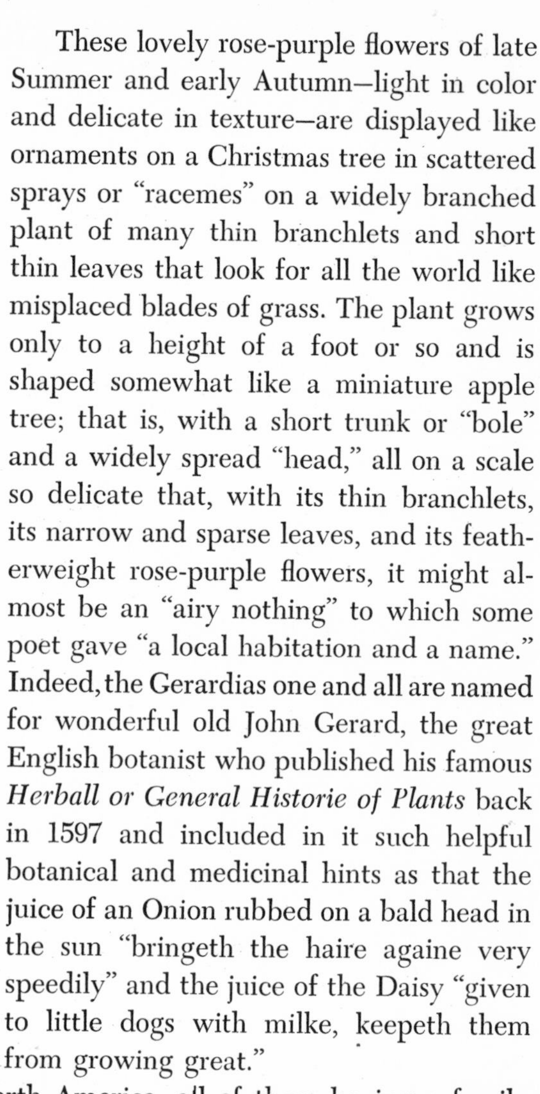

These lovely rose-purple flowers of late Summer and early Autumn—light in color and delicate in texture—are displayed like ornaments on a Christmas tree in scattered sprays or "racemes" on a widely branched plant of many thin branchlets and short thin leaves that look for all the world like misplaced blades of grass. The plant grows only to a height of a foot or so and is shaped somewhat like a miniature apple tree; that is, with a short trunk or "bole" and a widely spread "head," all on a scale so delicate that, with its thin branchlets, its narrow and sparse leaves, and its featherweight rose-purple flowers, it might almost be an "airy nothing" to which some poet gave "a local habitation and a name." Indeed, the Gerardias one and all are named for wonderful old John Gerard, the great English botanist who published his famous *Herball or General Historie of Plants* back in 1597 and included in it such helpful botanical and medicinal hints as that the juice of an Onion rubbed on a bald head in the sun "bringeth the haire againe very speedily" and the juice of the Daisy "given to little dogs with milke, keepeth them from growing great."

There are many species of Gerardia in North America, all of them having a family resemblance in flower shape and general delicate texture of the plants, but they vary much in size and color. The Woodland Gerardia is found from Maine to Michigan and, inland from the Atlantic coastal plain, south to Georgia and Louisiana. It grows in dry woods, thickets, and fields and blooms from August to October. Although the individual flowers —something less than an inch long—are narrowly bell-shaped, they do not hang as bells should but usually are held throat upward or horizontal. The outer rim of the corolla is 5-lobed with more than a hint of a 2-lipped formation. The delicate flowers fade by noon of the day they open, but new buds provide a fresh supply for succeeding days and the plants may be in bloom for the better part of three months. A similar member of the Gerardia group but slightly larger in every way is the Purple Gerardia (*Gerardia purpurea*) whose flowers may be 1½ inches long. The plant itself grows to a height of 3 feet or more and is more an inhabitant of moist soil and wet meadows than the Woodland Gerardia. It is found from New England to Minnesota and south to Florida and Texas and blooms from late July through September.

EARLY GOLDENROD; PLUME GOLDENROD

(*Solidago juncea*)

Leave to the botanists the tedious task of sorting out the hundred or more species of Goldenrod that are native to North America. The flowering sprays of this abundant group are known to everybody and feared by many persons as the cause of "hay fever," but the truth is that Goldenrod is no more guilty than any other plentiful plant that produces pollen. Medical research has revealed that, over most of the United States, the Great Ragweed (*Ambrosia trifida*) is the real guilty party in most cases, and it doesn't have the compensating virtue of the glorious beauty of the Goldenrod in late Summer and Autumn. Asters and Goldenrod make lovely the meadows and hillsides "when the frost is on the punkin and the fodder's in the shock."

The group name *Solidago* is derived from the same Latin word that gives us "solidify," to make whole, and refers to the healing powers that ancient physicians believed the plants to possess. John Gerard wrote in his famous *Herball* of the Goldenrod: "It is extolled above all other herbes for the stopping of bloud in bleeding wounds."

Goldenrod is well-named, because most of the stems are rodlike and serve nobly to hold up the attractive sprays of countless tiny golden flowers—with one notable exception in the case of the Silver-rod (*Solidago bicolor*) whose white or whitish flowers make it the pale member of this glowing group. You will find it growing among its golden brethren in dry ground over most of the United States east of the Rockies, and probably you will think it "a poor stick" in comparison with its richer relatives because its straight stem carries no flaunting flower spray. Its whitish flower heads merely cling somewhat forlornly along the upper portion of "rod." The Early or Plume Goldenrod shown here is found from New Brunswick to Saskatchewan and southward to Georgia and Missouri. It grows to a height of 3 feet or more in dry open ground, and its fine plume of golden flower heads may be found in bloom from late June to October. Remember that the Goldenrods are members of the great Composite Family and that the golden sprays are masses of flower heads that are, in turn, made up of tiny "ray flowers" and "disk flowers" best seen under a magnifying glass. But it's the general effect that is so colorful in our Autumn landscapes.

BONESET; THOROUGHWORT

(*Eupatorium perfoliatum*)

This sturdy plant with the medicinal name grows to a height of from 2 to 5 feet over most of temperate North America east of the Rocky Mountains and spreads its flat-topped clusters ("corymbs" to the botanist) of whitish flower heads for inspection from late July well into October. It grows in wet places generally—in swamps, along the fringes of streams, in ditches, on well-watered banks, and along woods roads where the overhanging trees keep the roadsides shady and moist. The grayish-white flower spray at the top of the plant may be as much as 6 inches or so in diameter and has something the appearance of a flat-topped white Goldenrod. But to the ordinary eye the most curious thing about the plant is the way the stem seems to grow right through the leaves, particularly the lower and larger ones that are completely joined at the base and reach out on opposite sides of the stem like a pair of narrow-based triangles from 4 to 8 inches long. The English name Thoroughwort often applied to this plant is a reference to this habit of the stem growing "thorough" or through the leaves, and so is the *perfoliatum*—Latin for "through the leaf"—of its scientific name. There are various explanations of how the plant came by the common name of Boneset. Some authorities have it that "herb doctors" declared that plants with united leaves like this one had the virtue of aiding to unite fractured bones. Another story is that an infusion made from the leaves of the plant was reputed to be good for the dengue or "break-bone" fever of warm climates; hence the name Boneset. In any event, "Boneset tea" made from the dried leaves was a standard home remedy for colds and fevers—or for warding off such ills—in New England a century ago. Modern doctors, however, order other treatment.

Aside from such disputed medical matters, the flower cluster of the Boneset plant is not particularly handsome but it does decorate the meadows and roadsides late in the season when many of the more beautiful and more delicate flowers have faded from the scene. It is another member of the Composite Family, but, unlike the Daisy and many others in that great group that are composed of "ray flowers" and "disk flowers," its little flower heads that make up the big cluster are composed only of tiny tubular "disk flowers." It's a small matter to the naked eye but it will loom larger under a magnifying glass, and the beginner who looks into such things will be making real progress.

WHITE SNAKEROOT

(*Eupatorium rugosum*)

This is a first cousin of the Boneset, ranges over approximately the same territory, grows to about the same height, bears somewhat similar clusters of white flower heads, and is much like the Boneset in many botanical details, yet it is easy for even a beginner in the field to tell them apart. In the first place, look at the leaves! They are notably different from the odd-shaped joined leaves of the Boneset through which the stem pushes its way upward. These are heart-shaped and held away from the stem by a stalk or petiole from ½ to 2½ inches long. The floral spray of the Boneset is flat-topped and rather compact in appearance, with the flower heads so close together that the general effect is fuzzy. The floral spray of the White Snakeroot is more open by far and rounded or even scattering. The flower heads are not lost sight of in the mass but stand out like little round white buttons that you might think you could count without touching. Aside from these differences easy to note, Boneset prefers to lift its head to the open sky for the most part, whereas White Snakeroot is largely a dweller in the woods or at least in shady places. It is a very hardy flower, and, though it may come into bloom in July, it will linger late in Autumn and is one of the last of the flowers to succumb before the onslaught of frosty October nights or the cold rains of November. Just as the first flowers of Spring are sought with special fervor, the last flowers of the year are looked upon with extra affection. By then most of the trees are bare along the hillsides. The migrating Whitethroat Sparrows are scratching for food among the dead leaves of the thickets. "The melancholy days have come, the saddest of the year." It's then that the White Snakeroot, still in sturdy bloom, gladdens the eye and cheers the heart.

Like all members of the *Eupatorium* group of the Composite Family, it has flower heads composed entirely of "disk flowers," and in this case they put on a good show in a small way. But here again you really need a magnifying glass to appreciate it. The name "Snakeroot," of course, comes from a belief of old days that an infusion made from the root of the plant was a cure for the ill effects of a bite by a poisonous snake. Every region where poisonous snakes are found has at least one "Snakeroot" and probably several at the very least. Names to the same effect are found in many languages on different continents. But the belief in modern medical circles is that there are better ways of treating the ill effects of bites by poisonous snakes than by drinking down an infusion made from any part of any one of these plants—or all of them put together.

JOE-PYE WEED; PURPLE BONESET

(*Eupatorium purpureum*)

When the wine-colored sprays of the Joe-Pye Weed begin to appear in rich woods, along the roadsides, in wet meadows, and almost anywhere in moist ground over most of temperate North America, Summer is on the wane and Autumn is just around the corner. The common name "Joe-Pye Weed" covers at least four species of *Eupatorium* that range practically from coast to coast, but they look much alike to the ordinary eye and the specific differences are details that the beginner can set aside until he becomes well acquainted with the group. The species shown here is common in rich woods, in thickets, and along shady roadsides over the eastern half of the United States and nearby Canada and grows to a height of from 4 to 8 feet on a stem as stiff and as straight as a lance. The leaves that grow in "whorls" or circles of 3's to 6's around the stem like spokes of a wheel are about 6 inches long, narrowly oval, pointed at both ends, and sharply toothed along the edges. The stem often carries a purplish tint and usually is dark purple at the "nodes" or where the leaf "whorls" branch out from it. The large rounded floral sprays at the tops of the stems vary in color from a wishy-washy white through a weak pink and on into a light lilac or pale purple, depending upon the particular plant, the place in which it is growing, and possibly local weather conditions. If you examine the floral sprays, you will find them made up of many little flower heads that are, in turn, gatherings of "disk flowers" according to the rule for the *Eupatorium* group. If this particular species prefers shaded territory, there are other Joe-Pye Weeds that prefer swamps, wet meadows, and river banks where they often provide a delicately tinted foreground for a picturesque landscape beyond. A hillside of Goldenrod above a swale of Joe-Pye Weed is truly a lovely combination of colors.

The Joe Pye after whom these flowers were named is supposed to have been an Indian medicine man who became friendly with the early colonists of Massachusetts and cured varied ills—typhus has been mentioned—by his skillful use of these plants. His medical secrets are now lost in a mist of legend, but Joe Pye himself, through the growing power of these tall plants, has achieved immortality of a kind, for his name will be preserved down the centuries as the great sprays of the Joe-Pye Weeds come annually into softly tinted bloom.

IRONWEED

(*Vernonia noveboracensis*)

This is still another member of the great Composite Family. As Wamba, the son of Witless, the son of an alderman, said—according to Sir Walter Scott in "Ivanhoe," though Wamba was speaking of another matter at the time: "Nomen est legio," meaning "Their name is legion" with Latin emphasis. So it is with the members of the Composite Family, and certainly the Ironweed can't be overlooked, because it is one of the tallest of the lot. When the Joe-Pye Weed is coming into bloom in low moist ground such as wet meadows, the fringes of brooks or streams, or the soggy borders of swamps, among those tall stalks bearing pinkish-purple sprays you may see here and there an even taller stalk carrying a wide floral spray of deep purple hue. That will be the Ironweed. There are half a dozen species of Ironweed fairly well distributed across the United States and southern Canada. They differ somewhat in size and flower color and in the shape of the leaves, but they look much alike to the ordinary observer and all of them are easily distinguished from the Joe-Pye Weeds—close relatives, by the way—among whom they often grow. The much deeper purple of the Ironweed flower spray is an easy guide because it stands out among the paler Joe-Pye Weed blooms. Another striking difference is in the way the leaves grow out of the stems. The leaves of the Joe-Pye Weeds are "whorled" or set in circles at intervals along the stem, whereas the leaves of the Ironweed are individualists. They come as they please and only rarely or accidentally grow opposite one another on the stem. In fact, they seem to grow out at all angles, but each one usually starts at an otherwise unoccupied point along the stem. A glance at the picture will make this plain.

The New York Ironweed, as this particular species is named, is common in moist open or moderately shaded ground in the Northeast and extends as far south as Georgia and as far west as Mississippi. It grows from 3 to 9 feet high and comes into full bloom in August and September, but in favored locations it lingers in bloom into October. At a distance it might be mistaken for one of the tall purple Asters in September, but, on a nearer view, the difference is quite plain because the Ironweed has only tubular "disk flowers" where the Asters have a center of tiny "disk flowers" surrounded by a colorful circle of flat "ray flowers."

NEW ENGLAND ASTER

(*Aster novae-angliae*)

The Asters are a wonderful group; sturdy, widespread, beautiful, and abundant almost everywhere in uncultivated ground. Botanists have found some 200 species in North America. They are members of the Composite Family along with the Joe-Pye Weed and the Ironweed, but, with their centers of tightly packed tiny "disk flowers" and their radiating fringes of colorful strap-shaped "ray flowers," they bear a much greater resemblance to such other members of that almost overwhelming family as the Fleabanes, the Black-eyed Susan, and the Common White Daisy. Most of the Asters come into bloom rather late in the season, flowering in Autumn days and displaying "ray flowers" of all hues from pure white to deep purple. There are white Asters that cover the shaded floors of the September woods. There are Asters of many different tints to brighten the country roadsides in harvest time. The hunter finds them in the swamps and on brilliant October hillsides when he is out with dog and gun. The early migrants among the birds go southward over a landscape that is sprinkled with a hundred kinds of Asters beneath them. Do not worry about trying to identify all the Asters in your area. They are far too many in number, and not only are the specific differences small in many cases but the species interbreed on occasions and cause confusion even among licensed botanists. It is enough for a beginner to know a few species and love the whole family. A general rule for recognition is: if it looks like a Daisy, it is an Aster or some close relative of that group. This diagnosis will do until a botanist comes along to settle the matter.

The New England Aster is one of the tallest and most beautiful of the apparently endless kinds of Asters found over most of the United States and southern Canada. It grows almost everywhere in waste open territory and along roadsides, but it seems to prefer moist ground and the fringes of swamps or water courses of any kind. It has a stout and hairy main stem that sometimes reaches a height of 8 feet, though about 5 feet would be closer to the average. The narrow, hairy leaves are from 2 to 5 inches long and are alternate —not opposite one another—along the stem. They have no stalks or "petioles" and appear to "sit on" the stem in a manner the botanists call "clasping." Near the top the stem sends out many branchlets in a spreading spray and the lovely flower heads with golden centers and rich purple rays are carried at the ends of the branchlets. Over their full range they bloom from August into October, and where they grow amid patches of Goldenrod the color contrast is spectacular.

BROAD-LEAF GOLDEN ASTER

(*Chrysopsis mariana*)

The Golden Asters—there are more than a dozen species in North America—look much like yellow Daisies, and, depending upon the species and local conditions, they grow from a height of a few inches to about 3 feet. The Broad-leaf or Maryland Golden Aster reaches a height of 2½ feet, has a flower head about 1 inch across, and is plentiful in sandy soil and open woods from New York to Florida and westward to Ohio and Texas. Most of the Golden Asters bloom from July to October, but the Broad-leaf usually waits until August to open its floral display. The golden-yellow flower heads are held up sturdily in a loose cluster (a "corymb") at the top of the stem, and where they grow in the New York and New Jersey seashore areas, they come into their golden prime about the time that the Summer vacationists are packing up to leave the beach and return to the city. If you roam the moors of Nantucket in August or September, you will find a different species of Golden Aster—the smaller, lower-growing, and narrow-leaved *Chrysopsis falcata* —brightening the footpaths and the fringes of the sandy rutted roads of that colorful region.

BRISTLY or STIFF-LEAVED ASTER

(*Aster linariifolius*)

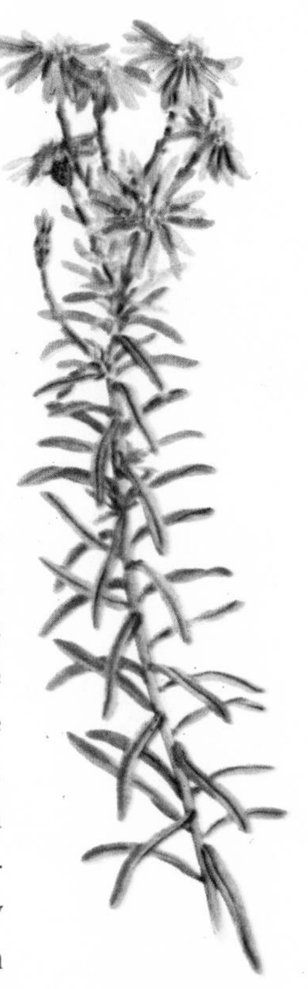

This particular flower deserves a medal if for no other reason than that it is one member of the confusing Aster group that is easy to identify. It may be found over the whole eastern half of the United States and as far west as Minnesota and Texas, pushing up its "stiffy and starchy" stalks to a height of from 6 inches to 2 feet. The narrow leaves, 1 to 1½ inches long and shaped like blades of grass, are really stiff and rough to the touch. The flowers are easy to gather for a bouquet because they appear in patches and each stem usually carries from 2 to 5 or 6 flower heads at the top, though not all of them open at the same time. Though the Bristly Aster is widespread, it is often quite local in distribution. You may find a whole field covered with it—in dry soil on open hillsides or roadsides—and no other patches for miles around. Another odd point is that the patches often migrate in a body. They die out in one spot and move on to another. They come into bloom in August and may be found flowering to October. The "ray flowers" may be lavender, pale blue, or almost white, and the yellow "disk flowers" turn red-bronze as they mature, a customary change with many of the Aster group.

CLOSED GENTIAN; BOTTLE GENTIAN

(*Gentiana andrewsii*)

This flower is easy to recognize but not so easy to find, and it is definitely difficult to come to any agreement on a common name for it. The scientific name remains soberly constant—the *andrewsii* is in honor of Henry C. Andrews, an English flower painter of about 150 years ago—but in different parts of its range or by different persons it may be called Closed Gentian, Blind Gentian, Bottle Gentian, Barrel Gentian, Fringe-tip Closed Gentian, or Closed Blue Gentian. Take your choice. There is no law covering the matter. The flowers really do look much like little narrow blue barrels fairly well sealed at each end. The stiff straight stem grows to a height of from 1 to 2½ feet with narrow fleshy leaves that "sit close" and come in pairs on opposite sides of the lower section of the stem. Near the top they are "whorled" or in a circle around the stem and provide what appears to be a green supporting bracket for the clusters of flowers 1 to 2 inches long that grow out of the "axils" or upper side of the leaf-joints. The plant prefers moist ground and is found—often in ditches or on wet roadside banks—over most of the eastern half of temperate North America from Quebec to Georgia. The flowers come into bloom from August into October and it requires the strength and persistence of the burly Bumblebee to force its way into the folded-over tip of the flower to gather pollen for food and, in the process, fertilize the flowers as it goes from one to another on its foraging trip. The Closed Gentian often escapes notice even where it is fairly common because it hides away in lush growths and the clusters of blue flowers do not catch the eye as they would if they were brighter in hue. So go slowly and look carefully if you want to find the Closed Gentian.

There are some two dozen species of Gentian in North America and many species in Europe and Asia. The group is named for King Gentius of Illyria, the country that Shakespeare chose as a setting for *Twelfth Night* and the region that we now known as Albania and Yugoslavia. Gentius is recorded in herbal history as the original discoverer of medicinal virtues in these plants. He reigned in the 2nd Century B.C. and came upon dire misfortune beyond the curative powers of any Gentian. His army was routed by the invading Roman legions in 168 B.C. and he and his family were led as captives in a triumphal march through the streets of Rome.

FRINGED GENTIAN

(*Gentiana crinita*)

Finis coronet opus! Let the end crown all and the last be the best! Here is a lovely flower that often carries its beautiful and delicately fringed petals into the frosted foreground of oncoming Winter. Blooming from late August into November, it ranges from Maine to Manitoba and from Georgia to Iowa, preferably in overgrown wet meadows where the turf is soft underfoot, where the Woodcock feed and the White-eyed Vireos nest, and where pushing young Willows, Alders, Viburnums, Panicled Dogweeds, and Gray Birches are eager to establish themselves. You may find it along brooks or the edges of swamps or even in roadside ditches, but do not look for it in meadows that have been mowed or on roadsides that have been trimmed with a scythe, for there it will have been cut down before its time if it springs up at all. It grows to a height of 2 to 3 feet, with the flowers carried much as candles are carried by a multibranched candelabrum. There is no need further to describe either the plant or the lovely tubular flowers of 4 fringed blue petals that are open to the Autumn skies. The petals alone are enough to catch the eye, gladden the heart, and identify the flower of which William Cullen Bryant wrote:

Thou blossom, bright with Autumn dew,
And colored with the heaven's own blue,
That openest when the quiet light
Succeeds the keen and frosty night;

Thou comest not when violets lean
O'er wandering brooks and springs unseen,
Or columbines, in purple dressed,
Nod o'er the ground-bird's hidden nest.

Thou waitest late, and com'st alone,
When woods are bare and birds are flown,
And frosts and shortening days portend
The aged Year is near his end.

Then doth thy sweet and quiet eye
Look through its fringes to the sky,
Blue—blue—as if that sky let fall
A flower from its cerulean wall.

I would that thus, when I shall see
The hour of death draw near to me,
Hope, blossoming within my heart,
May look to heaven as I depart.

FINIS.

An Introduction to Nature

PART 3

TREES

ILLUSTRATED BY MICHAEL H. BEVANS

AMERICAN YEW; GROUND HEMLOCK

(*Taxus canadensis*)

If the way to learn a subject is from the ground up, it seems sensible to start the study of trees by becoming acquainted with the American Yew or Ground Hemlock. You probably will have to bend over to get a close look at it. Throughout most of its range—from Newfoundland to Manitoba and south to Virginia, Kentucky and Iowa—it is a mere shrub of feathery evergreen foliage slanting upward a few feet from the forest floors where it flourishes, though on occasion it may reach a height of 5 feet or more. It would take some stretch of the imagination to call it a tree, but it grows among trees, appearing most frequently and abundantly in woods where tall evergreens predominate, and there its foliage, that justifies its secondary name of Ground Hemlock, may leave a beginner puzzled as to whether he is looking at a full-grown American Yew or a little Hemlock just starting out in life.

There are detailed differences that a botanist would point out in a jiffy, but the quickest way to settle the matter is to flip the branchlet over and look at the lower side of the leaf spray. The linear leaves or needles of the American Yew are green on both sides. They are a lighter green on the lower surface, or even a yellowish-green, but you can see plainly that they are green, whereas the Hemlock needles are decidedly silvery or pale gray on the lower surface. Once you make this comparison, you never again need be baffled by the superficial resemblance of the foliage of the lowly American Yew to that of any Hemlock, large or small.

One of the attractive features of this evergreen shrub is the bright red, berry-like fruit, curiously open at the outer end, that appears late in the season amid the dark foliage of some of the plants—the pistillate or "female" ones. The European Yew, which grows to a larger size and, according to English legend furnished the bows for Robin Hood and his merry men in Sherwood Forest, produces such quantities of pollen on the staminate or "male" trees that a branch shaken by the wind—or by hand—in the blossoming season will send clouds of the light-colored pollen into the air like smoke. That's why Tennyson in the *Holy Grail* had the monk Ambrosius say to Sir Percivale:

O brother, I have seen this Yew Tree smoke,
Spring after Spring, for half a hundred years.

BALSAM FIR

(*Abies balsamea*)

Almost certainly this is an old friend, known and cherished since childhood, though perhaps under another name. This is by all odds the favorite "Christmas tree" in North American homes at Yuletide. That's because it has two advantages over other evergreens that are used as Christmas trees. It holds its needles for a longer period after cutting than most of its rivals for the job, and it is superlatively aromatic. We have numerous native Firs, most of them inhabitants of the cooler regions of the Pacific Northwest, and they are a fragrant group as a whole. The crushed leaves, the bruised bark, or the punctured "resin blisters" will, in most cases, give off a pleasant odor. But the Balsam, as it is called, is by far the most pleasantly odorous member of this redolent group.

At any distance Firs and Spruces will look much alike to a beginner, but there is one difference that is easily noted. The cones of all our Firs grow upright on the branchlets, whereas the cones of Spruces hang down. Another point of difference can best be cleared up with the aid of a pocket magnifying glass. Spruce needles stripped from a twig leave little projections rough to the touch along the bare twig. If Fir needles are stripped in the same fashion, the "leaf scars" that remain on the twig will be tiny circles. If you wish to pursue the matter further under the magnifying glass, you will see that Spruce needles are squarish in cross section while Fir needles are narrowly rectangular.

The Balsam is a tree of medium size that ranges from Labrador to Yukon Territory and British Columbia and extends down into the United States on cool, high ground from New England to Minnesota. It reaches southward to Virginia along the Appalachian chain. The aromatic needles vary from ½ to 1¼ inches in length and the upright cones are from 1½ to 3½ inches long. Note how the seed scales drop off the cone axis, a mark of the Firs. By the way, the cones of the towering Douglas Fir (*Pseudotsuga taxifolia*) of the Pacific Northwest hang downward, but this is not a member of the *Abies* or "true Fir" group. These Douglas Fir cones are quite distinctive in that they have triple-tongued little "bracts" sticking out over the edges of the scales. No Spruce has cones like that, nor any other evergreen except a relative, the Big-cone Douglas Fir.

EASTERN HEMLOCK

(*Tsuga canadensis*)

This is one of the best known and also one of the easiest to identify of all the evergreens native to North America. It's like the Robin among birds or the common White Daisy among wild flowers. It is so familiar to most of us who roam the outdoors that it can be used as a standard of comparison in describing less common species or those more difficult to identify. There are other Hemlocks native to North America—the Western Hemlock and the Mountain Hemlock familiar to woodchoppers and lumber companies of the Pacific Northwest, and the Carolina Hemlock of the Allegheny ridges from southwestern Virginia to Georgia—but in ordinary conversation outside of lumber camps, lumberyards, or botanical conferences, the name "Hemlock" is usually taken as a reference to this species. In short, and without any law covering the matter, to the man in the street or the boy in the woods, this is *the* Hemlock.

There are few trees more attractive to the eye. This is a lovely, lofty evergreen of graceful pyramidal shape and feathery, dark foliage of linear leaves or needles about ½ inch long that spread out on either side of the branchlets to give a "flat" appearance to the leaf spray. Among the evergreens this is one of the distinguishing features of the Eastern Hemlock and another is the contrast between the dark green color of the upper side of a leaf spray and the pale gray or silvery sheen of the lower side. The tiny cones, rarely as much as 1 inch long, hang on the tips of the branchlets through the year and the brown cones of the previous season and the green cones of the current season often are found on the tree at the same time. The range of the Eastern Hemlock is from Nova Scotia and New Brunswick westward to Minnesota and south along the ridges to Georgia and Alabama. At maturity it may reach a height of 100 feet or so, with a trunk diameter of 4 feet or more, though such trees are exceptional. In general it is a narrowly pyramidal tree with a conical top like a church steeple. It prefers rocky hillsides and often forms imposing groves on the sides of steep ravines, but it is also found along roadsides, in dooryards, or planted for ornamental purposes on private or public ground. The cones of the other Hemlocks are larger than those of this species and the foliage not so flat in appearance. The Western Hemlock is the giant of the group and often reaches a height of 150 feet. This abundant tree of the Pacific Northwest is a fast grower and has become a real rival of the Spruces as a source of wood pulp for paper manufacturing and plastic industries.

RED SPRUCE

(*Picea rubens*)

As a whole, Spruces are a group of trees that are tall, dark, handsome, and almost forbidding in appearance where they extend in vast forests over the colder regions of the Northern Hemisphere. Most of the individual Spruce trees of North America are Canadian by birth and preferred residence. Where they extend down into the United States they begin to climb to enjoy cooler air, which means that they are found on the Rocky Mountain slopes of the West and the Appalachian ridges of the East. At lower levels the Spruces of this continent stick to Canada and the northern tier of the United States. There are two species, however, the colorful Blue Spruce, native to a portion of the Rocky Mountain region, and the imported Norway Spruce, that are widely planted across the country for decorative purposes, and these Spruces you may find wherever care and feeding will keep them alive.

To the beginner most Spruce trees will look much alike. Learning to distinguish one species from another will take some time and study. The immediate problem for the beginner is not how to distinguish one species of Spruce from another but how to know the Spruces from the Hemlocks and Firs. That's a fairly easy matter. In most of our North American species the Spruce needles are short, slightly curving, fairly stiff, and sharp-pointed and they grow in such fashion that the branchlets seem "armed at all points." Have you seen brushes with which the insides of bottles are cleaned? The "business end" of such a brush is a cylinder of bristles that stick out in all directions. That will give you some idea—a little exaggerated, perhaps—of how Spruce leaves are arranged along the branchlets. It's quite different from the comparatively flat or 2-ranked foliage of the Hemlocks and the upward sweep of the Fir foliage. There are other differences, such as the stubby, peg-like projections from which the Spruce leaves start and the way the cones of our Spruces hang below the horizontal while our Fir cones are carried erect on the branchlets. The Red Spruce, shown here, is an eastern species that ranges from eastern Canada south to North Carolina and Tennessee on high ground. The 4-sided needles, about ½ inch, are stiff and slightly curved, and the cones average about 1½ inches in length. The Spruces are the trees that furnish the bulk of the wood pulp used in the manufacturing of paper of all kinds, including the paper on which this is printed.

AMERICAN LARCH; TAMARACK

(*Larix laricina*)

The Larches or Tamaracks are an odd lot. They have linear leaves or needles and they produce cones like "the murmuring Pines and the Hemlocks," but they shed their leaves in the Autumn, which is the mark of the "deciduous" trees. Larch is the Old World name for the group, but Tamarack seems to be the choice on this side of the Atlantic. Under either name, this species is the most widespread of the group in North America and one of the hardiest trees on this continent. It ranges from Labrador to Alaska and from West Virginia on a slant across the United States to British Columbia. It likes wet ground and swamps, but it takes to the hillsides in many northerly portions of its range. It has been known to reach a height of 100 feet, but ordinarily it is a tree of medium size and at the northern limit of its range, which is approximately the "tree limit" of North America, it is little more than a ragged wind-blown shrub.

In the Winter it has a forlorn look like a dead Spruce, but the warmth of Spring brings out the clumps of 6 to 16 linear leaves, about 1 inch in length, that sprout in tufts from the tops of short spurs or "miniature stumps" along the branchlets. Unless you look closely you may miss the little staminate and pistillate flowers that ultimately produce the ⅝-inch cones along the same branchlets and put the tree and all other Larches or Tamaracks among the "Conifers" or cone bearers in the botanical world. In the early stages the developing pistillate flowers are attractive pink or reddish outgrowths along the tan branchlets, a feature that gave the tree the name of "Epinette Rouge" or "Red Spinelet" among French Canadians. The European Larch (*Larix decidua*), frequently planted for ornament in this country, has that same feature and among those who took note of it was Alfred Tennyson when he began one quatrain of *In Memoriam* with the line:

When rosy plumelets tuft the larch . . .

In the Pacific Northwest you will find the Western Larch (*Larix occidentalis*), the big brother of the American Larch and an important tree in the lumber industry. Its cones are about twice the size of those of the American Larch.

EASTERN WHITE PINE

(*Pinus strobus*)

The Pines are a widespread group of useful and, for the most part, graceful evergreens that range from coast to coast in North America and from the Gulf of Mexico to the Arctic wasteland. Many of our Pines have long, flexible, and odorous linear leaves or needles, but there is an easy way to distinguish even those that have comparatively short or stiff needles from any Yew, Fir, Hemlock, or Spruce. There are more than twenty species of Pine in North America but, with the exception of the Single-leaved Pine of narrow range in the Southwest, the linear leaves of all our Pines come in clusters or bundles ("fascicles" to the botanist) of from 2 to 5 needles each. The number of needles in a bundle, the varying lengths of the needles, and the shapes, sizes, and details of the cones, usually make it fairly easy to distinguish one species of Pine from another.

The needles of the Eastern White Pine and the Western White Pine come in bundles of fives, for instance, and so do the needles of the tallest of our Pines, the Sugar Pine of Oregon and California. But the range of the Eastern White Pine is from Newfoundland to Manitoba and south to Georgia and Iowa and over that area it is the only Pine to display needles 5 to a bundle. Where the Western White Pine and the Sugar Pine meet in Oregon and California, the enormous stout cones—up to 18 inches! —of the Sugar Pine are distinctive. The flexible, lustrous, and pleasantly aromatic needles of the valuable and beautiful Eastern White Pine are from 3 to 5 inches long and the drooping cones, looking somewhat like moldy cigars as they mature, may be from 4 to 10 inches in length. The early settlers and pioneers found great areas covered with pure stands of Eastern White Pine in the northern woods. Those trees are gone. They were used to build our civilization.

PITCH PINE

(Pinus rigida)

Though it may reach a height of 75 feet, the Pitch Pine more often is a much smaller, chunky tree holding stubbornly to wind-swept ground where few other trees could survive. It is found on offshore islands, sandy wastes, barren ground, and rocky ledges from Maine to Ontario and southward to western Georgia and the hills of Tennessee and Kentucky. Its rigid and usually curving needles, 3 to 5 inches long, come 3 to a bundle and its squat cones, 1 to 3 inches long and almost as broad as they are long, are armed with sharp prickles. After they shed their seeds, the empty cones, frequently found in clusters, may cling to the trees for years. A sticky pitch oozes out of buds and branches at the least provocation, or even with no provocation at all. Hence the name Pitch Pine.

LONGLEAF PINE

(Pinus australis)

Here is another Pine whose needles come 3 to a bundle and whose cones are furnished with sharp prickles, but there is little danger of mistaking this tree for any of its relatives. The shining needles that give it the name of Longleaf Pine are from 8 to 20 inches in length and as flexible as they are lustrous. On the old trees, which may reach a height of 120 feet, the foliage looks like graceful green drapery, but in the saplings the effect is even more artistic because at eye level each cluster of the extraordinary foliage seems to rise and fall away like a little green fountain. The stout cones are from 6 to 10 inches long and the orange-brown bark of the older trees is set off in irregular rectangles in a way to give the trunk something of a tiled appearance. The Longleaf Pine is found on the Atlantic Coastal Plain from Virginia to Florida and in the lowlands of the Gulf States, where it is as decorative as it is useful for timber and turpentine. There are other Pines of North America whose needles come 3 to a bundle, but always there are differences in leaf, cone, bark, or other detail by which you may know them.

RED PINE; NORWAY PINE

(*Pinus resinosa*)

The Red or Norway Pine and the Yellow or Shortleaf Pine are two tall trees of the eastern half of North America that usually produce their needles in bundles of twos, but there is no difficulty in distinguishing one from the other. The Red Pine is the northerly species and is found in dry woods from Newfoundland to Manitoba and south to West Virginia, Michigan, Wisconsin, and Minnesota. The Yellow Pine is the southerly species and occurs in dry, sandy soil from New York westward to Missouri and south to the Gulf Coast area. Where the ranges overlap, the Red Pine may be known by the fact that its 2-inch blunt cones are "unarmed" whereas the cones of the Yellow Pine, though similar in size and shape, have small but decided prickles. The Yellow Pine needles may be from 3 to 5 inches long but the Red Pine needles average about 5 inches long and may reach 6 inches or more in length. A considerable difference in the bark of the trunk, more easily seen than described, will soon become apparent to those who look closely at trees.

PINYON PINE

(*Pinus edulis*)

The scientific name of this little tree means "edible Pine." Not the whole tree, of course; just the pleasant-tasting seeds discarded by the broad, lumpy little cones about 2 inches in length no matter in what direction you measure them. The Pinyon Pine is native to the high ground—5000 to 10,000 feet altitude—of Arizona, New Mexico, Utah, and Colorado, but for the edible seeds that are marketed as "Pinyon nuts" or "Indian nuts" and also for ornamental purposes, it has been widely cultivated and is found in many sections of the United States. The needles average a trifle over 1 inch in length, are rather stiff, and usually come in bundles of twos, though bundles of threes also are found. There is a Single-leaf Pinyon of somewhat more westerly range and lower ground that reaches into southern California and also produces an edible seed for market. The feature of this tree, as its name implies, is that its needles, 1 to 2 inches in length, occur separately and not in bundles, which makes it unique among all our North American Pines.

BALD CYPRESS

(*Taxodium distichum*)

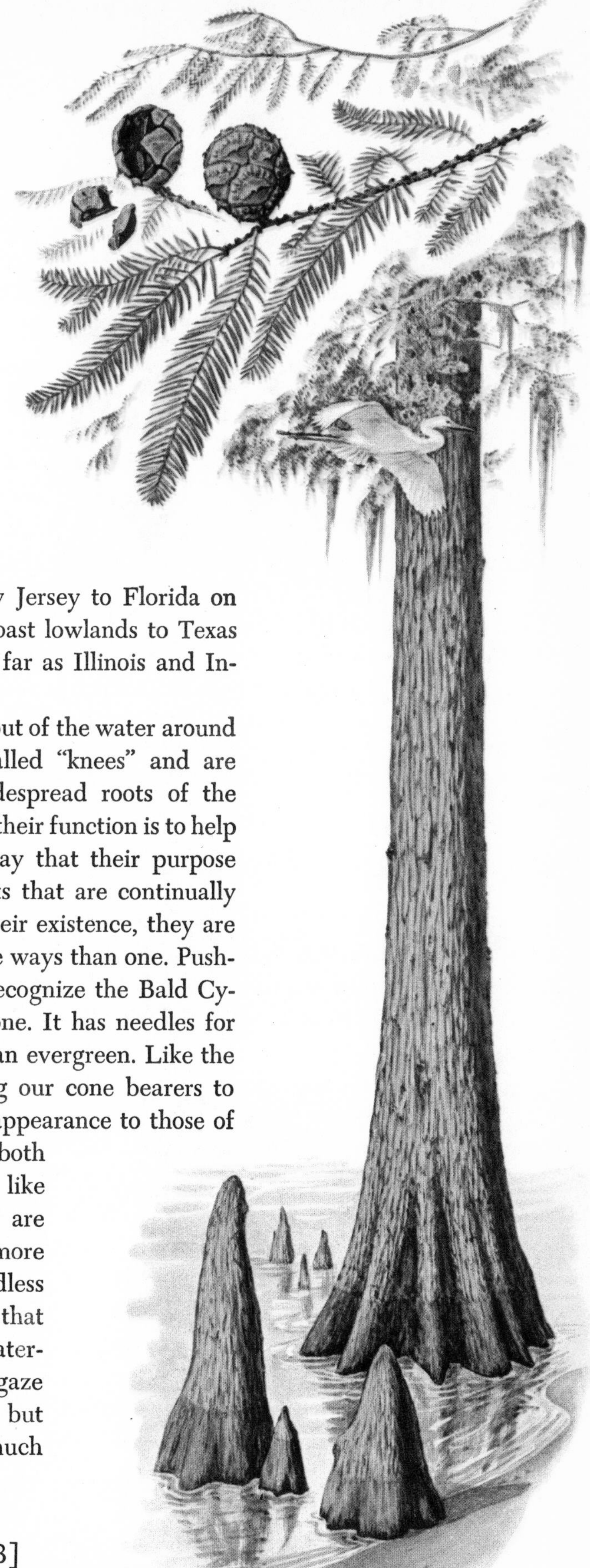

Put on boots or take to a boat if you wish to become acquainted with the Bald Cypress in its native haunts. There is no difficulty in recognizing the tree. The difficulty is in approaching it. Here and there you may find a few of these trees on fairly solid ground but, for the most part, the Bald Cypress is a towering tree of the southern swamps and usually is found with its flaring or buttressed trunk rising out of mud or shallow water and reaching skyward to a height of 80 or 100 feet, or even 150 feet in exceptional cases. It ranges from southern New Jersey to Florida on the Atlantic Coastal Plain, across the Gulf Coast lowlands to Texas and Mexico, and up the Mississippi Basin as far as Illinois and Indiana.

The sharp-pointed objects shown rising out of the water around the base of the tree in the illustration are called "knees" and are curious projections growing out of the widespread roots of the tree. Some persons hold to the opinion that their function is to help anchor the tree in soft ground and others say that their purpose is to provide an added supply of air for roots that are continually under water. Whatever the explanation of their existence, they are an added feature in a tree that is odd in more ways than one. Pushing through a swamp in a boat, you might recognize the Bald Cypress by the buttressed base of the trunk alone. It has needles for foliage and it produces cones, but it is not an evergreen. Like the Tamarack or Larch, it is an exception among our cone bearers to that extent. Its needles, somewhat similar in appearance to those of the Hemlock and green or greenish-yellow on both sides like those of the Yew, fall in the Autumn like the foliage of the Ash, or Maple. The cones are shaped as shown in the illustration and rarely more than 1 inch in diameter. But these are needless details. The Bald Cypress is a majestic tree that has no rival of similar appearance in its water-logged realm. You will know it on sight and gaze upon it with due respect. The wood is light but durable when exposed to the weather and is much used for casks, shingles, and railroad ties.

ARBOR VITAE; NORTHERN WHITE CEDAR

(*Thuja occidentalis*)

It isn't easy for a beginner to learn to distinguish the Arbor Vitae or Northern White Cedar from the Coast, Atlantic, or Southern White Cedar at a glance. There are other Cedars and Cypresses and allied Junipers across the country to add to the difficulty, but go slowly and cautiously among these evergreens of curious foliage and soon you will sort out the common species of your region. The Arbor Vitae in the wild is a narrowly pyramidal tree up to 50 or 60 feet in height with flat sprays of heavy foliage consisting of tiny leaves tightly braided along the branchlets. It is most easily recognized by the fruit, as shown, a narrow, upright cone ½ inch or so in length, opening at the outer end when ripe. This is a northerly tree found in wet ground from Quebec to Saskatchewan and extending down into the United States, climbing higher as it goes southward. It is common in cultivation as a trimmed hedge tree.

COAST or SOUTHERN WHITE CEDAR

(*Chamaecyparis thyoides*)

The foliage of this small to medium-size evergreen much resembles that of the Arbor Vitae or Northern White Cedar but the cones are quite different in character. All of the *Thuja* group have the little cylindrical cones that open from the outer end toward the base and all of the *Chamaecyparis* clan, including the great Port Orford Cedar (*Chamaecyparis lawsoniana*) of the Pacific Coast, have little globular cones that split toward the center in releasing the seed. As the various common names of this species imply, it is found in swamps and wet ground generally from southern Maine down the Atlantic Coastal Plain to Florida and across the Gulf States into Mississippi. That leaves little ground for confusion with the more northerly Arbor Vitae and, in the comparatively narrow region where their ranges overlap, the difference in the cones will easily distinguish one species from the other. The globular cones of the Coast, Atlantic, or Southern White Cedar are about ⅓ inch in diameter.

COMMON JUNIPER

(Juniperus communis)

There are Junipers of one kind or another from coast to coast over most of North America and they vary in size and shape from creeping shrubs to upstanding trees of picturesque appeal. They are evergreens and some of them display foliage rather similar in general appearance to that of the *Thuja* group or the *Chamaecyparis* clan mentioned on the opposite page, but you will recognize the Junipers easily because they are our only evergreens whose fruits are "berries" to the eye even if they are "cones with fleshy coverings" to the botanist. The stringy bark, the inner wood, the foliage, and the berry-like fruit of the Junipers are aromatic, much more so in some species than in others. The species shown here is a hardy shrub or small tree of rocky slopes, old pastures, and poor ground generally from Labrador to Alaska across Canada and all over the United States except the extreme Southwest and Southeast. The ½-inch needles are very sharp and, unlike most leaves, are gray above and green underneath. The pea-sized aromatic blue berry has a whitish bloom.

RED CEDAR

(Juniperus virginiana)

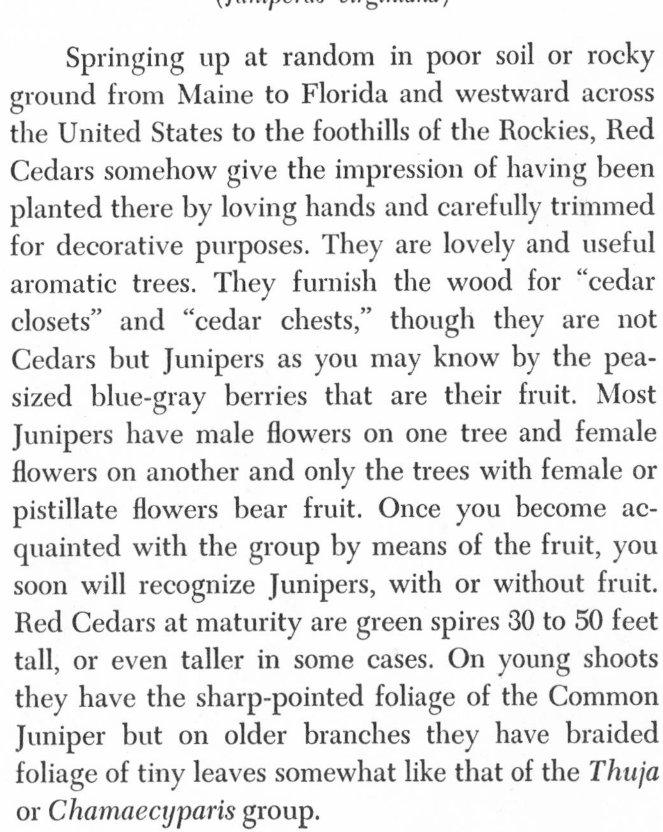

Springing up at random in poor soil or rocky ground from Maine to Florida and westward across the United States to the foothills of the Rockies, Red Cedars somehow give the impression of having been planted there by loving hands and carefully trimmed for decorative purposes. They are lovely and useful aromatic trees. They furnish the wood for "cedar closets" and "cedar chests," though they are not Cedars but Junipers as you may know by the pea-sized blue-gray berries that are their fruit. Most Junipers have male flowers on one tree and female flowers on another and only the trees with female or pistillate flowers bear fruit. Once you become acquainted with the group by means of the fruit, you soon will recognize Junipers, with or without fruit. Red Cedars at maturity are green spires 30 to 50 feet tall, or even taller in some cases. On young shoots they have the sharp-pointed foliage of the Common Juniper but on older branches they have braided foliage of tiny leaves somewhat like that of the *Thuja* or *Chamaecyparis* group.

REDWOOD

(*Sequoia sempervirens*)

The only rival of the Redwood on the face of the earth is its close relative and near neighbor of the Sierras, the Big Tree or *Sequoia gigantea.* These towering trees need no long technical description. To see them is to recognize them and to walk among them is an inspiring and almost overpowering experience. The great groves are meccas for thousands of tourists every year. In such places the massive trunks, reaching upward like great pillars to vanish somewhere in the dark canopy of evergreen foliage far overhead, lend an air of majesty—almost a touch of eternity—to the scene.

The Redwood is the tallest tree in the world, some of them reaching well over 300 feet in height. The Big Tree is bulkier of bole, greater in total tonnage, and of much longer life. It is believed that the Big Tree may reach an age of 4000 to 5000 years, but the longest life span of record for the Redwood is about 1400 years. The Redwood is much more abundant and is found along a 500-mile strip of the Pacific coastal area extending from southern Oregon to Monterey in California. The strip is roughly 30 miles wide, which means that it stretches from the ocean front inland to an altitude of 3000 feet on the slope of the coastal range of the Rockies. The Big Trees, so few and so much treasured that every grove is charted and named and each tree is counted and numbered, are restricted to a small section of the western slope of the Sierra Nevadas in central California from an altitude of 4300 to 8500 feet. The Redwoods are fed with moisture from the fogs that roll in from the Pacific Ocean. The Big Trees are watered by the eternal snows of the Sierras. The Redwood cones, shown here, are about 1 inch in diameter and the oval cones of the Big Tree are 2 or 3 inches long. That the tiny seeds in these cones produce such trees is almost incredible!

GINKGO; MAIDENHAIR TREE

(Ginkgo biloba)

This tree, imported from China, is found in rows along the streets and in the parks of many cities in the United States. It is easily recognized by the curious shape of its leaves and, when the leaves are off, by the short twigs that look like miniature stumps along the bare branches. There are male and female trees and the male is preferred for planting because the yellowish plum-like fruits that are produced in abundance by mature female trees litter the ground or the sidewalks beneath them. The crushed fruit has a bad odor and a worse taste but the kernel of the ½-inch round stone inside is sold for food in China and Japan. Fossil prints of Ginkgo leaves have been found, indicating that it must have existed millions of years ago just about as it does today. The name Maidenhair Tree is a reference to the shape of the leaves, somewhat like Maidenhair Fern divisions.

BLACK WILLOW

(Salix nigra)

Without any question, a beginner will be lost among the more than 100 species of Willow that as mere shrubs or trees up to 100 feet in height are found in various sections of North America. The best that the novice can do is to learn to know a Willow from any other tree, scrape an acquaintance with a few species, and leave the others to later study with a field guide or botanical textbook. As a rule, all Willows bear either male or female catkins and the female or pistillate catkins produce tiny and narrowly pear-shaped pods containing seeds with silky down attached. Willows are commonly found in moist ground and along water courses and long, narrow leaves are a badge of the tribe. The Black Willow, pictured here, may be found as a shrub or a tree up to 60 feet more in height from New Brunswick and Quebec across the continent to the foothills of the Rockies and southward as far as North Carolina, Tennessee, Alabama, and Arkansas. The leaves are 2 to 6 inches long and the expanded Spring catkins from 1 to 3 inches in length. On the lower twig, shown here, note the tiny fringes at the base of the leaves. These are the "stipules" found on many Willows, especially on shoots.

PUSSY WILLOW

(*Salix discolor*)

About the only time the ordinary passerby recognizes a Pussy Willow is in the early Spring when the famous catkins are on display, though it is more or less common as a shrub or small tree in moist ground or along ponds, streams, and lakes from Labrador to Alberta and south to Virginia, Kentucky, and Missouri. It is also much planted for ornament and the bare branchlets are sold by florists in late Winter to purchasers who put them in water at home and watch the flower buds burst open and the glorious catkins come into full bloom. Here is a chance to put a magnifying glass to good use by looking through it at the pollen-laden staminate catkins at the peak of production. You can do this conveniently at home, but you may have to compete with the early bees that are working on the flowers if you try it outdoors. The leaves that come later are from 1½ to 4 inches long, bright green above, whitish on the underside, and quite variable in shape, but on the average much broader than the typical long, narrow leaf that marks the Willow clan from a distance.

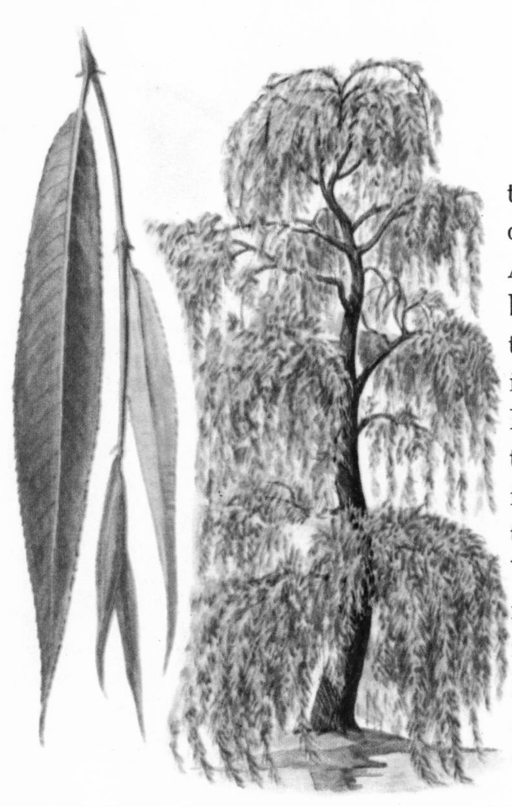

WEEPING WILLOW

(*Salix babylonica*)

This is a tree that has spread from its native China to temperate regions all over the world because of its ornamental value. It was introduced into Europe from Asia and from Europe to North America where it may be found almost anywhere in moist ground from Quebec to British Columbia and southward to the Gulf of Mexico. Its greenish-yellow catkins are not at all spectacular. In fact, most persons at any distance probably mistake them for early foliage. The striking feature of the Weeping Willow, of course, is the extraordinary length of the thin, pendulous branchlets clothed with typical narrow Willow leaves 4 to 5 inches in length. The trees may reach a height of 70 feet, with a full, round crown carried by a stout trunk as much as 6 feet in diameter. By a lake, or hanging over a stream, the effect is decidedly attractive to the eye. One reason for the abundance of the Weeping Willow is that it is easily propagated by slips and a fast grower when it takes root.

EASTERN COTTONWOOD

(*Populus deltoides*)

This is one of the most widespread trees in temperate North America and may be found, mostly in lowlands and along water courses, from the Atlantic Coast to the foothills of the Rockies and from southern Canada to the Gulf of Mexico. It is one of the many Poplars native to this continent and has the faults and virtues of others of the clan. It springs up readily and is a fast grower but, like most fast growers, it is not a strong tree and often suffers breakage from storms. The Cottonwood may attain 100 feet in height and its network of fine, fibrous rootlets that reach out a long way for moisture enables it to flourish where many other trees could not survive. For this reason it is often a valuable shade tree where shade is at a premium.

The Poplars are close relatives of the Willows, as is indicated by the much similar way in which they display their flowers and produce their winged seeds. The Poplar flowers, like those of the Willows, are arranged in catkins that appear before the leaves are out, and the staminate and pistillate catkins are on different trees. The pistillate or female catkins produce strings of seed capsules that eventually turn loose tiny seeds with fine, white, cottony, thread-like attachments that aid their distribution by the wind. But where the Willows as a group are noted for long, narrow leaves on very short stalks, the Poplars have broad leaf blades held well away from the branchlets by long "petioles." In most species of Poplar there is a curious flattening of the petiole that produces a shimmering effect in the foliage. This is explained in detail in the description of the Quaking Aspen on the next page.

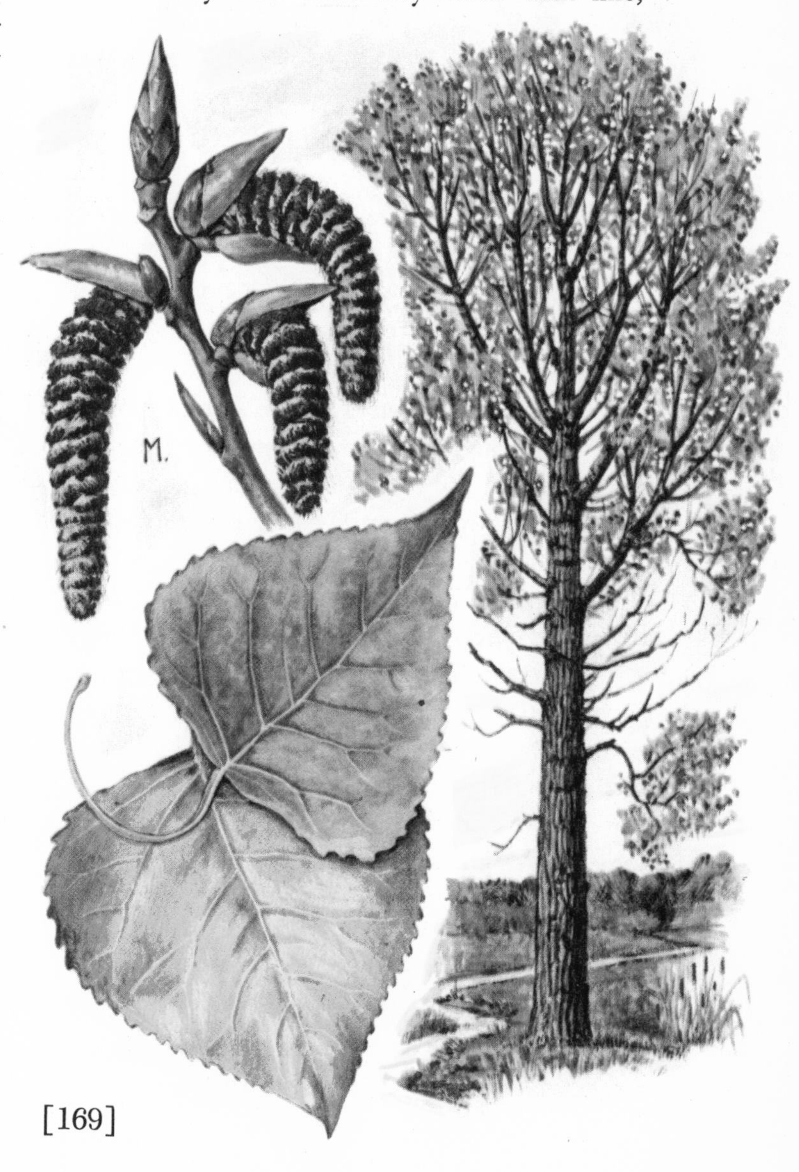

Among the Poplars you will recognize the Cottonwood by its triangular leaves, 3 to 7 inches long, petiole included, with the blades sharp-pointed and toothed, as shown. Other distinctive features are yellowish twigs and conical Winter buds about ½ inch long and quite gummy. The male catkins, 3 to 5 inches long, are fuller and rounder than the pistillate catkins that eventually lengthen to the cottony "necklace" stage that accounts for the name, Necklace Poplar, sometimes applied to this species. The catkins usually are so numerous that they litter the ground.

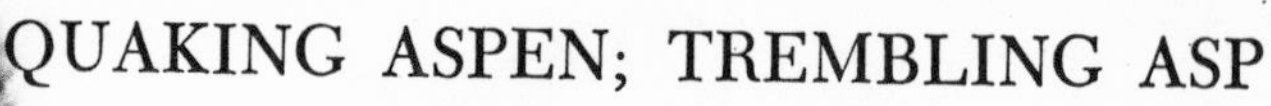

QUAKING ASPEN; TREMBLING ASP

(*Populus tremuloides*)

Whether it is called Quaking Aspen or Trembling Asp, the name comes from the way the shining leaves quiver in the slightest breeze. This is due to a gradual flattening of the leaf stalk or "petiole" in a vertical plane from the branchlet to the base of the leaf blade. Thus the leaf blade is not only lightly held in place, but the flattened surface of the petiole, at right angles to the plane of the leaf blade, offers another purchase for any breeze that may be stirring. The long-petioled leaves are 1½ to 3 inches in diameter, almost round in outline though the tip is pointed, and rather shiny above and below. This member of the Poplar group spans the continent but is rather a northerly species and is not found in the Gulf States. It springs up quickly on burnt ground and in its younger years has a bark greenish-white or cream in color. Popple is still another name for this tree.

LARGE-TOOTHED ASPEN

(*Populus grandidentata*)

Though this member of the Poplar clan is well named and may be distinguished by the large teeth of the leaves that measure 2½ to 4 inches in length, it is more easily recognized by the white, cottony covering of the lower surface of the leaves in their younger state. This gradually wears off on the larger trees but in saplings it is persistent. The leaves of the White Poplar, introduced from Europe, have a similar cottony lower surface but the teeth are fewer, shallower, and more blunt. The Large-toothed Aspen is largely a tree of the Northeast, but it stretches across lower Canada to Ontario and Minnesota and down the high ground of the Appalachians to Tennessee. Like the Quaking Aspen and the Cottonwood it is found frequently on burnt ground, but it is more persistent and sturdier than the Quaking Aspen and often reaches a respectable age and height of 80 feet or more.

LOMBARDY POPLAR

(*Populus nigra italica*)

We can leave to the botanists the question of where this variety of Poplar originated and why it produces only male catkins. What everybody knows is that untold numbers of Lombardy Poplars line the highways and canal banks of the lowlands of Europe and that the tree is extensively planted for ornamental or other purposes all across temperate North America. If you have a clear view of a Lombardy Poplar, you can recognize it a mile or more away. That's because it is the only broad-leaved tree or non-evergreen that grows in such a narrow, upright fashion. It has a tall, straight trunk and numerous branches that, reaching outward but little, curve sharply upward to parallel the trunk. The appearance of the tree as a whole is that of a towering column of shimmering greenery in Summer and bare branches in Winter.

If anything more than the shape were needed to identify the Lombardy Poplar, the leaf would do it. It has the typical long stalk or "petiole" of the Poplar group but the leaf blade is a triangle, broader than it is high. The leaves vary in size but if the blade is 2½ inches high, it probably will be more than 3 inches in width near the base. Since the tree bears no female catkins, it produces no seed, but that's a small matter because the roots send up shoots—a common custom among Poplars—that are easily cut and planted to start a new generation on its way skyward.

This tree often escapes from cultivation and, with its habit of sending up numerous shoots, it sometimes gets beyond control and becomes a local nuisance. But in its proper place it can be a useful and artistic addition to a landscape. Veterans of European campaigns of the World Wars of modern times will remember the picturesque rows of Lombardy Poplars they so often glimpsed in low, flat country and that gave notice of a road, a river, or a canal in the distance. In the Metropolitan Museum of Art in New York City there is a painting that finds high favor with most visitors, particularly those who love tall trees. It is a canvas by Homer D. Martin showing a row of Lombardy Poplars along the Seine below Paris. The tall trees loom against a blue sky and are reflected in the waters of the river in the foreground. The artist called it "View on the Seine" but the more popular name for it is "Harp of the Winds."

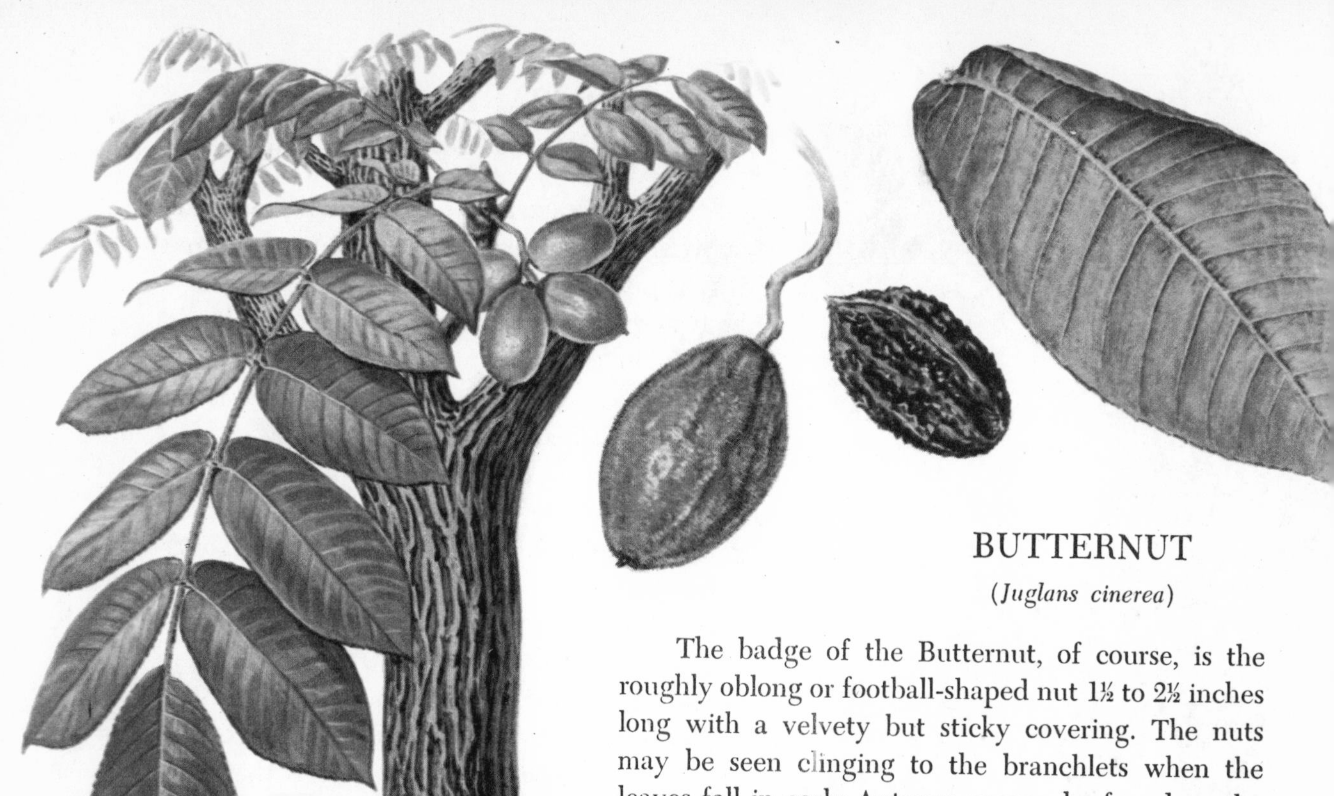

BUTTERNUT

(*Juglans cinerea*)

The badge of the Butternut, of course, is the roughly oblong or football-shaped nut 1½ to 2½ inches long with a velvety but sticky covering. The nuts may be seen clinging to the branchlets when the leaves fall in early Autumn or may be found on the ground under the tree. Aside from that, the Butternut is a medium-sized tree that branches in a somewhat aimless manner and often loses limbs in strong winds. You rarely find Butternut trees of upright character, noble bearing, and fine foliage. Most of them look shiftless in shape and attitude and appear to be merely loitering where they grow. The bark is brownish-gray with straggling vertical grooves in it, and the rather sparse foliage, light green at first, turns yellowish in a vague way as Summer progresses. The trees are never strong and usually linger out a comparatively short life in a crippled condition. The nuts are delicious if it doesn't bother you to have your fingers deeply stained in removing the husk to get at the meat of the matter.

What makes the Butternut of special interest at this point is that it has compound leaves and is the first such tree to be met in this book, though there are many in the woods. In describing the Larch (Page 13), it was explained that a "deciduous" tree is one that loses its leaves in Autumn and, after standing bare all Winter, comes out with a new full crop of leaves in Spring. Roughly speaking, a leaf is the part that falls off a deciduous tree in Autumn. There will remain a "leaf scar" at the parting point and a bud formed there for the production of the shoots of the following year. The Butternut leaf in the picture might seem to be a group of leaves to a beginner, but it is a single leaf made up of a number of divisions called "leaflets" growing opposite one another along a central axis. This arrangement is called "pinnate" and the Butternut leaf is "pinnately compound," from 15 to 30 inches long, with 7 to 17 leaflets from 2 to 4½ inches long and, curiously enough, shaped somewhat like the nuts in outline. The Butternut is found in rich woods, on open slopes, in pastures, and along roadsides over most of temperate North America east of the Rockies.

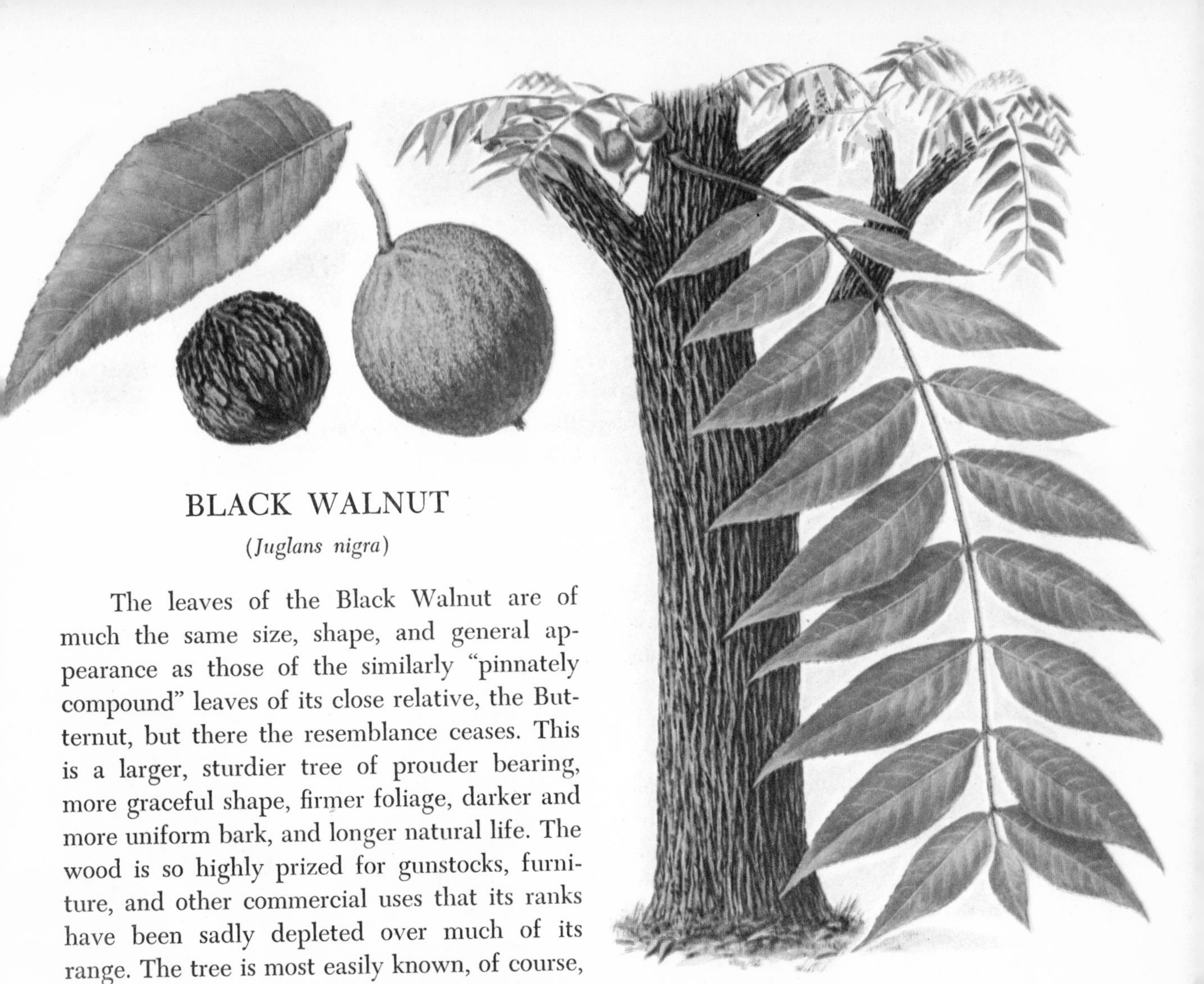

BLACK WALNUT

(Juglans nigra)

The leaves of the Black Walnut are of much the same size, shape, and general appearance as those of the similarly "pinnately compound" leaves of its close relative, the Butternut, but there the resemblance ceases. This is a larger, sturdier tree of prouder bearing, more graceful shape, firmer foliage, darker and more uniform bark, and longer natural life. The wood is so highly prized for gunstocks, furniture, and other commercial uses that its ranks have been sadly depleted over much of its range. The tree is most easily known, of course, by the nuts enclosed in the spherical green husks about 1½ or 2 inches in diameter. These fruits may appear singly or in clusters of twos and threes. The husk is firm and smooth and quite different from the sticky, hairy, wrinkled husk of the Butternut, but it will give the same iodine-like stain to your fingers if you pull it apart to get at the approximately spherical and roughly ridged nut inside. The meat is delicious, but the shell is so thick and hard that it's no easy matter to come at it, which is why the English or Persian Walnut (*Juglans regia*) with its much thinner shell and larger meat content is the species cultivated by the nut growers of the warmer parts of the United States.

The compound leaf of the Black Walnut is from 1 to 2 feet in length and the 11 to 23 leaflets, 2 to 5 inches long. The leaflets are often lopsided at the base and you will note that the sharpening toward the tip is more gradual than it is in the leaflets of the Butternut. The Black Walnut is a hardy tree that is found in the wild from Massachusetts to Minnesota and southward to the higher ground of the Gulf States. In the Southwest and in California there are some other native species of Walnut that may be recognized as such by the resemblance in fruit and leaf to the larger, better-known, more widespread and much more useful Black Walnut that stands as a family favorite in many a farm pasture or rural dooryard.

BITTERNUT HICKORY

(*Carya cordiformis*)

If you live east of the Mississippi, you probably can find half a dozen species of Hickory in your home territory. They are an eastern group as a whole, though some species are found well west of "the Father of Waters" and Texas has a good assortment. All the Hickories have compound leaves of much similar pattern and produce more or less edible nuts. Staminate and pistillate flowers appear on the same tree after the leaves in Spring, the staminate or male flowers as catkins in drooping clusters of threes, and the pistillate or female flowers in little spikes along the branchlets above. The Hickories are distinguished, one from the other, by easily noted differences in leaves, buds, bark, and the nuts they bear. The Bitternut is one of the most widespread of the group and is found high and low, in wet ground or dry, in open fields or in woods, from Maine across Ontario and Michigan to Minnesota and south to the Gulf States.

The compound leaf of the Bitternut is fairly typical of the clan. The leaflets are sharply toothed in a small way, are practically "sessile" or sitting tight along the leaf axis, and increase in size toward the terminal leaflet. The Bitternut leaves are from 6 to 10 inches long and usually have 7 or 9 leaflets, shaped as shown. The nuts are about 1 inch in diameter and, though the husks fall away readily and the shells are not hard to crack, the contents have a flavor that has fairly earned the name of Bitternut for this species.

Even the beginner will not have much trouble in distinguishing the Bitternut from other Hickories. For one thing, all through the leafless season the Bitternut flaunts bright yellow buds to the Winter winds, a gay touch of color displayed by no other native Hickory. Another difference is that the bark of the Bitternut is much smoother than that of its close relatives. It's a clear, smooth gray bark lined with vertical blackish streaks interwoven in an attractive pattern. On older trees it eventually becomes ridged in a mild way. The Bitternut is an abundant and hardy tree, and a rapid grower that may reach a height of 100 feet, but as lumber it doesn't have the toughness of others of the clan.

SHAGBARK HICKORY

(*Carya ovata*)

The outstanding feature of this tall and stalwart tree is the shaggy bark that explains the common name by which it is known over a range that extends from Quebec and Maine across Ontario to North Dakota and south to the Gulf Coast region. The only other native tree with somewhat similar bark is the Big Shellbark Hickory (*Carya laciniosa*) that is found over about half of the same range. Where the two species grow in the same area there are differences in bark and leaf that are easily noted. For instance, the bark on the trunk of this species seems to be more "at loose ends," so to speak. The rather broad, ragged, plates of gray bark of the Shagbark curl away from the trunk at the edges, particularly the lower end. The longer and narrower loose strips of the Big Shellbark do not flare out in that fashion. Another point of difference is that the compound leaves of the Shagbark, 8 to 20 inches long, usually have only 5 leaflets, as shown in the illustration, whereas the larger leaves of the Big Shellbark, 12 to 24 inches long, usually have 7 leaflets. The fruit runs to the same scale. Husk and all, they may be 2 or 2¼ inches in diameter, with the Big Shellbark products averaging just a bit the larger. The husks are thick and the shells of the nuts are hard to crack, but it's worth the trouble because the flavor of the meat is delicious.

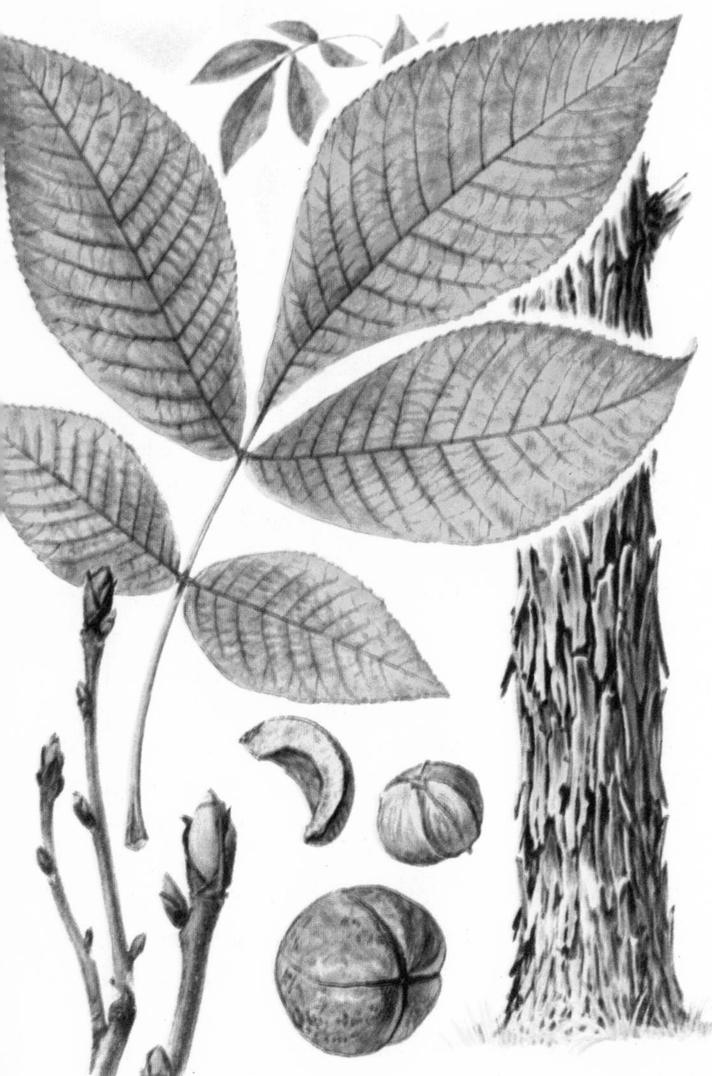

Hickory lumber is noted for its toughness and the Shagbark furnished much of the wood that was turned into spokes for wheels when wagons were the common carriers of goods and passengers in this country. It is now much in demand for the handles of axes and other tools. The wood is heavy, even for a Hickory, and a cubic foot of it, dried, weighs just a bit over 52 pounds. It shares with some others of the Hickory clan the honor of being used as firewood in the production of "hickory-smoked hams" and other such delicacies. If you come across this tree in Winter, note the large, cream-colored terminal buds with the darker "bud scales" that protect them. There are numerous other Hickories native to this continent, but you can sort them out in time by taking note of the details of bark, bud, and fruit and the size, shape, and number of the leaflets of the compound leaves.

PECAN

(*Carya illinoensis*)

This is the largest of our native Hickories and there are reports of trees in the wild up to 160 feet in height, with tremendous trunks and a wide crown of foliage. Originally an inhabitant of the lowlands of the Mississippi Basin, it is now cultivated well beyond its natural range for the commercial value of the thin-shelled, oblong-cylindrical nuts of fine flavor that it bears in abundance. The compound leaves are from 9 to 20 inches in length, with 9 to 15 leaflets about 4 inches in length and much alike in shape, thus differing from the other Hickories whose leaflets usually increase much in size and change somewhat in shape toward the outer end of the compound leaf. The nuts, in thin husks that are easily removed, grow in clusters of 3 to 11 and by their shape definitely identify the tree for anyone who may be in doubt.

HOP HORNBEAM

(*Ostrya virginiana*)

This tree, common in hardwood forests over the eastern half of temperate North America, often is overlooked. It never grows to great size and its leaves, 2 to 5 inches long and shaped as shown, are not distinctive. The light-colored fruit clusters, which look like the hops used in brewing and give the tree its name, often are at least partly concealed by the heavy, drooping foliage of late Spring or early Summer. The easiest way to make the acquaintance of the Hop Hornbeam is to look for it in Winter when you will know it by its gray-brown bark seemingly fashioned of papery vertical strips, its many long, thin, drooping branchlets and, at the tips of many of the branchlets, clusters of 2 or 3 tiny staminate catkins held stiffly at divergent angles. These Winter catkins, about ¾ inch long, expand and droop, as shown, in Spring to furnish the pollen to fertilize the female flowers that come with the unfolding of the leaves.

HORNBEAM; IRONWOOD; BLUE BEECH

(Carpinus caroliniana)

This small and often slanting tree of rich woods and moist, shady ground found over the eastern half of North America is easily recognized at any time of year by the smooth, tight bark of wavy and twisting blue and gray bands that give the trunk and branches the appearance that accounts for the names Ironwood and Blue Beech applied to it in some regions. The thin but strong branches reach well out horizontally and support numerous graceful, drooping branchlets. The leaves have about the same shape, size, and general appearance as those of the Hop Hornbeam, including the many sharp little teeth that look almost like fringes. The catkins of Spring turn into the distinctive fruit, as shown, drooping clusters of stiff, leaf-like "bracts" with little seed nutlets at the centers. These clusters hang on the trees long after the leaves have fallen in the Autumn and are an additional mark of identity, though the distinctive bark usually settles the issue at once.

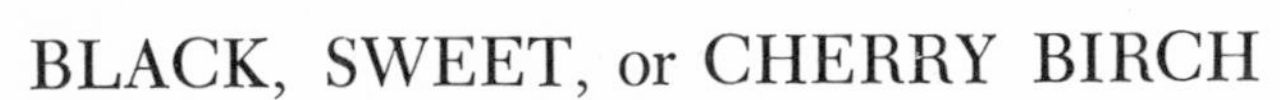

BLACK, SWEET, or CHERRY BIRCH

(Betula lenta)

To the ordinary observer and for practical purposes most of our Birches are distinguished one from the other by the color of the bark. Thus we have White, Gray, Red, Yellow, and Black Birches, as well as a few other less common Birches of narrower range. The Black Birch has dark bark somewhat similar to that of the Cherry Tree, which accounts for another of its common names, but Sweet Birch is a logical name for it. This is the tree with the strong wintergreen flavor from root to branchlet. If you lay the axe to a Black Birch, the air is fragrant as the chips fly. The tree, which grows to a height of 70 to 80 feet, is common in rich woods from Maine and Quebec to Ontario and southward to the uplands of Georgia and Tennessee. The leaves, shaped as shown, are 2½ to 5 inches long and have fringe-like teeth. Through the Autumn and Winter the bare branchlets carry not only the little upright seed-filled cones or "strobiles" of the season but the pendent and tightly sealed staminate catkins that, through whirling snows and icy blasts, wait patiently for the warm summons of returning Spring.

YELLOW BIRCH

(*Betula lutea*)

This is much like the Black Birch in leaf, branch, and fruit, but the yellowish sheen to the rather loose and laterally peeling bark on the trunk makes it easy to recognize the Yellow Birch in the woods. You might even think that the bark had been lightly buttered here and there. There are minor differences in the leaves and fruit of the Black and Yellow Birch but, to a beginner, the resemblances will be more easily noted than the differences. The Yellow Birch twigs even have a pleasant wintergreen flavor, though to a lesser degree than the Black Birch twigs. On the average, this is a larger tree than the Black Birch and it likes higher and cooler territory. It is found from Quebec to Minnesota and southward on high ground to North Carolina and Tennessee. The seed "cones," like those of the Black Birch, hang on for months and provide food for many birds in Winter.

RED BIRCH; RIVER BIRCH

(*Betula nigra*)

At first sight a beginner might mistake a Red Birch for a Yellow Birch because of the shaggy, peeling bark, but in this species the tint is red instead of yellow and the curling patches are smaller and more numerous upward along the trunk. If in doubt, look at the leaves. The leaf blades of the Yellow Birch, like those of the Black Birch, are well rounded or even "scalloped" or heart-shaped at the base, while those of the Yellow Birch start out at an angle away from the base. Some call them "diamond-shaped," but that's going a little too far. A still more helpful matter to the beginner is that the Red Birch and Yellow Birch do not commonly mix with one another. Between them they cover the whole eastern half of temperate North America from the Gulf States well into Canada, but the Red Birch is the southerly species and the Yellow the northerly resident. Where their ranges overlap the Yellow Birch is on high ground and the Red Birch on low ground, often on river banks, which accounts for its secondary name of River Birch. The leaves of the Red Birch, as you will note, are more coarsely toothed than those of the Yellow Birch. The seed "cones" ripen in June and fall away quickly.

WHITE BIRCH; PAPER BIRCH

(*Betula papyrifera*)

This is one of the most striking and beautiful trees in North America. It prefers a cool climate and its natural range is the high ground in the northerly section of the United States and northward to the Arctic Circle. It grows to be a fairly tall tree and it stands out in the woods because of the contrast in color between its white bark and the dark bark of the surrounding trees. There are very few native trees with which it could possibly be confused, even at a distance. One is the Sycamore, whose upper limbs sometimes have a clear cream-white bark that catches the eye from far away; but the Sycamore rarely invades the cool northerly region in which the White Birch flourishes, and in the few areas where they may be found on common ground, it is no problem at all to distinguish one from the other on closer inspection. The mottled trunk of the Sycamore is nothing like the clear white trunk of this tree and there are, of course, notable differences in leaf, flower, and fruit.

But Gray Birch and White Birch often are confused by novices in the woods. Both trees are Birches with white bark, so there is some ground for confusion at first sight. There are, however, two details that easily distinguish one species from the other. The leaves of the Gray Birch are decidedly triangular in outline with the stalk or "petiole" in the middle of the flat base line. The White Birch leaves, 1 to 4 inches long, are shaped, as shown, with the base line of the leaf blade gently curving away on each side of the petiole. But leaves often vary in shape and if there is any doubt in your mind about the identity of the tree, rub your hand over the white bark of the trunk. If it is a Gray Birch, your hand will come away clean. If it's a White Birch, the palm of your hand will be covered with a white powdery substance that coats the bark and adds a final velvety touch to its beauty. The handsome bark of this species peels laterally in strips and discloses a lovely red-brown or sometimes fawn-colored inner bark. Outer and inner bark were used by the Indians in the making of canoes and in more modern times they have been fashioned into writing paper, picture frames, and souvenirs of all kinds. You may occasionally encounter other white-barked Birches, native or imported, but this and the Gray Birch are by far the most common. Learn them first.

GRAY BIRCH

(*Betula populifolia*)

This is the small Birch that springs up in great numbers in neglected fields and burned-over areas and on embankments and filled ground in the northeastern section of the United States and adjacent Canada. It is rarely more than 30 feet in height, pyramidal in its younger days but usually slim and slanting if it survives to grow more than 20 feet tall. It has thin, drooping branchlets; the triangular leaves that distinguish it from the true White Birch are lustrous and long-petioled, and they shimmer and waver in light breezes like those of the Quaking Aspen. The white bark of this tree does not peel in the manner of the White Birch and the trunk is marked with triangular dark patches, particularly beneath the branching points. It's a tree of fast growth and is very common over its range, but its range is narrow, its life is short, and it is often crippled by ice storms.

COMMON ALDER

(*Alnus serrulata*)

The Alders are a group of shrubs and trees closely related to the Birches, as may be noted by the catkins and fruiting cones or "strobiles" they produce and which, remaining on the leafless branches in Winter, serve as an easy guide in becoming acquainted with them. That is, you will find it an easy matter to know an Alder when you see one, but which species is a matter to be taken up later with more experience. On the Pacific Coast the Red Alder may be a tree 90 feet tall, but in the East most of the Alders are shrubs like the much-branched Common Alder whose leaves, catkins, and fruiting cones are shown here. This species, which grows to 15 feet or more in height, is found in swamps and wet ground generally from Nova Scotia south to Florida and southwestward to Oklahoma.

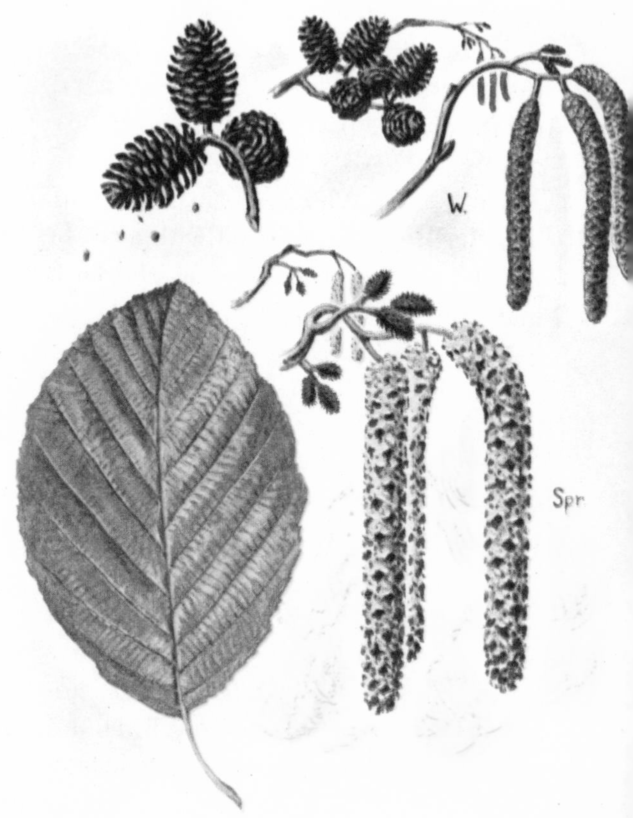

BEECH

(*Fagus grandifolia*)

You can't mistake a Beech if you see one, and it is common in the woods over most of the eastern half of the United States and adjacent Canada. Furthermore, it has been extensively planted for decorative purposes and you may find it flourishing almost anywhere in temperate North America. The clear, smooth, tight-fitting, light gray bark of the trunk and branches of the Beech is as well known as the red breast of the Robin. A mature Beech is tall, broad, handsome, and useful. The wood is used for furniture, tool handles, salad bowls and many other purposes. Beechnuts are on the diet list of many birds and mammals. They were the favorite food of the immense flocks of Passenger Pigeons that, we are told, "darkened the skies" as they flew over this country a century ago and have since vanished from the face of the earth. Of the countless millions of Passenger Pigeons that once were found in North America, no single descendant survives.

Beeches tend to form groves in many localities but they also are found interspersed with other trees such as Oaks, Maples, Birches, and Ashes in mixed forests. The leaves are 3 to 6 inches long, shaped as shown, with prominent veins and sharp teeth that are really the outer ends of the veins. If you look carefully just after the leaves unfold in Spring, you will find the inconspicuous flowers. The staminate or male flowers hang in a fluffy cluster on a thin stalk 1 inch or more in length and the pistillate or female flowers appear in stubby, upright clusters along the branchlets. The beechnuts are something like miniature chestnuts in their bristle-covered, short-stalked little husks that eventually open from the outer end and drop the tasty fruit to the ground below, where it is found and deeply appreciated by many forms of wildlife. In the Winter, looking at the long, thin, sharp-pointed buds of the Beech, you will understand Thoreau's reference to them as "the spearheads of Spring." The Copper Beech so often seen in cultivation is a color variety of the European Beech, which closely resembles our native species but has a bark darker in tone. Nurserymen also have developed a Weeping Beech and several other varieties. But all these are easily recognized as Beeches by those who know our native Beech. Look in Beech groves for Beechdrops, stiff, brown-stalked flowering plants parasitic on Beech roots.

CHESTNUT

(*Castanea dentata*)

From Maine to Minnesota and southward on high ground to Florida and Mississippi, the children of today have been deprived of a birthright. Long ago over the same area there was no finer sport for youngsters than to go hunting for chestnuts on a crisp Autumn morning when frost had opened the big burs with the fierce prickles on the outside and the rose-velvet lining on the inside. The opened burs above meant that there were chestnuts to be found below. Searching in the grass and among the fallen leaves was a great game in which there was competition for quality as well as quantity in treasure-trove. "Oh, boy! Look at this one!" "Bet I find a bigger one!" They were shining brown, silky, and beautiful. You could eat them on the spot or take them home and serve them up boiled, roasted, or mashed. The flavor was delicious whether they were raw or cooked.

If youngsters prized the tree for the nut crop it produced, lumbermen looked on the Chestnut with high favor for other reasons. It provided wood of the finest kind for many commercial purposes and it was rich in the tannin used in the tanning industry. In the open, it was a stalwart tree with a broad crown. Some pasture Chestnuts were 80 feet or more in height and about as broad as they were tall. But the almost incredible fact is that the great Chestnut trees that flourished so widely in this country only a half-century ago have vanished, every last one of them! "Going for chestnuts" of an October morning on a hillside bright with Autumn foliage is no longer a radiant reality but a fond memory of days that are no more.

What happened was that an imported fungus struck the trees at their tops and slowly crept downward, killing them inch by inch while scientists tried in vain to halt the slaughter. From the roots of the gaunt skeletons came numerous shoots but, when such shoots became saplings 15 to 20 feet tall, the blight cut them down. To this day the deceptive cycle goes on and often you will find, springing from old roots, Chestnut saplings bearing leaves, as shown, 6 to 9 inches long, with pin-point teeth that distinguish them from Oak leaves of similar size and shape. You might even find saplings with golden, flowering plumes or possibly a few burs. If so, gaze upon them fondly. These saplings are the Peter Pans of the tree world. Our joy in them is mixed with sadness. They can never grow up.

WHITE OAK

(*Quercus alba*)

Then here's to the Oak, the brave old Oak,
Who stands in his pride alone!
And still flourish he, a hale green tree,
When a hundred years are gone!
(H. F. CHORLEY, 1808–72.)

Oaks are mighty trees with virtues that have been enshrined in mottoes, maxims, and proverbs. "Tall Oaks from little acorns grow." "Little strokes fell great Oaks." "Strong as an Oak." "Hearts of Oak." There are Oaks in all pleasant lands north of the Equator and there are dozens of species in North America. Furthermore, they hybridize in a way to puzzle the expert at times, which means that a beginner can lose his way among the Oaks in no time at all. However, a start can be made by learning how to recognize some of the more common species of different regions of this continent.

Our native Oaks seem to fall naturally into two divisions called the White Oaks and the Black (or, if you prefer, Red) Oaks. The important or scientific distinction is that the species in the White Oak group have flowers that produce acorns in a single season. In the Black Oak group the acorns are not "full grown" or "ripe" until the second year of their existence. The unimportant but very helpful difference to the beginner among trees is that, as a rule, the ends of the veins of the leaves in the Black Oak group stick out as harmless spines or tiny, hair-like bristles.

Look at the leaves of this White Oak. There are many lobes, but not a bristle tip at the end of any one of them. Of course, that quick test at a glance merely tells the beginner that the leaf puts the tree either in the White Oak or the Black (or Red) Oak group. Tracking down the species is more difficult and often requires a study of three kinds of evidence; the bark, the leaf and the acorn. The difference in bark often is hard to discern and leaves are quite variable in size and shape. The best evidence is the acorn. The White Oak is one of the tall, broad, and brawny trees of the forests of North America from the Atlantic Coast to the foothills of the Rockies. The leaves are variable but usually they have 5 to 7 deep lobes and are 4 to 9 inches in length. The cylindrical acorns are about ¾ inch in length and the cup is quite shallow, covering only the lower quarter or third of the acorn. These are the details to note when tracking down any species of Oak. The staminate flowers of the Oaks, hanging in drooping catkins, are much visited by insect-seeking warblers on Spring migration.

MOSSY-CUP OAK; BUR OAK

(*Quercus macrocarpa*)

This shows how helpful the acorn can be in identifying the Oaks. Where you find a large, roundish acorn deeply set in a broad, gray, heavily beaded cup with an astonishing silvery fringe at the rim, you will know immediately that you have come upon a Mossy-cup or Bur Oak. These striking cups may be as much as 2 inches in width, but 1¼ inches would be about average. You might note that the leaves are deeply lobed near the base and broader and more solid toward the tip, but the acorns are as good as a signboard on the tree. The Mossy-cup Oak ranges from Nova Scotia to Manitoba and south to Texas, but it is not common in the Northeast and is rarely found on the Atlantic Coastal Plain south of Delaware. It flourishes best in the river basins of the interior and is said to reach a height of 150 feet or more in the Wabash Valley. Its ability to withstand the cold Winters of Manitoba proves that it is one of the hardiest of our Oaks.

CHESTNUT OAK; ROCK OAK

(*Quercus prinus*)

A glance at the leaf will tell you why this is called the Chestnut Oak but you can see that the wavy teeth of this leaf are blunt or rounded and quite unlike the sharp teeth of the Chestnut leaf. The name Rock Oak, applied to it in some areas, is due to its fondness for rocky slopes over a range that extends from Maine to upland Georgia, with a scattering representation from Ontario and Michigan south to the Ohio Valley. The acorns are about 1 inch long, narrowly oval, and one third to one half enclosed in a thin cup. This is an Oak of only medium height but it grows to a great age and on older trees the heavy vertical ridges on the lower part of the trunk help to identify the species. The beginner must be warned, however, that there are other Oaks with somewhat similar leaves and acorns and even the botanists are not in complete agreement as to how they should be separated and named. This species is offered as a sample of the group.

LIVE OAK

(*Quercus virginiana*)

This cherished tree of the Deep South is found from Virginia down the Atlantic Coastal Plain into Florida and across the Gulf Coast region into Texas and Mexico. It is rarely more than 50 feet in height, but where it grows in the open it carries a widespread crown of shining foliage and the horizontal reach of some of the branches is remarkable. It is called Live Oak because the lustrous leaves remain on the tree through the Winter and do not drop off until the new crop is coming along in Spring. Thus it has a "live" appearance when other Oaks seem "dead" in their leafless Winter sleep. The unlobed leaves are mostly narrowly oval in shape and from 1 to 4 inches long, but they vary considerably in shape and size in different regions. The dark acorns, shaped as shown, and up to 1 inch in length, are borne on longish stalks or "peduncles" with from 1 to 5 acorns in a cluster. There are other Oaks with unlobed leaves but the species can be sorted out by leaf and acorn details.

COAST LIVE OAK

(*Quercus agrifolia*)

The comparatively few native "live" or evergreen Oaks are inhabitants of the warmer sections of North America. The Emory Oak (*Quercus emoryi*) of the Southwest, the aptly named Canyon Live Oak (*Quercus chrysolepis*) of the mountain valleys from Oregon to Mexico, and the Coast Live Oak whose holly-like leaves and bullet-shaped acorns are shown here, are three such species. All of them have unlobed leaves, usually with spiny teeth, but each may be distinguished by the size and shape of the leaves and acorns. The Coast Live Oak is found along the coastal area from San Francisco southward into Lower California. Where the sea winds whip it with salt spray on exposed headlands it is stunted and scraggly, but on inland hillsides or the forested uplands it grows to a height of 80 or 90 feet with widespread branches. The leaves are from 1 to 4 inches long and the curious acorns vary from ¾ inch to 1½ inches in length. The California White Oak (*Quercus lobata*) has somewhat similar acorns even longer and thinner than these, but the deeply and bluntly lobed leaves bear no resemblance to those of this species.

RED OAK

(*Quercus rubra*)

This is truly one of the great trees of field and forest over most of the eastern half of the United States and adjacent Canada. It is among the tallest of our native Oaks and probably the hardiest of that stalwart clan. It ventures well into Canada, farther north than most Oaks of this continent, and flourishes in regions where the snows are deep, the winds icy, and the temperature readings low for many months of the year. It is a fast grower and seldom is bothered by blight or insect pests. It bears acorns in profusion and, because they have a bitter taste that causes squirrels and other animals to neglect them as an article of diet, they remain on the ground to produce saplings in great numbers. For these and other reasons the Red Oak is one of the most common Oaks over its range. It averages 70 to 80 feet in height at maturity, usually has a stout trunk clear of branches for some distance above the ground, and is one of the most valuable timber trees of North America. It is also a fine shade tree whose worth is appreciated not only in this country but in Europe where it has been planted more extensively than any other native American Oak.

Such are some of the virtues of this tall, strong, and handsome tree. There are varying explanations of how it came by the name of Red Oak. Some say it's because of the reddish inner bark. Others think the name refers to the reddish twigs, the red tinge to the leaves as they unfold in the Spring, or the deep red color they turn in the Autumn. You can tell from the typical leaves shown above that there is considerable variation in its foliage. Saplings sometimes have enormous leaves but on mature trees the many-lobed, bristle-tipped leaves are 4 to 8 inches long, deep green above and yellowish-green underneath. There are other Oaks with somewhat similar leaves but note that the shape of the Red Oak leaf is broadly oval and that the clefts of the lobes, at the deepest, are well out from the midrib. But Oak leaves are tricky in many species and, on the average, the acorn is a better clue. The Red Oak acorn, shaped as shown, is about 1 inch long. As you can see, it's a fine stout acorn set in a particularly shallow cup. There is no other acorn like it over most of the range of the Red Oak.

BLACK OAK

(*Quercus velutina*)

Most persons refer to this species as the Black Oak but it also is known as the Yellow Oak, the Yellow-barked Oak and the Quercitron Oak in different parts of the country. You can take your choice or follow local option but, to simplify matters, it will be called the Black Oak here. It is one of our tallest Oaks and a common one over much the same range as that of the Red Oak except that the Red Oak extends further in a northerly direction and the Black Oak goes all the way down to the Gulf Coast, which the Red Oak does not. The many-lobed, bristle-tipped leaves of this species vary greatly in shape and size, even on the same tree. On mature trees they may be anything from 3 to 12 inches in length, some of them deeply cleft between narrow lobes, others with narrow clefts between broad lobes, and still others with only shallow indentations like the lower leaf in the illustration. In general, however, they tend to be "heavy-headed" or obovate in outline, broader beyond the middle than toward the base, and deeply lobed.

The acorns are the most reliable guide in tracking down this species. They aren't much to look at but they run fairly true to form. Shaped as shown, they average about ⅝ inch in length and not much less than that in width. Note that the cup covers half or more of the acorn and is "raspy" around the rim. Another feature of this species is the yellow inner bark that furnishes tannin for use in the tanning of leather and a yellow dye used in the textile industry.

There are some sixty or so species of native Oak in North America and a few introduced species including the Cork Oak (*Quercus suber*) of the Mediterranean area whose spongy outer bark furnishes the corks for bottles. Maples, Elms, Birches, and other such groups have leaves that run somewhat to a general pattern for the group. But not the Oaks! They display leaves in an astonishing assortment of shapes and sizes. Even the general rule that bristle-tipped leaves indicate Oaks that take two years to ripen their acorns is merely a "rule of thumb" that doesn't hold in the case of the Coast Live Oak and a few other species that have spiny-tipped leaves and ripen their acorns in a single season. But these variations in size and shape of leaves, along with the acorns, help to track down the different Oaks.

PIN OAK

(*Quercus palustris*)

This is an Oak of medium size that is more or less common in lowlands and moist ground generally, from Massachusetts to Iowa and south to North Carolina and Oklahoma. The bark is dark and, for an Oak, rather smooth and tight-fitting. The leaves are 4 to 6 inches long and deeply lobed, and the acorns are delightfully neat little things in flat cups, shaped as shown, and about ½ inch long or broad. The bristle tips of the leaves show it to be one of the Black (or Red) Oak group. The name Pin Oak comes from its numerous slender branchlets. The *palustris* in its scientific name comes from the Latin word for a swamp and refers to its fondness for wet ground, but it is a sturdy tree and can live in dry ground if planted there. The slender branchlets and the drooping curve of many of its branches make this an Oak that can be recognized as far as it can be seen in the leafless season. The small leaves, the slender branchlets, and the neat little acorns are the marks of the Pin Oak.

SLIPPERY ELM

(*Ulmus rubra*)

This is the Elm with the savory and slippery inner bark that is turned into lozenges for the drugstore trade. It grows throughout most of the eastern half of temperate North America but is usually passed over as "just another Elm" by the ordinary wayfarer. However, if you look closely, you may recognize it by the large leaves that are covered on the upper surface with hairs that are stiff to the touch no matter which way you rub your fingers over them. They are typical Elm leaves, alternate on the branchlets, sharp-toothed, and lopsided at the base, as shown, but they are 4 to 8 inches long, which is above average for Elms. The seed "wafers" of other native Elms have a fringe of tiny hairs around the rim but the Slippery Elm does not. In the Winter a good mark of the Slippery Elm is the covering of long rusty hairs on the dark oval buds that stand out along the gray twigs. But the sad truth is that this tree is safe only when it goes unrecognized.

AMERICAN ELM

(Ulmus americana)

The original range of this lovely tree of classic shape and graceful bearing extended only from the Atlantic Coast to the foothills of the Rockies, but it has been so extensively planted that it now may be found in abundance everywhere in temperate North America. It's a tree of the wild that has become almost domesticated by popular demand. It's a delight in our dooryards and a solace in our cemeteries. It ornaments our public parks. It stands as guardian of our city streets and as warden of our village greens. Go for an auto ride almost anywhere in this country and most of the Oaks, Maples, Pines, Hickories, and other trees that you see along the way will be growing where the seed settled on the soil. But most of the American Elms that you see will be growing where somebody planted them by hand. These trees are truly things of beauty and if not "a joy forever," a joy for at least a century unless the dread Dutch Elm disease gets in its deadly work.

Oliver Wendell Holmes, the genial "Autocrat Of The Breakfast Table," had a great love for the noted Elms of New England and drove many a mile to inspect some famous ones and put his tape measure around their trunks. If you haven't done so, read his account in "The Autocrat" of one such expedition; the hearsay report of a tremendous Elm, the setting out, the fear of disappointment, the heartthrob at the first distant sight of a swelling crown of foliage, the arrival, and the absolute awe at the grandeur of the great tree! For a tree lover, that is a thrilling adventure story.

The American Elm leaves, shaped and toothed as shown, are 2 to 6 inches long. They average a bit smaller than the leaves of the Slippery Elm, are not as rough to the touch on the upper surface and are more lopsided at the base. The fruiting wafers of this species are slightly smaller than those of the Slippery Elm and they have a fine fringe of tiny hairs around the edges. There are other native Elms and a few imported ones, like the English and Scotch Elms that have been widely planted. All of them have characteristic Elm leaves and fruits but they may be distinguished by differences in leaf, bark, or branches as well as details of flowers and seed "wafers." This species, however, is the loveliest of all.

HACKBERRY; SUGARBERRY

(*Celtis occidentalis*)

We have a number of native species of Hackberry in North America, but this is by far the most widespread and when you have learned to know this one on sight you will have little difficulty recognizing its close relatives. This species may be found from the Atlantic Coast to the Rockies and from the Gulf States to the Canadian Border and even beyond it in Ontario and Quebec, but it isn't fond of cold weather or long Winters and it thins out or disappears at high altitudes and along the northern border of the United States. You will know it by its gray bark curiously ridged or sprinkled with warty growths, its sharply toothed leaves 2 to 5 inches long, shaped as shown, and often studded with light patches caused by a fungus, and by the fruit that accounts for the name of Hackberry or Sugarberry. These berries or "drupes," purple-black when ripe, are about ⅓ inch in diameter.

RED MULBERRY

(*Morus rubra*)

The White Mulberry of Asia, whose leaves are the diet of the silkworm, was planted in the American Colonies in the hope that the silk industry could be fostered here. The tree took root but the silk industry did not. The result is that the White Mulberry is now more common than our native Red Mulberry in some Atlantic States. The Red Mulberry, found from New England across Ontario to the Dakotas and south to the Gulf Coast, is a bigger and better tree in every way. It has larger leaves, much better fruit, and a longer fruiting period much appreciated by many kinds of birds. The White Mulberry crop comes and goes in a couple of weeks but the Red Mulberry carries fruit through many weeks of Summer. On the young shoots you will find the curiously lobed leaves that are a mark of the Mulberry clan. The ordinary heart-shaped leaves are 2 to 6 inches long. If you pluck a leaf, you will see a drop of milky juice appear at the point of separation from the twig; another family trait.

OSAGE ORANGE; BOWDOCK

(*Maclura pomifera*)

This relative of the Mulberries that can be anything from a much-twisted shrub to a well-rounded tree 60 feet in height has a fruit mass the size and shape of an old-fashioned cannon ball, a feature that leaves no doubt as to its identity when these greenish-yellow spherical objects from 3 to 5 inches in diameter strew the ground underneath the tree in early Autumn or cling to the bare branches after the leaves have fallen. If you break open one of these pebbly-surfaced spheres, you will find it something like a compact cauliflower in texture—but not in taste! Incidentally, in breaking it open, you probably will find your fingers sticky from the milky juice oozing from the cuts or bruises in the vegetable matter. It is not, of course, a single fruit but innumerable fruits joined together to form this lumpy globular mass of seeds and fleshy coverings and attachments. Staminate and pistillate flowers appear on different trees. Since the fruit masses are a picturesque feature of the species, the pistillate or female trees that produce the fruit are preferred for planting. It seems a great waste that the fruit isn't good eating but it is rarely used for food by bird or beast, and no child who has tasted it ever is eager for a second helping.

Aside from the spectacular fruit clusters, the Osage Orange of either sex may be known by the brownish-yellow or orange-yellow bark of the many curving branches, the shining leaves 3 to 5 inches long, shaped as shown in the illustration, the thorns that are a real menace along its branches, and the milky juice that appears where you break off a leaf, a bud, or even a thorn. The milky juice is common to the Mulberry family but the thorns are an added feature in the Osage Orange. It is native to Missouri, Kansas, Oklahoma, Arkansas, Louisiana, and northeastern Texas, but it has been widely spread by cultivation and now may be found almost anywhere in the United States. These trees are frequently planted to form hedges and, if trimmed low, the curving branches with their sharp thorns form an almost impenetrable barrier. The Osage Indians of its native territory extracted a yellow dye from the wood of this tree and also used it to make bows for hunting and warfare. For that reason the early French settlers of Louisiana gave the tree the name of "Bois d'arc" or Bow Wood. In time the French "Bois d'arc" was corrupted to Bowdock, a name that still survives in some areas. Another name for it is Mock Orange, which is unfortunate because that is also a common name for two different species of flowering shrub. Such confusion shows the value of scientific names that remain constant all over the world for all plants and creatures under the sun.

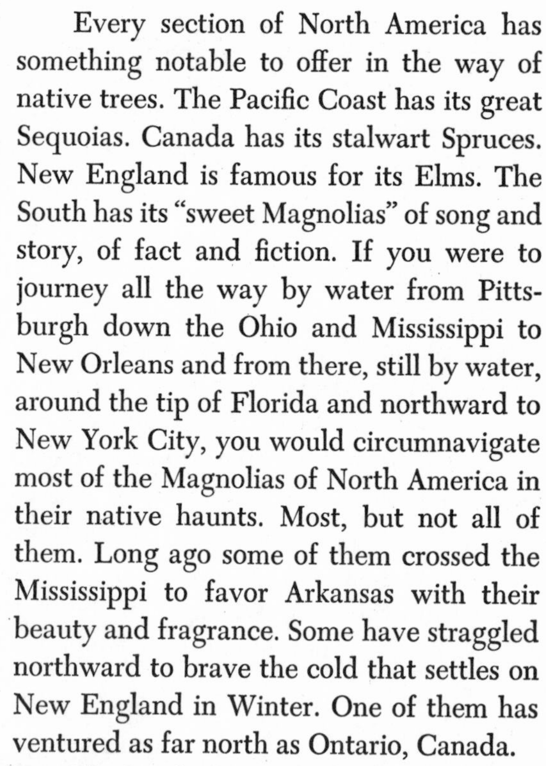

SWAMP MAGNOLIA; SWEET BAY

(*Magnolia virginiana*)

Every section of North America has something notable to offer in the way of native trees. The Pacific Coast has its great Sequoias. Canada has its stalwart Spruces. New England is famous for its Elms. The South has its "sweet Magnolias" of song and story, of fact and fiction. If you were to journey all the way by water from Pittsburgh down the Ohio and Mississippi to New Orleans and from there, still by water, around the tip of Florida and northward to New York City, you would circumnavigate most of the Magnolias of North America in their native haunts. Most, but not all of them. Long ago some of them crossed the Mississippi to favor Arkansas with their beauty and fragrance. Some have straggled northward to brave the cold that settles on New England in Winter. One of them has ventured as far north as Ontario, Canada.

The lovely Swamp Magnolia or Sweet Bay is a tree that reaches a height of 50 to 60 feet in the swamps and lowlands of the South, but it decreases in size northward and is a thin, small tree at the northern limit of its range, which is the Gloucester region of Massachusetts. Some historians say that the original Swamp Magnolias of the Gloucester area were brought from the South by loving hands and planted where they or their descendants have flourished to such an extent that they gave their name to a seaside Summer resort that grew up nearby and is now Magnolia, Massachusetts, a residential area dotted with magnificent homes overlooking the sea. However, the trees are hardy enough to have made their way that far northward without helping hands and probably did.

In the matter of flower and leaf, this is the smallest of our native Magnolias, on which account it is known as the Small Magnolia in some regions. It is also called the Swamp Bay, the Sweet Bay, the Beaver Tree, and the Laurel Magnolia. Its somewhat leathery and narrowly oval leaves are 3 to 6 inches long, shining green above, and a soft whitish-gray underneath that helps to identify the tree when flowers and fruit are missing. The leaves are evergreen in the South, but they go with the Winter winds in the North. The cream-white, cup-shaped flower of 6 to 9 petals is 2 to 3 inches across before the petals sag, and the lumpy red fruiting cone or seed cluster characteristic of the Magnolias is about 1½ inches in length. This species offers a good example of the value of a scientific name for a tree or, in fact, any plant. It has many common names and varies in size from a shrub to a 60-foot tree over its range, but the scientific name remains constant throughout.

CUCUMBER TREE

(*Magnolia acuminata*)

This member of the Magnolia group owes its common name to the fact that its lumpy fruit in the green stage looks something like a cucumber. This is the hardiest and the tallest of the native Magnolias, reaching a height of 100 feet under favorable conditions and pushing as far north as Canadian ground where the Province of Ontario dips down among the Great Lakes. It is found from that region southward to the Gulf of Mexico and there is no difficulty in distinguishing it from any of the other Magnolias at any time of year because this species has ridged bark on its trunk whereas the other Magnolias have a smooth gray bark somewhat like that of the Beech.

You have to look sharp to find the flowers in late Spring because they are not striking in color and often are concealed by the leaves that, shaped as shown, are rather thin in texture compared to other Magnolias and are 6 to 10 inches long. The flower petals are 2 to 3 inches long and the lumpy cylindrical fruit containing the seeds is about the same length, turning from green to a dull red as it ripens. Eventually the bright red seeds slip out and dangle on thin threads before they fall to the ground, a common trait in the Magnolia clan. The Umbrella Tree (*Magnolia tripetala*), so called because its huge leaves (up to 2 feet long) are clustered around the tips of the branches in umbrella fashion, is cultivated as far north as New England. It is a fine shade tree and has handsome white flowers of good size, but the odor will never be enshrined in perfume and offered for sale in the best shops.

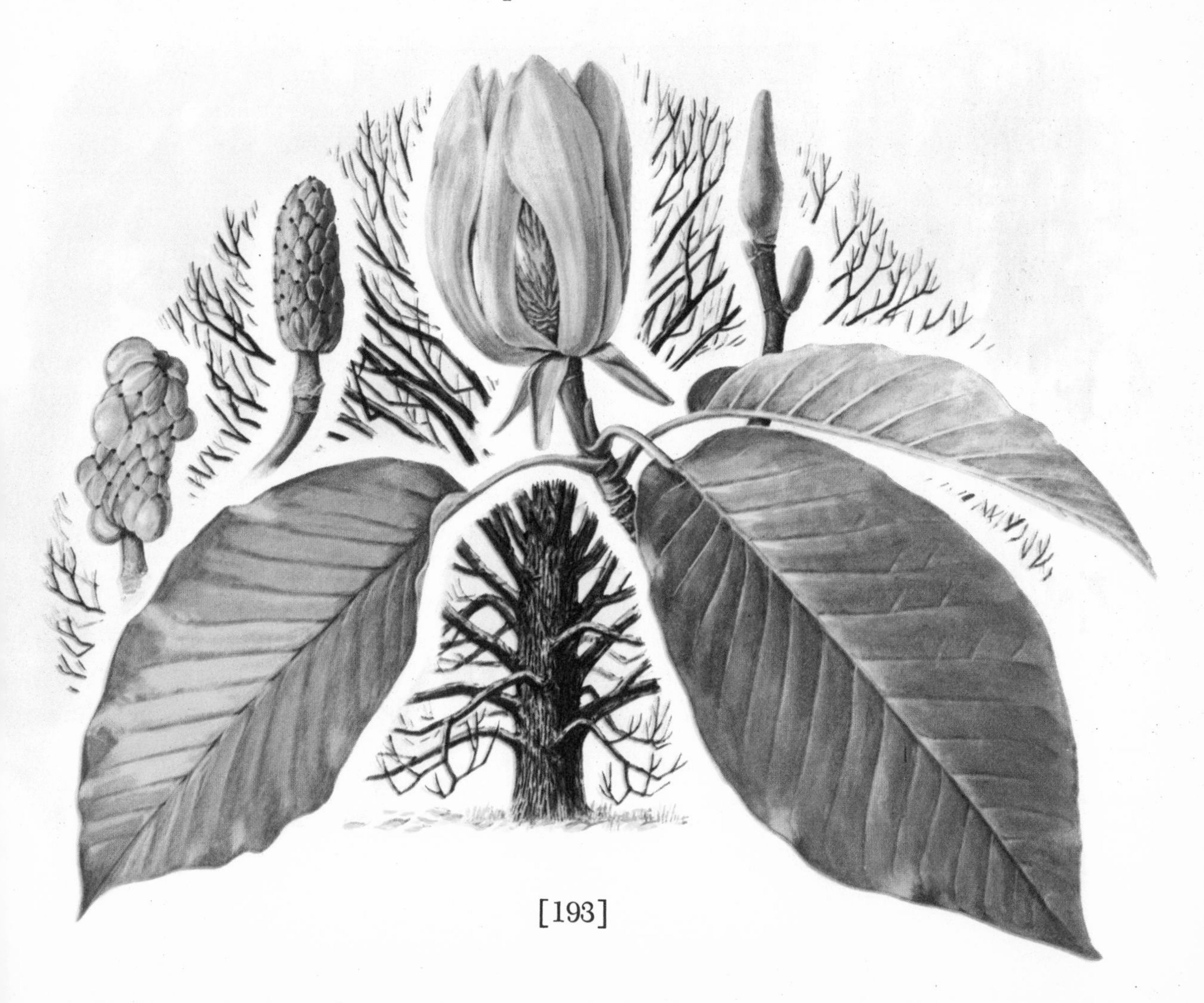

TULIP TREE

(*Liriodendron tulipifera*)

Here is a tall and stalwart tree that is not only magnificent in bulk but distinctive in almost every particular. It has a trunk like a Greek column, a lovely flower, an odd-shaped leaf, conical clusters of winged seeds that stand out against the cold sky in late Autumn, and reddish-brown Winter buds that look like miniature thumbless leather mittens. The young bark of branches and saplings is smooth and green, but the old bark of the great cylindrical boles of the big trees is deeply fissured and a rich brown in color. By the towering trunk alone you may know the tree. But the leaves, too, are in a class by themselves. We have no other native tree of North America with such square or broadly indented tips, and the way the young leaves unfold in Spring is a delight to watch. They are coiled in the bud and folded along the midrib in such fashion that as they emerge they look like tiny taximeter flags coming to the upright position

If anything else were needed to identify the Tulip Tree, the abundant flowers that cover it during May and June would do it easily. They vary to some extent, but in most of them the basic green of the 6 petals is crossed by a bright orange band with yellow borders. The petals are about 2 inches long and the later conical clusters of winged seeds or "samaras," 2 to 4 inches long, are held upright at the tips of the branches long after the leaves have disappeared. In fact, a few ragged husks may persist until Spring. Purple Finches and other seed-eating birds get some of the tiny seeds with their 1-inch wings but most of them are carried away by the Winter winds. Tulip Trees are found from Rhode Island across southern Massachusetts, New York, and Ontario to Wisconsin and southward to the Gulf Coast region. For some strange reason this tree is called the Yellow Poplar in the lumber industry. The wood is light and is used for such things as crates, boxes, and radio and television cabinets. In late Summer the greenery of the Tulip Tree begins to turn to gold in spots and patches in a way to recall a lovely line by Gerard Manley Hopkins: "Glory be to God for dappled things."

PAWPAW

(Asimina triloba)

This shrub or small tree, noted for its odd-looking edible fruit, loves the shade and is found in the undergrowth of woods from New York and Ontario to Nebraska and south to the Gulf Coast. The leaves, shaped as shown, are from 6 to 12 inches long. The showy purple flowers of 6 petals are about 1½ inches in diameter. The fruits, which may be single or 2 or 3 in a cluster, are 3 to 5 inches long and look much like fat little sausages or stubby bananas with rounded ends. They are green at first but turn brown as cool weather ripens them, and the interior contains scattered dark seeds about 1 inch long surrounded by a custard-like sweetish pulp that many persons find delicious. It is often sold in the market. Another way of spelling the name is Papaw and another name for it, a tribute to the fruit, is Custard Apple.

SASSAFRAS

(Sassafras albidum)

The legend is that no two leaves of the Sassafras are alike. Of course, that isn't true. Though the leaves are quite variable in shape and size, there are usually enough of the "mitten" type to make it easy to recognize a Sassafras whether it is a sapling a few feet high or a tree 80 or 90 feet tall with a rugged trunk of deeply grooved brown bark. It sprouts so readily that thickets of Sassafras saplings often are found on the roadside or along the edge of a wood. Your sense of smell will help you identify this tree. Root and branch, flower and fruit, all are highly aromatic when crushed or bruised. The pistillate and staminate flower sprays grow on separate trees, and the pistillate turn into the handsome ⅓-inch fruit, as shown, and are eagerly eaten by birds. The branchlets, twigs, and buds are green in Winter. The Sassafras is found from southern Maine across lower Ontario to Iowa and southward to the Gulf Coast region. Sassafras tea was once supposed to cure all ills.

SPICEBUSH

(*Lindera benzoin*)

The best time to become acquainted with the Spicebush is in the early Spring when, in wet woods and thickets and along stream borders from Maine to Michigan and southward to North Carolina and Kansas, it displays countless clusters of waxy little yellow flowers on dark branches still bare of leaves. It is more of a shrub than a tree and usually occurs in clumps in shady moist ground, with the individual stems radiating outward and upward on a slant to a height of 4 to 15 feet or so. The smooth leaves that appear later are 2 to 5 inches long, about half as wide, and tapering at both ends. The fruit, which ripens in late Summer, is a small partially flattened red "drupe," as the botanists call it, enclosing a single stone. You probably will prefer to call it a berry. The real feature of the Spicebush, and a sure means of identification at any time of year, is the delightful citronella-like odor that comes from any part of the plant under pressure.

WITCH-HAZEL

(*Hamamelis virginiana*)

This is the slanting shrub or small tree of shady ground, including the undergrowth of woods over practically the whole of the eastern half of the United States and adjacent Canada, that so often is cut down and ground up to produce the witch hazel of the drugstore trade. It has several other distinctions. The curious flowers of 4 twisting linear petals like tiny yellow ribbons about ¾ inch in length appear in Autumn and hang on the bare branches after the leaves have fallen. The fruit are nutlets in blunt, little ½-inch capsules that do not ripen until the following Autumn and then by contraction they "explode" and fling the tiny nutlets to the ground some distance away. The leaves are variable but usually broadly oval in shape, 2 to 5 inches long, and wavy or bluntly toothed in outline.

SWEET GUM; BILSTED

(*Liquidambar styraciflua*)

This is a tall, handsome tree native to and flourishing best in the southeastern portion of North America and in most cases it can be recognized without an upward glance. That is, unless somebody has been around lately cleaning up with a rake. The Sweet Gum, or Bilsted as it is called in many parts of the South, produces numerous green male and female flowers that generally pass unnoticed and an abundance of horny-coated or "beaked" fruiting spheres about 1 inch in diameter that can't be ignored. These globular clusters of seed capsules dangle from the branchlets on thin stalks or "peduncles" long after the leaves have fallen, and eventually fall themselves to litter the ground as dry brown husks with deep pits where the seeds have disappeared from their cells. There the husks lie until they rot away, which is not a rapid process. On a well-kept lawn, of course, measures have to be taken, usually with a rake and a bushel basket.

When the tree is in foliage it is easily recognized by the long-petioled leaves with blades that are about 6 inches in diameter and star-shaped in outline. On many Sweet Gum trees the smaller branches have corky "wings" or ridges running along them, but this is an individual matter. Some trees display no such ridges on their branchlets and others have them in astonishing abundance. The name Sweet Gum is due to a sticky substance, said to be pleasant to chew, that oozes from cuts made in the trunk or branches. With its attractive gray bark, its distinctive leaves that turn a beautiful combination of crimson and orange in Autumn, and the persistent seed clusters that furnish fine food for Goldfinches, Pine Siskins, Bob-whites, and other birds, the Sweet Gum is an admired and cherished tree over its natural range from the Gulf Coast north to Missouri and Illinois and northeastward to New York and southern New England. You may find it elsewhere under cultivation but it can't stand long periods of low temperature and ordinarily is not hardy as far north as the Canadian Border. It is lumbered for its light, strong wood used in making furniture.

SYCAMORE; BUTTONWOOD; PLANE TREE

(*Platanus occidentalis*)

The most colorful feature of this high, wide, and handsome tree is the bark. A short distance above ground the pebbly brown bark on the massive bole of a big Sycamore becomes a mottled, dappled, or piebald combination of rich brown and cream-white patches, with here and there a splash of pale green. This picturesque pattern extends out some distance along the larger branches, but on the smaller branches the bark is so light in color that, where it shows through the greenery of Summer, the branches look as though they had been whitewashed. This is one of the largest of our native broad-leaved trees and it may reach a height of 150 feet or more under favorable conditions. Over its natural range, which extends from southern Maine across Ontario to Nebraska and south to the Gulf States, it prefers the open country to the forests and the lowlands to the uplands. It flourishes best along natural waterways and the towering masses of foliage and shining branches of rows of great Sycamores often mark the windings of rivers of the rolling regions of the Midwest.

The large, handsome leaves might be mistaken, at a quick glance, for the foliage of some of the Maples, but there are some differences that are immediately noted. In the first place, the Sycamore leaves grow alternately along the branchlets and not opposite one another as do the leaves of all Maples. In the second place, you will see that the swollen base of the leaf stalk or "petiole" is a hollow cap for the bud of next season that will be uncovered when the leaf drops to the ground in Autumn. The leaf blades, lobed and toothed as shown, are 4 to 9 inches in diameter. The little clusters of staminate and pistillate flowers that appear just after the leaves unfold in Spring usually escape notice, but the spherical brown seed clusters, about 1 inch in diameter, dangle on wiry stalks from the bare branches for all to see through the Autumn and Winter. The California Sycamore usually has 2 to 5 seed balls on each hanging stalk. The imported London Plane Tree, much planted in our parks, generally has 2 on a single stalk. Otherwise, these trees look much alike to the ordinary eye.

AMERICAN MOUNTAIN ASH

(*Pyrus americana*)

These small trees, more often seen in cultivation than in the wild, are easily identified by the compound leaves, the sprays of white flowers in Spring, and the fruit clusters that often cling to the bare branches well into the Winter. The species pictured here is found as a large shrub or small tree from Newfoundland to Manitoba, seeping down into the United States from Maine to Minnesota and running down the high ground of the Appalachians to Georgia and Tennessee. The only difficulty for the beginner is that a more northern species (*Pyrus decora*) and the European Mountain Ash (*Pyrus aucuparia*) look much like this one and may be encountered over much of the same territory. However, the three species may be sorted out later by noticeable differences in the details of flowers, leaves, fruit, and buds. In this species the leaves are about 10 inches long with 11 to 17 leaflets, and the decorative fruits, highly prized for food by many birds and some animals, are about ⅕ inch in diameter.

SERVICEBERRY; SHADBUSH

(*Amelanchior arborea*)

It might help the beginner to know that the scientific name of this species means "tree-like member of the Amelanchior group." The numerous Amelanchiors of many sizes and species found readily over most of temperate North America are probably more familiar under the name of Shadbush or Shadblow because along the Atlantic section of their range they flower about the time the shad run up the river to spawn. The white or occasionally pinkish flowers come just before the leaves and have 5 strap-like petals, a mark of the clan. The fruit is berry-like, varying in size and color according to the species. The Serviceberry, illustrated here, may be anything from a shrub to a tree 60 feet tall and ranges from New Brunswick to Minnesota and southward to the Gulf States. The leaves are 2 to 4 inches long, the petals about ½ inch long, and the reddish-purple fruit about ⅜ inch in diameter and rather tasteless.

DOTTED HAW; DOTTED THORN

(*Crataegus punctata*)

The Haws of North America are a group of innumerable species of very thorny shrubs or small trees that grow singly or in clumps and have crooked, twisted, and sometimes interwoven branches, Spring clusters of 5-petaled white or pink flowers of the apple-blossom type, and Autumn fruit like tiny apples or rose hips, usually red, orange, yellow, or some combination of such colors. The Dotted Haw, shown here as a sample of the bewildering group, is common in pastures and on dry, open hillsides from Maine and Quebec to Minnesota and south to western Georgia and Tennessee. It has slightly curved thorns 1 to 2 inches long, leaves 2 to 3 inches long, and the fruit covered with dots accounts for its name. But sorting out all the species is an impossible task for a novice. In the words of King Lear: "Oh! that way madness lies; let me shun that."

BIRD CHERRY; FIRE CHERRY; PIN CHERRY

(*Prunus pennsylvanica*)

Three widespread Wild Cherries of North America are this species and the two that follow. To the beginner they may look somewhat alike, especially in the sapling stage, but there is no difficulty in distinguishing one from the other if a little attention is paid to details of leaf, flower and fruit. For instance, this species produces its ½-inch white flowers in "umbels" or "corymbs," which means that the flowers and later the ¼-inch red cherries are on individual stalks or "pedicels" an inch or so in length, as shown. This immediately sets it apart from the Wild Black or Rum Cherry and the Choke Cherry that flower in cylindrical "racemes," an arrangement in which the individual flowers and consequent fruit appear on short stalks along and around a central axis. The illustration shows why some persons call this the Pin Cherry. It is called the Bird Cherry because of the fondness birds have for its tart fruit and is known as the Fire Cherry in some regions because it springs up quickly in burnt areas. It is a northerly species, common across Canada and much of the northern section of the United States. At best, it is a small tree with a short life span. However, the tart fruit is tasty and the tree serves as useful cover until better trees take over.

CHOKE CHERRY

(*Prunus virginiana*)

This common shrub or small tree is found over practically all of habitable North America east of the Rockies and furnishes fruit that is eaten by man, bird, and beast; but it should be avoided until it is fully ripe and loses the astringent or "puckery" effect on the mouth, from which effect it derives its name. Its long cylindrical clusters or "racemes" of white blossoms on short stalks along a central axis are quite similar to those displayed by the Wild Black Cherry, but the duller and more leathery leaves of the Choke Cherry, 2 to 5 inches long, have the wider part of the blade beyond the middle, which is not the case with the lighter and shinier leaves of the Wild Black Cherry. The easiest way to distinguish the Choke Cherry from the Wild Black Cherry is to glance at the ripe or ripening fruit. The 5-pointed flower calyx sticks to the developing fruit in the Wild Black Cherry, but there is no sign of it on the fruit of this species.

WILD BLACK CHERRY; RUM CHERRY

(*Prunus serotina*)

This is a valuable timber tree, as well as a source of tasty fruit, over the eastern half of temperate North America. In the sapling stage the bark is smooth and reddish-brown, but on the stout trunks of old trees it is dark gray and flaky. There are many species of Wild Cherry in North America but this and the Choke Cherry are the only ones that flower in cylindrical clusters. The illustration shows quite clearly the calyx that adheres to the fruit in this species and makes it an easy matter to distinguish it from the Choke Cherry. Once this difference is fixed in mind, the beginner will note differences in shape, texture, and general appearance of the leaves and will soon know the Wild Black Cherry from the Choke Cherry at a glance. The name Rum Cherry goes back to colonial days when the fruit of this species was used to flavor rum. It is said that the wilted leaves of the Wild Black Cherry are poisonous to cattle.

KENTUCKY COFFEE TREE

(*Gymnocladus dioica*)

Keep your eyes open for this tree because you never know where you will encounter one. Originally native in rich woodlands over a limited area of eastern and central North America, it has been planted to such an extent that now you may find it almost anywhere in the United States and southern Canada. It is common in public parks and on private estates and the offspring of such plantings often go over the fence and escape to the wild. The clusters of little flowers, wan white in color, are easily overlooked amid the foliage of late Spring, but the bark of the trunk and larger branches is distinctive, the leaves are truly remarkable, and the fruit pods are eye-catching curiosities that make most Kentucky Coffee Trees no trouble at all to identify with these odd objects clinging to the stark, gaunt, blunt branchlets through the leafless months of the year. Some of the trees bear only staminate or male flowers, and thus do not produce fruit, but more often the odd pods are hung out as a sign for all to see through Fall and Winter.

These pods are flat, leathery, and mahogany-colored, from 4 to 10 inches long and about 2 inches in width, and each one contains 2 or more blackish seeds about the size of lima beans. The Kentucky Coffee Tree is a relative of the lima bean, and of the string and butter beans and garden peas as well. All these and many other vegetables, flowers, and trees belong to the great Pulse, Pea, or Legume group, a large and famous family of the plant world that the botanists call the Leguminosae, the badge of which is the bean-type fruit.

Where the big pods of the Kentucky Coffee Tree are missing in the leafless season, it isn't difficult to recognize the tree by its blunt branchlets and the peculiar gray bark of a flaky appearance as though it had been daubed on with a palette knife by some painter of the French Impressionist school. The leaves that appear quite late in Spring are doubly compound and really astonishing in size. They may be 3 feet long and 2 feet wide and have 100 or more 1½-inch leaflets, as shown in the illustration.

HONEY LOCUST; HONEY-SHUCK

(Gleditsia triacanthos)

As the long seed pods show, this is another member of the Legume group. It is also the thorniest large tree in North America. The Haws, to be sure, are thickly armed with stiletto-like thorns pointing in all directions, but the Haws are shrubs or small trees, whereas the Honey Locust that is now found over most of the eastern half of the United States and adjacent Canada is a stalwart tree at maturity and sometimes is well over 100 feet in height. On many of the larger Honey Locusts the dark gray bark, sandpapery in texture, is covered with fearsome compound thorns almost down to the ground, but on other trees the lower trunk is clear and the "barbed wire entanglements" begin with the main branches and continue all the way out to the many, crooked, thin, drooping branchlets that are a feature of the tree. There is one variety that has no thorns at all, but it is an oddity and rarely encountered except in cultivation.

The compound thorns are only one notable feature of the Honey Locust, or Honey-shuck as it is known in some regions. The leaves are quite distinctive, too. They may be doubly compound, like those of the Kentucky Coffee Tree though in a much smaller way, but most of them are merely compound and they usually sprout in clusters along the branchlets. They average 8 or 9 inches in length and have 7 to 10 pairs of narrowly oval leaflets about an inch long. But the most striking feature of this tree and the one that accounts for its name of Honey Locust is the long, twisting fruit pod that contains not only numerous flat oval seeds but a sweet pulpy substance with a flavor not unlike that of honey. When ripe in early Autumn, these twisted, ribbon-like and fairly stiff pods are a darkish red-brown in color, 8 to 18 inches long, and about 1 inch wide. Some of them cling to the bare branches long after the leaves have vanished but many fall with the leaves to litter the ground and become tasty food for cattle, rabbits, squirrels, birds, and other creatures of the wild. Those neighborhood children who know a good thing when they see one will open the pod, discard the seeds and chew on the pod for the sake of the sweet substance that coats its inner surface. Try it yourself. It's good.

REDBUD; JUDAS TREE

(*Cercis canadensis*)

Because of its attractive flowers, many persons know the Redbud as a cultivated shrub or small tree over most of temperate North America, but in the wild it is found in the undergrowth of rich woods from New Jersey to Nebraska and southward to the Gulf Coast. It really has red buds in Winter; and in the Spring, before the leaves appear, it produces abundant clusters of rose-purple flowers that seem to grow right out of the dark bark of the branches. That's the time of year when it is easiest to track down the Redbud in the wild, but it may be recognized later by the roundish heart-shaped leaves that measure 3 to 5 inches in any direction or by the 3-inch beans that are its seed pods and that cling to the branches through the Autumn. The flowers of the pea type and the beans show that it is a member of the great family of "Legumes." The name Judas Tree comes from the legend that it was on a Near Eastern tree of this type that Judas hanged himself and that its flowers, white at the time, turned color with shame and have blushed ever since. Look for the flowers as the birds come north in Spring.

YELLOWWOOD; VIRGILIA

(*Cladrastis lutea*)

This is an exceptional tree in several respects. It is rare in the wild over its narrow, native inland range and common in cultivation over the greater part of the United States. It is a tree of medium size that is highly prized for the lavish supply of drooping clusters of cream-white, pea-type flowers in late Spring. The fruit pod is a light, thin bean 3 to 4 inches long and, as it often clings to the bare branches through the Winter, it is an aid in recognizing the tree. The bark is smooth and gray like that of the Beech and underneath it the wood is a bright yellow that even a shallow incision will show. The compound leaves are about 1 foot long; the 2-inch oval leaflets are not usually opposite one another along the axis. And next year's buds are under the petioles!

COMMON LOCUST; BLACK LOCUST

(*Robinia pseudo-acacia*)

If a farmer calls a tree a Locust without any further description, this is the species he means. From its original narrow range along the Appalachians, it has spread by cultivation and escape over the eastern half of the continent. It grows to be a tall, narrow tree of picturesque appeal, with twistingly corrugated brownish-gray bark, graceful and delicate compound leaves and, in Spring or early Summer, drooping clusters of sweet-smelling, cream-white, pea-type flowers that, along with the 3-inch beans they ultimately produce, prove its membership in the Pulse or Legume family. The leaves may be a foot or more in length with 7 to 21 oval leaflets 1 to 1½ inches long. The tree grows quickly, provides valuable timber, and has other good qualities, but it also has faults. It carries stout and sharp little thorns on its branches, spreads rapidly where it isn't wanted and is desperately stubborn in resisting eviction from such places.

WAFER-ASH; HOP TREE

(*Ptelea trifolia*)

This is a common enough shrub or small tree from Quebec to Nebraska and south to the Gulf States, but it generally escapes notice unless the dry seed clusters catch the eye where they cling late in the year after the leaves have fallen. These "wafers"—circular samaras to the botanist—are about ¾ inch in diameter and the product of a spray or "compound cyme" of greenish-white little flowers that appear in June or July. The compound leaves are long-stalked or "petioled," as shown, and the 3 leaflets, pointed at both ends, may be 2 to 6 inches long. The crushed leaves smell something like the hops used in brewing, which explains the name Hop Tree sometimes applied to it. The branches of the Wafer-Ash are favorite places of deposit for the linear whitish egg masses of one of the odd-looking "Brownie Bugs," the triangular *Echinops binotata.* The parent insects often are found on the Wafer-Ash and, if you carry a pocket magnifying glass, it is worth while taking a look at them.

AILANTHUS

(*Ailanthus altissima*)

The name Ailanthus is alleged to mean "Tree of Heaven" in some Moluccan dialect and is a reference to the height of 100 feet it sometimes reaches in Asia, to which it is native; but in North America, where it is now widespread, it doesn't grow to any such commanding height nor has it gained any such high-flown title. In fact, because of the offensive odor of the staminate flowers, the crushed leaves, or the bruised bark, it is often inelegantly called "Stinkweed." It is a hardy tree, growing on almost any kind of ground and springing up quickly in vacant city lots. The clusters (panicles) of greenish-yellow staminate and pistillate flowers are produced on separate trees. The pistillate clusters have no offensive odor and produce masses of colorful seed-carrying "samaras" 1 to 2 inches in length, which are yellow with a crimson blush. The compound leaves may be 2 to 4 feet in length with 11 to 31 leaflets, 2 to 5 inches long, and shaped as shown.

STAGHORN SUMAC

(*Rhus typhina*)

This is the most widespread of the three harmless and handsome Sumacs—the Staghorn, the Smooth, and the Dwarf or Wing-rib Sumac—that are found in abundance over most of eastern North America. They are much similar in general appearance and fruiting habit and their compound leaves turn a brilliant crimson that adds color to the Autumn fields. It's the soft brown hairy growth on the younger branches that gives the name Staghorn to this species. The inconspicuous little flowers come in pyramidal clusters and the pistillate clusters turn into attractive cone-shaped masses of tiny seeds enclosed in hairy coverings. The compound leaves may be 2 feet or more in length with numerous leaflets, shaped as shown. They differ decidedly from the Ailanthus leaflets in that they are sharply toothed in a small way, and furthermore a drop of milky sap will appear if you pluck a Sumac leaflet. The Smooth Sumac will be known by its smooth branchlets and the Dwarf Sumac by the "wings" along the leaf axis between leaflets.

POISON SUMAC

(*Rhus vernix*)

To offset three friendly, handsome, and harmless Sumacs, there are three nasty members of the group. They are the Poison Sumac, the Poison Ivy, and the much similar but more southerly Poison Oak. The only good thing about Poison Sumac is its comparative scarcity over a range that covers the eastern half of the United States and adjacent Canada. It's a shrub or small tree up to 25 feet in height and is found almost exclusively in swamps or wet ground. The compound leaves are 1 to 2 feet long and the 7 to 13 leaflets, 2 to 3 inches long, are red-veined, shiny above and smooth along the edge. The flower and fruit clusters are more open than those of the harmless Sumacs and the sprays of off-white or soapy-looking little berries or "drupes" usually hang on through the Winter and help to identify the species. However, some plants do not fruit, so try to learn the whereabouts of the Poison Sumac when it is in leaf—and then keep away from it. As a skin irritant it is worse than Poison Ivy.

POISON IVY

(*Rhus radicans*)

It might be a good idea to have the first lesson in botany consist of teaching a child to recognize Poison Ivy because it is found almost everywhere in temperate North America and ignorance of its appearance has caused much suffering to countless victims. It is a shrub or climbing vine that is easily recognized when in foliage by its long-stalked compound leaves made up of 3 shiny leaflets, shaped as shown. The leaflets, 1 to 4 inches long, may be smooth-edged or bluntly toothed. It's a good thing to note all the details and become thoroughly familiar with the variations in the leaflets so that the plant may be recognized the more easily. It flowers and fruits much like the Poison Sumac but the clusters are more compact and the Poison Ivy berries or "drupes" are not shiny but a dull gray. Where you see such clusters of dried fruits in Fall or Winter on a shrub or along a climbing vine, keep away!

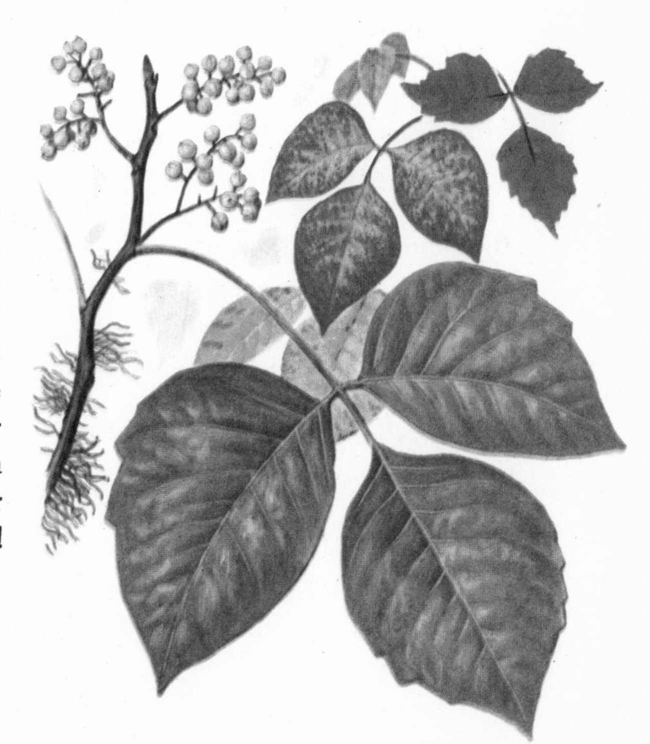

AMERICAN HOLLY

(*Ilex opaca*)

The Holly wreath, made of this or the much similar European Holly, conveys the Christmas spirit far and wide in happy homes. The American Holly is found as a thick shrub or a tree up to 50 feet or more in height with a tight-fitting, dappled gray bark, evergreen foliage consisting of thick, leathery, spiny-tipped leaves 2 to 3 inches long and, in season, the attractive red berries or "drupes" about ¼ inch in diameter that contrast so brilliantly with the dark green foliage. Though it grows as far north in the wild as the coastal region of Massachusetts, it is more at home in the South and reaches its greatest size well below the Mason-Dixon line. It flourishes in moist woodlands from the Gulf States to Illinois and Indiana and is common through the Atlantic States northward to New Jersey. It has numerous close relatives in North America, including some with red berries and others with yellow or black fruit, but none with the combination of red fruit and spiny-tipped evergreen leaves that distinguish this species.

BLACK ALDER; WINTERBERRY

(*Ilex verticillata*)

Of a gray day in November or December, the beautiful little black-tipped red berries or "drupes" along the dark branchlets of the Black Alder lend a welcome touch of color to a stark and leafless landscape. Seldom growing to tree size, it usually is found as a shrub 6 to 12 feet high in swamps, wet meadows, and along the shores of ponds and lakes from Newfoundland to Minnesota and south to Georgia and Missouri. It is a true Holly or *Ilex*. The common name of Black Alder comes from the fact that it often grows among Alders and its leaves, shaped as shown and about 2 inches long on the average, turn blackish in Autumn. The greenish flowers come after the shrub is in full leaf and few persons notice the inconspicuous little staminate and pistillate clusters that appear in the angles or "axils" where the leaf stalks emerge from the branchlets. In fact, few persons recognize or pay any attention to the Black Alder or Winterberry until the bright red berries, about ⅕ inch in diameter, catch the eye in Autumn.

BLADDERNUT

(*Staphylea trifolia*)

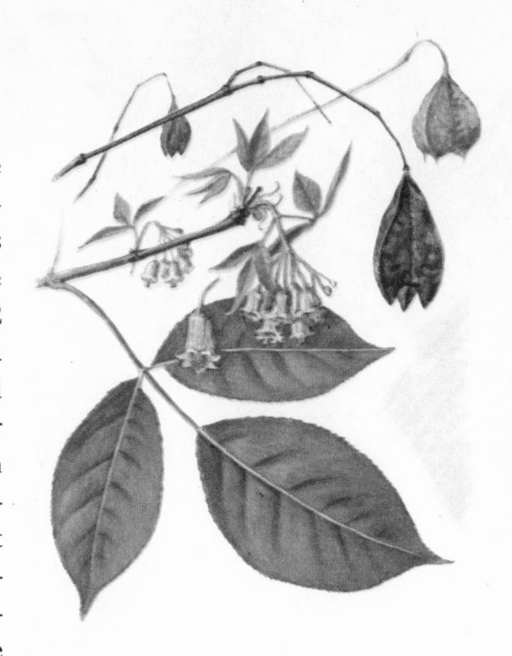

This shrub or small tree probably would be completely overlooked were it not for the persistent seed pods that cling to the leafless branches through Autumn and early Winter and challenge attention in the form of inflated capsules about 2 inches long, usually divided into 3 sections with a seed in each section. It is found in rich woods and thickets and occasionally along forest borders or roadsides from Quebec to Minnesota and south to Georgia and Oklahoma. It is often seen in cultivation for the sake of the curious "bladders" that earn it the common name of Bladdernut. The compound leaves grow opposite one another and usually consist of 3 oval leaflets 2 to 3 inches long. The 3 leaflets account for the *trifolia* of its scientific name. The *Staphylea* comes from the Greek for "a bunch of grapes" and refers to the somewhat grape-like drooping clusters of small 5-petaled white flowers in Spring and the consequent pendent pods that catch the eye later.

NORWAY MAPLE

(*Acer platanoides*)

We have many native Maples in North America but this species, introduced from Europe because of its handsome appearance, regular habit of growth, and disease-resistant qualities, is now a common sight to "city folk" over most of the United States. It has been planted extensively along city streets, highways, parkways, driveways, and byways in all directions. Its wonderful sprays of flowers in Spring would be admired by millions except for the fact that they are light green in color and most persons mistake them for early foliage. The large 5-lobed leaves may be 7 inches wide and the "keys" or "samaras" that show it to be of the Maple family are set at the widest angle of all Maple keys. The bark of the trunk is regularly ribbed somewhat like that of the White Ash. A clinching detail for recognition is the drop of milky juice that appears at the base of the leaf stalk or "petiole" when plucked from the branchlet. But the bark, flower sprays, and keys should be enough.

SUGAR MAPLE

(*Acer saccharum*)

The great Maples of North America, a noble family with many tall, handsome, and useful representatives, flourish in field and forest from the Atlantic to the Pacific and from Mexico to the Arctic Circle. They are among the finest of our "hardwoods" and produce good lumber, including the "curly maple" and "bird's-eye maple" cherished by woodworkers. A family trait is that the leaves grow opposite one another on the branchlets but the real badge of the clan is the fruit, the Maple "key" that is really 2 winged seeds joined together in growth.

The stalwart Sugar Maples that sometimes reach a height of 100 feet or more are found from the Gaspé Peninsula to Manitoba and south to the Gulf States, but they are at their best and most abundant in the mixed forests of the Great Lakes States, New England, and southern Canada. Incidentally, this is the tree that gave Canada its emblem, the Maple Leaf. It is also the tree that in the northern part of its range, produces the sap that, through spile and bucket and boiling down amid the wild winds and late snows of March and April, becomes the maple syrup and maple sugar of commerce. Where "sap boiling" is a regular Spring custom, a grove of these Maples—usually referred to as a "sugar bush"—is a valued possession.

For the most part it is not particularly difficult, even for a beginner, to distinguish one species of Maple from another, but it so happens that there is a Black Maple (*Acer nigrum*) found over much of the range of the Sugar Maple and the resemblance is such that some botanists still insist that it is merely a variety of the Sugar Maple. In any event, they have the same sweet sap and similar keys but the leaf of the Sugar Maple, 3 to 8 inches broad, usually is 5-lobed, as shown, and firmly flat in contrast to the usually 3-lobed Black Maple leaf that tends to be droopy at the edges. The name Black Maple refers to the bark, which is darker than that of the Sugar Maple and not as coarsely ridged or plated. Also, the Black Maple prefers rich bottomland while the Sugar Maple is a climber and likes slopes and well-drained uplands. The greenish-yellow flowers of the Sugar Maple are not presented in flamboyant clusters like those of the Norway Maple but hang modestly and almost shyly on thin stalks or pedicels 2 to 4 inches long amid the early foliage.

RED MAPLE

(Acer rubrum)

This is a Maple of medium size found mostly in swamps and wet ground over the eastern half of the United States and adjacent Canada. Twice a year the Red Maple puts on an advertising campaign to attract public notice and advertise its name. In early Spring, long before its leaves appear, it hangs out untold numbers of beautiful little red flowers that, before very long, turn into "keys" that are strongly tinted with red. Furthermore, the young leaves appear on red stalks or "petioles," though this often escapes notice, just as do the red twigs and the red buds it displays through the Winter. But again in Autumn it calls attention to itself in a spectacular way. It is so often found in swamps that many farmers call it the Swamp Maple and one of the first signs of Autumn is the turning of the leaves of the Red Maples in the swamps. They turn red, of course; a bright red that is in striking contrast with the sober green foliage still worn by most of its neighbors.

It's rather helpful to the beginner when a tree lives up to its common name as the Red Maple does in eastern North America and as the Big-leaf Maple does along the Pacific Coast with its enormous leaves up to 12 inches or more in width. The leaves of the Red Maple are quite modest in size, averaging about 4 inches in width. They are usually 3-lobed and appear to be so even when they are 5-lobed because the 2 lower lobes, when present, are more like mere bumps than distinct lobes. They are smaller than the 3-lobed leaves of the Black Maple and much more toothed along the outlines of the lobes. The bark also helps to distinguish the Red Maple. On older trees the lower bark of the trunk is dark gray and somewhat pebbly or wrinkled and ridged, but higher up and on the branches it is a smooth and light gray that, sighted through gaps in green foliage, often looks almost white.

By the way, keep your eyes open for the Sycamore Maple (*Acer pseudoplatanus*), an introduced species widely planted as a shade tree not only in the East but along the Pacific Coast. It has large, thick, 5-lobed leaves and its flowers and keys hang down like bunches of grapes.

SILVER MAPLE

(*Acer saccharinum*)

It's the silvery lower surface of the foliage, which shows in striking contrast to the sober green of the upper surface when the wind tosses the branches about, that gives this tree its name. It's a weak sister among the Maples. Though it often grows to be a fairly large tree, it is never a strong one and often loses limbs in storms. It is common, mostly in moist ground, from New Brunswick to Minnesota and south to the Gulf States. You will know it by the slashed appearance of its much-toothed, deeply-cut, 5-lobed leaves about 5 inches in diameter, its long drooping branchlets that curve up sharply toward the tips, the widespread keys, and the flaky gray bark of the trunk. There are other Maples, native and imported, that are not shown in this book but all may be recognized as Maples by their opposite leaves and the "keys" that are the badge of the clan.

BOX ELDER; ASH-LEAVED MAPLE

(*Acer negundo*)

This is a Maple that, in most places, lives under an assumed name. It's a small and friendly tree that likes to be near water, but it is much cultivated and may be found in good ground almost anywhere in temperate North America east of the Rockies. Over this wide range it is commonly called the Box Elder and certainly its compound leaves would never lead the ordinary person to link it with the familiar Maples of the countryside, but the typical Maple "keys" that are its fruit settle the issue. These keys, produced only on the trees that bear pistillate flowers, hang in thick clusters, as shown. The compound leaves, which have the family trait of growing opposite one another on the branchlets, may have 3, 5, 7, or 9 leaflets and the leaflets may be sparsely toothed or even lobed. The bark of the trunk and branches is brown and only slightly ridged. The foliage, though variable, is quite distinctive.

HORSE CHESTNUT

(Aesculus hippocastanum)

Under a spreading chestnut-tree
The village smithy stands;
The smith, a mighty man is he,
With large and sinewy hands;
And the muscles of his brawny arms
Are strong as iron bands.

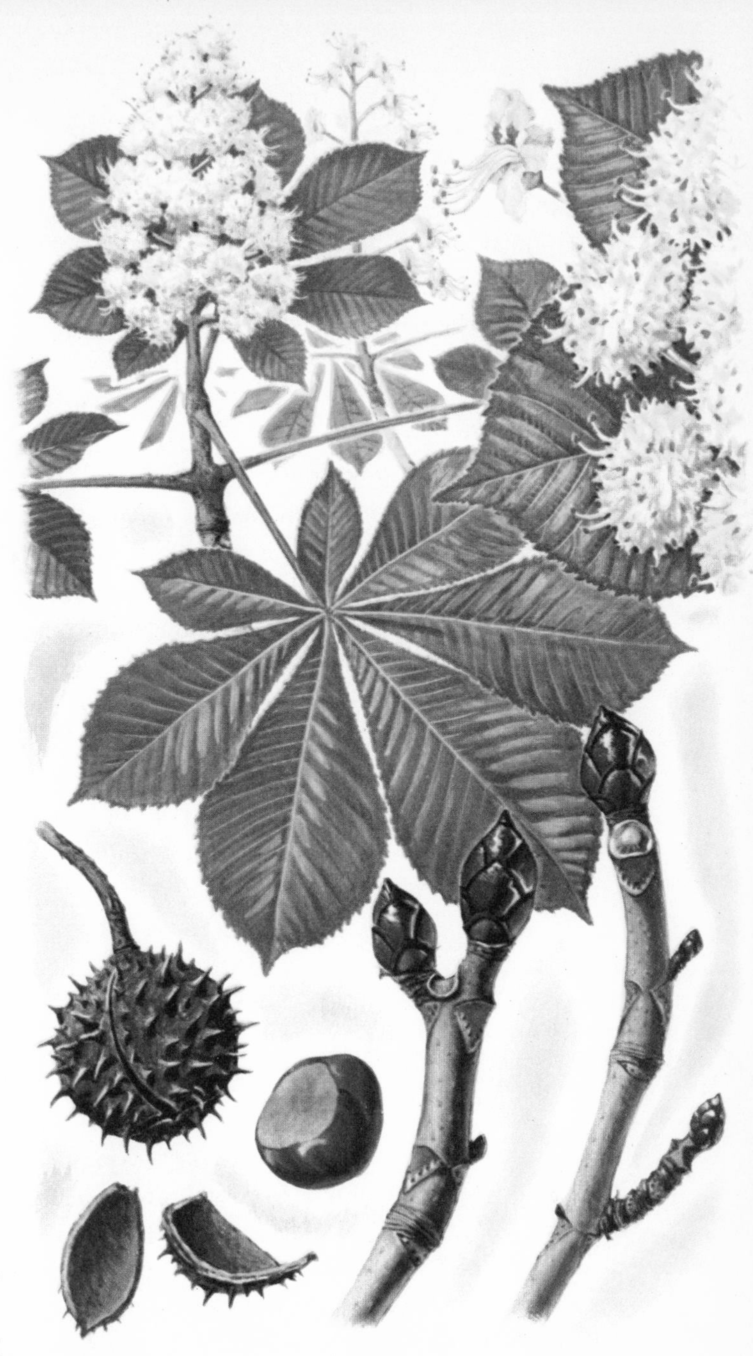

So wrote Longfellow a century ago when the village blacksmith shop was a center of activity and a clearing house for local news. The inspiration for the verse was a blacksmith shop that the poet passed in going to and from his Cambridge home when he was teaching at Harvard. The popularity of the poem brought many persons to see the "village smithy" and some visitors were surprised to find that the "spreading chestnut" of poetic fame was not our native and noble Chestnut but the Horse Chestnut pictured here. This tree of southwestern Asia and ancient days in Greece followed the march of civilization across Europe, where it now may be seen along the streets and in the parks of many great cities, and was brought to North America about 200 years ago to flourish in much the same way here.

It belongs to a group, including our native Buckeyes, that has much similar flower clusters, "palmately" compound leaves growing opposite one another on the branchlets, and the curiously marked fruit called "horse chestnuts" or "buckeyes" typical of the group. However, there are differences that are easily noted. If in doubt, the color of the flowers, the number, shape, and size of the leaflets in the compound leaves, the shape, size, and prickliness or lack of it in the coverings of the fruit pods, and the gumminess or lack of it on Winter buds will enable you to track down the species. For instance, the Horse Chestnut usually has 7 radiating leaflets in its compound leaves whereas the Buckeyes usually have 5, and the Horse Chestnut leaves average larger, with the central leaflet sometimes 10 inches or more in length. The upright clusters of white flowers flecked with red, the very prickly pods, and the very gummy Winter buds are other features of the Horse Chestnut.

OHIO BUCKEYE

(*Aesculus glabra*)

This illustrates what was stated of the Buckeye group on the previous page. You may encounter one or more of our five or six native species of Buckeye almost anywhere from New York to California and southward to the Gulf States and they vary in size from shrubs to tall trees. The Ohio Buckeye, also called the Fetid Buckeye because the bruised bark or crushed foliage gives off a bad odor, is usually a small tree with long-stalked leaves, greenish-yellow flower clusters, and fruit husks that are mildly prickled or roughly pebbled. The "buckeyes" are about 1 inch in diameter and the leaflets of the compound leaves 3 to 6 inches long. The illustration shows 5 leaflets, which is the common rule among Buckeyes, but sometimes you will find 6 or 7 leaflets. You will also find other species of Buckeye with red, yellow, or even purple flowers, leaflets of different size, and fruit husks of different texture and shape.

WESTERN SOAPBERRY

(*Sapindus drummondii*)

This is a native tree of the Southwest that often is confused with the naturalized Chinaberry or Pride-of-India Tree (*Melia azedarach*) found in dooryards or along village streets in the warmer portions of the United States, particularly the Southeast. The confusion is caused by the much similar clusters of dried yellowish berries or "drupes," about ½ inch or more in diameter, that cling to the trees through the Winter. However, there are differences easily noted. The flower clusters of the Soapberry are white or greenish-white, whereas the slightly larger flower clusters of the Chinaberry usually are purple or pale lilac. The compound leaves of the Soapberry, about 1 foot long, have 9 to 19 leaflets, shaped as shown, and smooth along the edges. The larger leaves of the Chinaberry are doubly compound and the leaflets are toothed or lobed. The berries of the Soapberry will produce a lather if crushed in water.

BASSWOOD; LINDEN

(Tilia americana)

The American Basswoods are the counterparts of the European Lindens and either name will serve well enough to identify the trees, though Basswood seems to be the preference of farmers and woodsmen who find them in the wild on this side of the Atlantic. There are three or four species native to the eastern half of temperate North America and several European species have been much planted along city streets, in public parks, and on suburban lawns for shade or decorative purposes. To the ordinary eye all these different species are much similar in general appearance and the beginner will do well to forget about specific differences for a time and be content to learn to recognize one and all Basswoods or Lindens as such at first sight. This is a very easy matter over a considerable portion of the year because of the odd way in which the clusters of flowers and subsequent fruit hang from the approximate centers of what look like very narrow leaves but are "bracts" to the botanist. The illustration shows this plainly and the fact that the clusters of dried, pea-like nutlets often hang on the trees after the leaves have fallen is a further aid in identification.

The species shown here is by far the most widespread and abundant of our native Basswoods and in late Spring or early Summer it is laden with delightfully fragrant clusters of little cream-colored flowers that are nectar and ambrosia to Honeybees. At such times you can actually locate the tree "by ear" because of the hum made by the myriad bees in their activity around the flower clusters. The beekeepers in some regions pay tribute to these trees by referring to the early season, light-colored product of the hive as Basswood honey as distinguished from the later and darker product they call Buckwheat honey. But a closer bond between the bees and the trees is that the light wooden frames in which honey is sold in the comb are made of Basswood. The heart-shaped, sharp-toothed leaf blades of this species may be as much as 8 inches long but average about 5 inches in length. The dark bark of the trunk and branches, reddish twigs, and dark red buds help to identify the Basswood or Linden in Winter. It is a fine shade tree and is much planted along city streets.

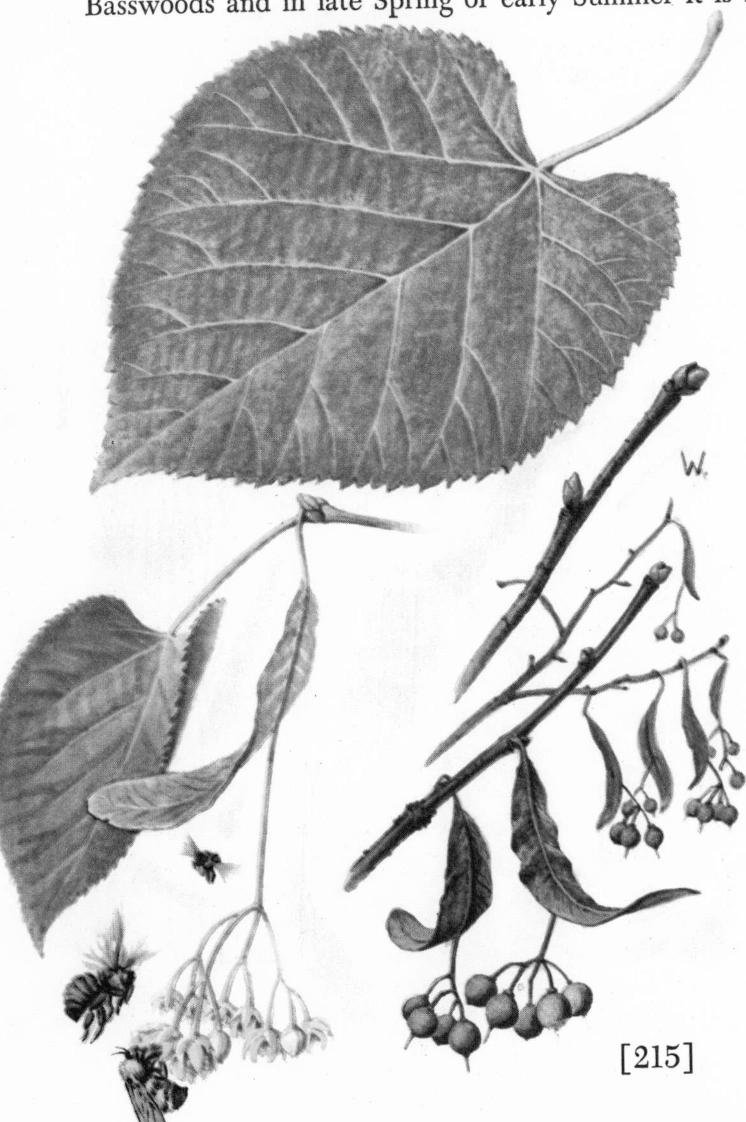

SOUR GUM; TUPELO; PEPPERIDGE

(*Nyssa sylvatica*)

This in an interesting and attractive tree even though it never grows beyond medium height. It is variously known as Sour Gum, Black Gum, Tupelo, Pepperidge, Hornpipe, Beetle-bung, and Snag Tree and possibly has a few other local titles over a range that extends from Maine to Michigan and south to the Gulf States. It prefers wet ground and often is found in or along the borders of swamps, but it can and does thrive on slopes and good upland territory. The leaves, shaped as shown, are 2 to 5 inches long and such a lustrous green on the upper surface in Summer that they fairly glisten where the sunlight strikes them. In the Autumn they turn a deep rich red so distinctive that the tree can be recognized at a distance by that feature alone.

For the beginner, of course, the easiest way to recognize the Sour Gum is by the fruit that usually is produced in abundance, though some trees bear only staminate or male flowers and produce no fruit. You will note in the illustration that the oval, berry-like "drupes," about ⅓ inch long and blue-black when ripe, appear on long stalks and may be single or as many as 4 to a cluster. They really do not have much "meat" on them because the stone inside takes up so much room. Furthermore, they have a slightly acid taste. But apparently this makes no difference to the Robins, Mourning Doves and other birds that flock to the feasting when this fruit ripens in the early Fall.

In the leafless season you may recognize the Sour Gum by the deeply corrugated dark gray bark of the trunk that, on mature trees, contrasts sharply with the smooth light gray bark of the many short branches that stick straight out horizontally or, in many cases, slant downward. The famous Cotton Gum (*Nyssa aquatica*) of the southern swamps, a close relative, is a bigger tree with a buttressed trunk, odd-shaped leaves and fruit an inch long.

FLOWERING DOGWOOD

(*Cornus florida*)

Everybody can recognize the Flowering Dogwood when it's in bright bloom in the Spring, but there are some things about this popular small tree that often are overlooked or perhaps not known by the average observer. The flowers, for instance, are not what they seem. The 4 broad, notched, cream-white or occasionally pink divisions that catch the eye and that most persons take to be petals are something quite different. If you wish to see them in an earlier stage, look at the picture of the bare branchlets as you find them in the colder months when the leaves are off. Each tiny, pear-shaped, sharp-tipped object is a future flower group enclosed by a wrapping of 4 "bracts" as the botanists call them. The wrappings hold tight until "Spring unlocks the flowers to paint the laughing soil" as Reginald Heber put it. Then the wrappings unfold, expand, and change color to form a handsome frame for the true flowers, the little greenish-yellow objects in the small circle in the center.

If you look at the true flowers, you will find that they have 4 petals and it's well to keep this in mind because there are many species of native Dogwood in North America and only a few have the colorful bracts that make this species notable over the eastern half of the United States and adjacent Canada. The more northerly midget member of the clan, the Dwarf Cornel or Bunchberry (*Cornus canadensis*) has similar bracts and the Pacific Dogwood (*Cornus nuttalli*) which grows to be a tree of good size, usually has 6 such colorful bracts, but where these are missing, the 4 petals of the little Dogwood flowers distinguish them immediately from the 5-lobed Viburnum flowers that grow in similar clusters and often are found side by side with the Dogwoods. The fruits of the Dogwoods are berry-like "drupes" that are fine food for many birds. Those of the Flowering Dogwood are, as shown, bright red in color, black-tipped, and somewhat oval in shape. The colorful bracts in the Spring, the bright berries of early Autumn, and the tiny, pear-shaped Winter packages of future flower clusters mark the Flowering Dogwood.

RED-OSIER DOGWOOD

(*Cornus stolonifera*)

This is one of the many native species of Dogwood that usually go unrecognized because at first glance they look nothing like the well-known Flowering Dogwood. In fact, they look more like Viburnums and, since they often are found in company with Viburnums and produce similar flattish clusters of little cream-white flowers, there is some excuse for confusion. But when in bloom, the flowers tell the tale. The tiny Dogwood flowers have 4 petals. The little faces of the Viburnum flowers are distinctly 5-lobed. Later you may note how the veins of the Dogwood leaf curve sharply toward the tip along the edge of the leaf. The name of this species comes from the deep red or wine-purple color of the stems and branches, a feature particularly noticeable in northern Winters. The Silky Cornel or Kinnikinnik (*Cornus amomum*), another of the clan, has much similar colorful branches but in that species the pith is brown; in the Red-osier it is white. Such are the details that help the beginner to sort out the Dogwoods.

PERSIMMON

(*Diospyros virginiana*)

From Pennsylvania to Iowa and south to the Gulf States the Persimmon is well and favorably known for the smooth, round, orange-colored, edible fruit that it produces. It takes a touch of cold weather to ripen the fruit and anyone who "jumps the season" does so at the risk of setting his or her teeth on edge. The leaves of the Persimmon, shaped as shown, and quite shiny on the upper surface, are 3 to 7 inches long. The tree is ordinarily of medium size but in the Mississippi Basin some Persimmons have reached 100 feet in height. The bark of the older trees is ruggedly corrugated and looks even more like alligator hide than the bark of the Sassafras. A feature of the Persimmon is that the fruit clings to the tree long after the leaves have fallen and the dried calyx of the flower likewise clings to the fruit until it meets its fate, consumption or dissolution. The Persimmon may be found in New York and New England but it is primarily a southern tree.

WHITE ASH

(*Fraxinus americana*)

There are Red, White, and Blue Ashes but this combination of colorful names has no patriotic or narrowly geographical significance. It's true that the Red, White, and Blue Ashes are native residents of the United States but they live and thrive in Canada, too. Few regions of temperate North America are without some representative Ash and many areas can boast half a dozen or more species and varieties. The hardy Black Ash pushes northward almost to the shores of Hudson Bay. The Water Ash sticks to the southeastern portion of the United States. The Oregon Ash prefers the Pacific Coast for residential purposes.

For the beginner, sifting the Ashes (no offense!) will be quite a task and will take some time and study. A good start can be made by becoming acquainted with the White Ash, one of the outstanding members of a fine tribe, a tall and shapely tree of clean limbs and lovely foliage. It's a good shade tree for lawns and also one of the most valuable timber trees in the forests of North America. When you know the White Ash, you will have no trouble in recognizing other Ashes as Ashes, but there may be some difficulty in tracking down the species or variety.

There are three things by which the Ashes may be known. The first is that they have compound leaves. The second is that these compound leaves grow opposite one another along the branchlets. The third item is the typical winged seed that usually is produced in abundant clusters except on those trees that bear only male or staminate flowers and, happily, they are in the minority. The White Ash, which is found from Quebec to Minnesota and southward to Georgia and Texas, has a trunk with grayish-brown bark with a neat network of narrow ridged hollows running up and down. The compound leaves, 8 to 15 inches long, have 5 to 9 leaflets, shaped as shown, and 2 to 6 inches long. Note that the leaflets have stalks about ½ inch long. The "samara" or winged seed is 1 to 2 inches long. The various species of Ash are distinguished by differences in detail of bark and bud, leaf and branch, flower and seed, but all Ashes have opposite compound leaves and the typical winged seeds of the tribe that, by the way, are much liked by many birds.

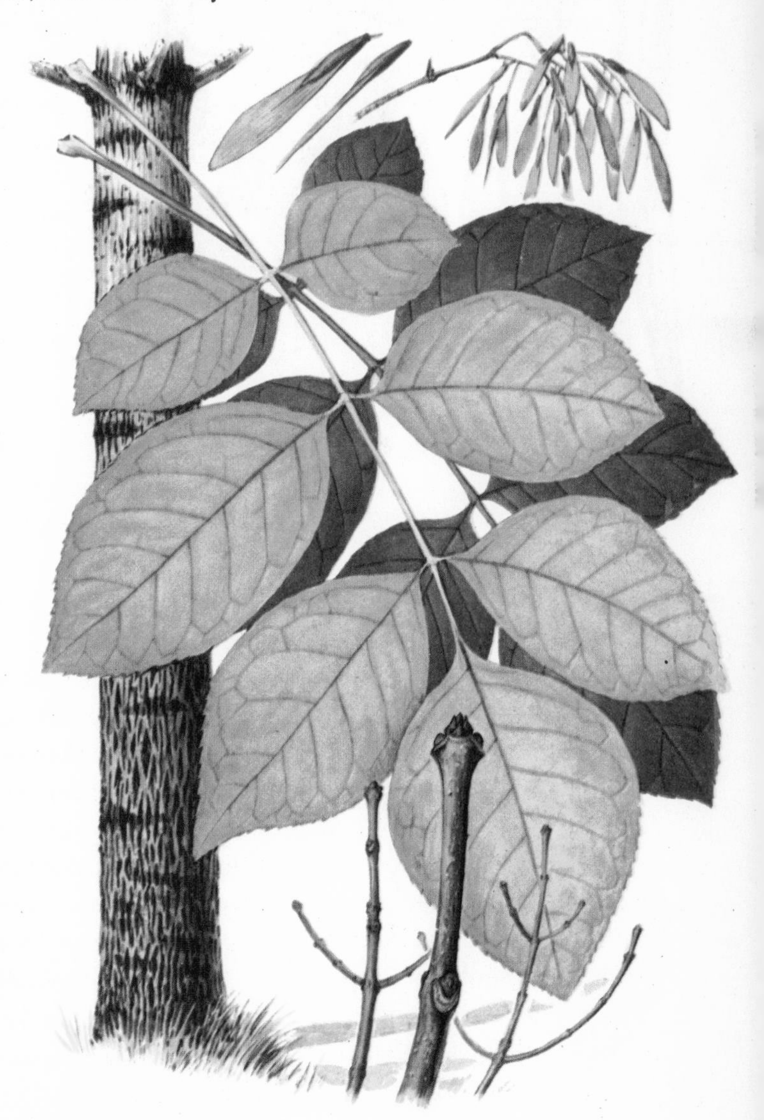

COMMON CATALPA; INDIAN BEAN

(*Catalpa bignonioides*)

The Catalpas are medium-sized trees with huge broad leaves, pyramidal clusters or "panicles" of 2-lipped, bell-shaped, showy white flowers, and seed pods that look like long, thin beans but are capsules that eventually split open and release innumerable winged seeds. The dried capsules or their twisted remnants usually cling to the tree through most of the Winter. The leaves are 6 to 12 inches long and the seed capsules sometimes reach 20 inches in length. In this species the throat of each flower is streaked with yellow and much dotted with purple. In the very similar Western Catalpa (*Catalpa speciosa*), the leaves are a bit larger and much more pointed at the tip, the seed capsules are thicker, and the fewer flowers in the more open clusters have little or no purple spotting in the throat. The introduced Paulownia has somewhat similar large leaves and pyramidal flower clusters but the flowers are pale blue. In the leafless season the Paulownia may be known by its oval, empty seed pods and coming flower sprays in velvet bud.

BUTTONBUSH

(*Cephalanthus occidentalis*)

This is a common to abundant shrub in swamps and wet ground generally and grows to tree size only in the southern part of its broad range that extends from the Atlantic to the Pacific in temperate North America. It has crooked or curving branches and the shiny and narrowly oval leaves, 4 to 7 inches long, are late in appearing in Spring. However, there is no need to go into details of bark, bud, or leaf because the flower and seed clusters are easy marks by which the shrub may be known. The round clusters of little cream-colored flowers are about 1 inch in diameter and they appear on long stalks or "peduncles" in late Spring or Summer. They quickly condense to spherical seed clusters, about ¾ inch in diameter, that turn brown as the seed ripen and hang on through most of the Winter. You can't miss them.

NANNYBERRY

(Viburnum lentago)

Every section of temperate North America has on display one or more of our many native species of Viburnum, all of which have such traits in common as simple leaves that grow opposite one another along the branchlets, flattish clusters or "compound cymes" of little 5-lobed mostly white or cream-colored flowers, and fruit in the form of small, 1-seeded berries or "drupes." Most of our Viburnums are shrubs but a few reach tree size, including the Nannyberry that ranges from Quebec to Manitoba and south to Georgia and Colorado and may be anything from a large shrub to a tree 30 feet or more in height. The flowering clusters are 2 to 5 inches in diameter and the berries, about ½ inch long, are blue-black when ripe. The leaves, shaped as shown, are minutely sharp-toothed and 2½ to 5 inches long. A much similar species, the Black or Sweet Haw (*Viburnum prunifolium*) has smaller leaves and flower clusters and is more southerly in range, reaching down to the Gulf Coast.

SOUTHERN ARROWWOOD

(Viburnum dentatum)

This and another species of Arrowwood (*Viburnum recognitum*), more northerly in range, are shrubs up to 10 feet or so in height that are commonly found in moist ground and along the borders of swamps, ponds, and streams from New Brunswick to Ontario and Michigan and south to South Carolina and Tennessee. The distinction between the two species is based on the amount of hairiness on the twigs, the "petioles," and the leaves, and a difference in the type of groove in the seed or stone of the fruit, but the beginner can let that go until later and lump the Arrowwoods together for the time being. The clusters of little white or cream-colored 5-lobed flowers are from 1 to 4 inches in diameter and the ripe berries or "drupes," about ¼ inch long, are blue-black. The leaves, shaped and toothed as shown in the illustration, have stalks or petioles about 1 inch long and leaf blades 1 to 4 inches long. If you go walking in wet ground, you are sure to run into Arrowwood.

MAPLE-LEAVED VIBURNUM

(*Viburnum acerifolium*)

This is a shrub up to 6 feet in height that is found in the undergrowth of dry or rocky woods from Quebec to Minnesota and south to Georgia and Tennessee. It is called Dockmackie in some regions but Maple-leaved Viburnum is the perfect name for it. From the shape, size, and texture of the leaves, it might be mistaken for an infant Maple but the flowers and fruit prove it to be one of the Viburnums. The leaves are 2 to 4 inches broad and the flat sprays or "cymes" of little cream-colored or sometimes pinkish 5-lobed flowers are 1 to 4 inches in diameter. The small, ovoid, 1-seeded berries or "drupes" that come later are purplish-black when ripe. The Arrowwoods, the Nannyberry and the Maple-leaved Viburnum are just a few of the many Viburnums native to North America but an acquaintance with them will give the beginner a knowledge of the flowering and fruiting processes of the group and other species will soon be recognized.

RED-BERRIED ELDER

(*Sambucus pubens*)

Everybody knows the common "Elderberry" (*Sambucus canadensis*), the familiar roadside shrub with the compound leaves, the flat sprays of cream-colored flowers much like those of the Viburnums, and the later abundance of dark, juicy fruit often served up in tarts or pies or turned into "Elderberry wine." This is a taller, wilder, and red-fruited relative that may be found blooming much earlier in cool woods over most of temperate North America. The flower and fruit clusters in this species are not flat but rather pyramidal in shape. Other differences are that the Common Elder leaves have 5 to 11 leaflets whereas the Red-berried Elder more often displays only 5 to 7 typical Elder leaflets, shaped and toothed as shown. When leaf and fruit have gone, the brown pith of the stem or branch will distinguish this species from the Common Elder, which has white pith.

EUCALYPTUS; BLUE GUM

(*Eucalyptus globulus*)

Where you find any Eucalyptus in North America, you have reached cultivated ground because these are imported trees. There are scores of species of Eucalyptus in that vast region of the Southern Hemisphere known as Australasia. Just about a century ago, more than a dozen species were introduced into California and of that group the Blue Gum has been most successful in making itself at home on North American soil. It is a common sight almost anywhere at low altitude in California and has been much planted in Arizona and New Mexico as well as all along the Gulf Coast from Texas to Florida. A fast grower, at maturity it is a very tall and rather slim evergreen with willow-like leaves 6 to 12 inches long and brown outer bark that peels off in long straggling strips to expose the gray inner bark in a way to suggest the dappled or piebald bark of the Sycamores. The funnel-shaped whitish flowers, about 1½ inches broad, appear in the leaf axils along the branchlets and ultimately produce the curious seed capsules, shaped as shown, and up to about 1 inch across the top. Bark and bud as well as leaf, flower, and fruit contain an aromatic oil that is often used for medicinal purposes.

* * * * *

Reader, this is as far as we can go together. But let neither of us stop learning because we have come to the end of a book. We never can come to an end of the wonders and beauties of Nature. The more we know of such matters, the greater enjoyment we find in living. As we close this book let the last words be from Milton:

To-morrow to fresh woods, and pastures new.

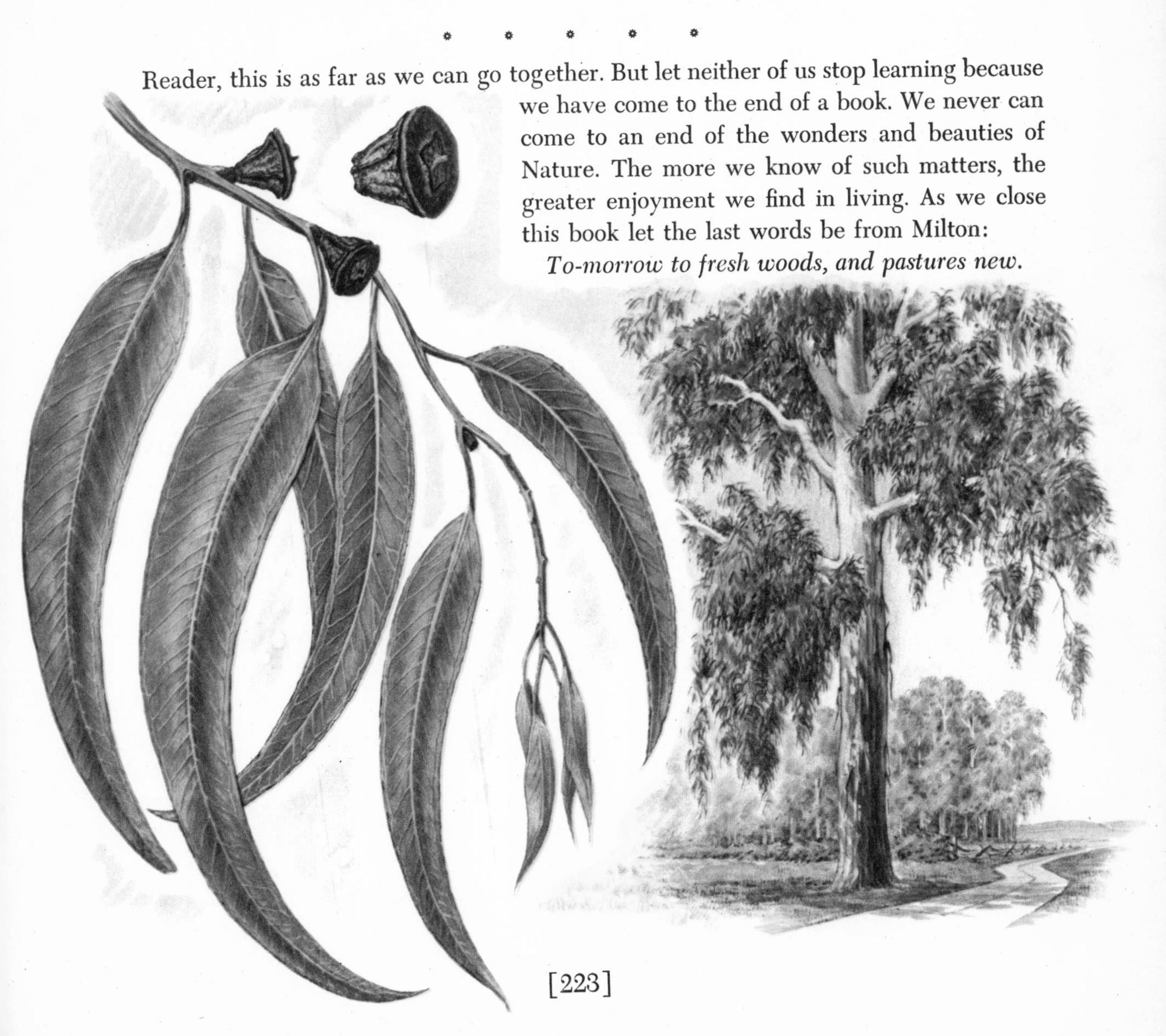